THE UNWRITTEN RULES
OF PhD RESEARCH

Gordon Rugg and Marian Petre

Open University Press

Open University Press
McGraw-Hill Education
McGraw-Hill House
Shoppenhangers Road
Maidenhead
Berkshire
England
SL6 2QL

email: enquiries@openup.co.uk
worldwide web: www.openup.co.uk

and Two Penn Plaza, New York, NY 10121–2289, USA

First published 2004

A catalogue record of this book is available from the British Library

ISBN 0 335 21344 8 (pb) 0 335 21345 6 (hb)

Library of Congress Cataloging-in-Publication Data
CIP data applied for

Typeset by RefineCatch Limited, Bungay, Suffolk
Printed in the UK by Bell & Bain Ltd, Glasgow

Contents

Preface

One of the most frequent laments of the postgraduate researcher is: 'Why didn't someone tell me that earlier?' There are innumerable things which nobody bothered to tell you, or to write in the books, and which could have saved you from large amounts of confusion, depression, wasted effort and general tears and misery if only you had been told them earlier.

The authors have spent more than their fair share of time with desperate beginners, explaining the basic principles of research over cups of coffee. This book is an attempt to cut down their caffeine overload. It explains the basic craft skills and ground rules of the academic world in general, and research in particular. Its focus is the vitally important things that the standard textbooks don't bother to mention on the sweet assumption that they can be left to the readers' lecturers and supervisors.

If you are doing a PhD or an MPhil then this book is intended to help you to do the best research possible with the minimum of wasted effort. It is also intended to help you use your research as part of your career development and self-development so that you don't end up on graduation day, certificate in hand, wondering just what the hell to do next and realizing that you've just spent several years moving painfully in the wrong direction.

The authors' backgrounds are varied. Their academic credentials include PhDs, publication of various journal papers and encyclopaedia articles, advanced research fellowships, a couple of journal editorships, refereeing for major journals and fund-giving bodies, and raising between them over a million pounds of research funding. Their students still talk to them, and sometimes say nice things about them.

A challenge!

Readers of an observant turn of mind may notice that, although we have used brief quotations at the head of each chapter, we have not given any indication of the source of those quotations. Readers of a cynical turn of mind may wonder whether we hadn't got round to it by the time the manuscript went into print; such suspicions are not only unworthy, but also wrong. The reason for the missing sources is that they are an opportunity for you to test your new skills in tracking down obscure and incomplete references. We are offering a prize for this.

The prize (to begin with the question most likely to interest impoverished PhD students) involves more glory than fortune; it's Gordon's much-loved personal copy of Thucydides, as mentioned in several places in this book, complete with Post-it place markers from the Research and Scholarship lectures. Just in case you're wondering whether it's an extremely valuable first edition, the answer is that it's a battered Penguin paperback with a retail value of about 50 pence. If this isn't sufficient inducement, the publishers are also prepared to throw in a large box of chocolates. This competition is intended to be a source of gentle amusement in spare moments, not something on which to spend huge amounts of time.

Your mission is to track down as many as possible of the sources for the quotations below, then document them properly as a set of references, using the most recent version of the Harvard referencing style, and laying them out as you would the reference section at the end of your thesis. We have used only some of the quotations from the book, out of consideration for those readers whose sensitivities are too refined to confront the horrors surrounding, for instance, the Pnakotic manuscripts or Evingolis' application of schema theory. Keen readers are of course welcome to try and track down the sources of all the quotations.

The winner will be the person who tracks down the most quotation sources from the list below. If there's a tie, we'll bribe a copy-editor to go through the relevant entries and award the prize to the entrant with the fewest typos. If there's still a tie after that, we'll choose one at random, and give the others due recognition (but no tangible prize . . .)

Please send your entries to: enquiries@openup.co.uk with 'Competition Entry' clearly marked in the subject line. The closing date for entries is 31 December 2004.

The quotes

. . . *it were insidious to particularize; but I must acknowledge the politeness of Mons. La Hire, of the royal French artillery, who volunteered his services in setting and firing the train to the magazine, and who was somewhat bruised and singed.*

. . . *take this woman out of Bren-paidhi's way, or face administrative procedures.*

He wrote in a complicated style, overloaded and lacking in charm. Not that he was indifferent to language and its nuances; on the contrary, correct use of language was for him a moral question, its debasement a symptom of moral breakdown.

. . . *I shall publish such papers on the cryptogams of Kamschatka that no one will ever set the mark of intelligence upon my head again.*

Still, it gave the facts – some of them – and apart from being dated 'off Barcelona' in the customary way, whereas it was really being written in Port Mahon the day after his arrival, it contained no falsehood . . .

Only yesterday I learnt, to my surprise, that you trice puddings athwart the starboard gumbrils, when sailing by and large.

. . . *he was no more consistent than other men, and in spite of his liberal principles and his dislike of constituted authority he was capable of petulant tyranny when confronted with a slime-draught early in the morning.*

About this book

What it is, what it's not, and how to make best use of it

. . . I had said much, but found that my words had been given scant attention.

We've spent a lot of time helping PhD students with problems, and advising potential PhD students who want to avoid problems. Most of these people have read books with titles like *How to get a PhD*; most of them have been given good advice by supervisors and potential supervisors. The problems don't come from the books and the advice – most of the books on this topic range between good and excellent, and most of the advice we've heard reported to us has been sound. The problems usually come from what's absent from the books and the advice. This book is intended to fill at least part of that gap.

Most of the problems we've dealt with involve what's known as tacit knowledge in the broad sense – things that nobody bothers to tell you explicitly, either because they assume you know them already, or because they are so familiar to them that they completely forget that other people don't know them, or because they don't think they are worth mentioning. Book writers usually assume (correctly, in our opinion) that these things are better dealt with informally by supervisors. In an ideal world, this would happen, but in practice supervisors are human (i.e. overworked, forgetful, distracted and imperfect). What we've done is to write down an overview of these unwritten rules, so that the situation makes more sense to you. You can then ask your supervisor about how things work in your discipline, and (with luck) get some solid, specific guidance.

For PhD students, the main problems in our experience fall into two main categories. One is 'big picture' knowledge about how the academic system works, and why it works that way. For instance, what are some classic career paths in academia? Why is academic writing so dry? Why do some people get lectureships in good departments before they've finished their PhD, whereas others are still struggling to find any job ten years after their doctorate? What counts as a 'good' department anyway, and why? Many students are too embarrassed to show their ignorance by asking questions like these; more students are too focused on the immediate problems of the PhD to think of asking them until it's too late.

The second category involves what are known as 'craft skills'. These are usually low-level skills, normally viewed as not sufficiently important to be worth mentioning in textbooks – tricks of the trade which are usually taught informally by supervisors or other mentors. These range from quite specific information (e.g. 'How many references should I have in the first paragraph of something I write?') to quite general rules of thumb (e.g. 'How can I get a reasonable brief overview of this topic that my supervisor's advised me to read about, without spending six months wading through the literature?') The specific skills, and the specific answers, vary across disciplines; however, once you are aware of the basic concept of craft skills, you can then find out what the craft skills are in your chosen area, and learn them.

Each section of this book deals with an area of tacit knowledge which is important to PhD students. Some fairly specific topics, such as how to handle criticism, are relevant in more than one place (for instance, handling criticism is relevant to writing, to presentations and to the viva). Some more general topics, such as writing, manifest themselves in different ways at different stages of your PhD (which is why this book is structured around topics, rather than in chronological order of what will happen to you in your PhD). Each section begins with a description of the topic, and is illustrated with examples and anecdotes. Where an anecdote is dubious or apocryphal, we've said so; the others, including the bucket dropped on one author's head, are true, even when improbable. These verbal descriptions are intended to help you understand what the issues are, and why things are the way they are; the anecdotes are there to illustrate the underlying points and to help you remember them.

Understanding is all very well, but isn't much consolation when it's the day before your first seminar presentation and you're worried about whether there's something blindingly obvious that you've forgotten. We've therefore included a fair number of checklists, bullet points and the like, so that you can check that you've remembered the key things.

That's the main body of the book. Our advice is to read it first from start to finish (since you'll do that anyway, and there's not much point in giving advice which will be ignored). The best thing to do next is to read it in more detail, starting with the topics furthest away from you in time – first, the section on what to do after the PhD, then the sections on the viva and on writing up, and so on. The reason for this is that most students are so focused, understandably, on the immediate problems surrounding them that they rarely look more than one step ahead. This is all very well in the short term, but it usually stores up long-term problems. What happens, for instance, if you're in a discipline where you need to be the author of at least two journal papers, and to have at least two years of part-time lecturing experience, to be shortlisted for a full-time lectureship? If you don't discover this until the last six months of your PhD then you'll have problems if you want to go straight on to a lectureship; if you know about it early, then you can start getting the right things on your CV in good time.

One important thing to keep in mind when reading this book is that disciplines vary. This is why we use words such as 'usually' quite a lot. The precise indications of quality in a CV will be different between, say, history and geology, but the underlying concepts usually remain the same – for instance, the concept of a strong CV as opposed to a weak one. This book is intended to help you understand what these underlying concepts are, so that you can find out what form they take in your discipline, and then make sure that you have the right indicators of quality in your written work, in your presentations and in your CV.

Books about getting a PhD usually end with a bibliography. This one doesn't. There are some classic books which are useful to students in pretty much any discipline, such as Huff's *How to Lie with Statistics*, and standard guides to English grammar. You can find these in the bibliographies of pretty much any book on getting a PhD, and we didn't think that there was much point in duplicating them. After these classics, things get trickier. Different disciplines have very different core reading, as we discuss in detail in the section on reading, and we didn't think that we would improve the world by putting together a compendium of core readings from assorted different disciplines – if you're doing a sociology PhD, for instance, you probably wouldn't be terribly interested in the classic texts on igneous geomorphology. Some authors include selections of books which they find useful, and which they believe other people would find useful too. We've decided not to do this, though not without misgivings. The reason is that most of the books we'd like to recommend are pretty idiosyncratic, and it usually takes a considerable time to get through to students just why we're serious about recommending that they read, say, part of Thucydides' *History of the Peloponnesian War* (especially if they're doing a PhD in an area such as computer science). For the time being, therefore, we're planning to use these texts only in face-to-face supervisions.

What we've done instead is to include a considerable amount of guidance about searching the literature, so that you can find the key texts that you need for your PhD for yourself, with (we hope) the minimum of wasted time and effort. We have also included a list of terms which we think you might find useful. These are generally our own idiosyncratic terms or terms informally used in one or more discipline which haven't made their way into most textbooks, such as 'eyeballing the data'.

On the subject of informality, we have deliberately used an informal style throughout this book. This is not the style which we use for other venues, such as when writing journal articles, so don't be tempted to use this style in your own written thesis. We have also alternated between using full abbreviations (e.g. Ph.D.) in some specific contexts, and common shorter versions (e.g. PhD) in the main body of the text. The shorter abbreviation is a lot less fiddly when writing a large document like this book, but in formal contexts you need to show that you know the correct version, and to use that consistently.

We've deliberately omitted a variety of other things, such as how to use statistics, on the grounds that these are well covered in other books, and this one is quite long enough already. We hope you find it useful and enjoyable.

Acknowledgements

. . . it were insidious to particularize; but I must acknowledge the politeness of Mons. La Hire, of the royal French artillery, who volunteered his services in setting and firing the train to the magazine, and who was somewhat bruised and singed.

We would like to thank all the people who helped us with the writing and publishing of this book – they know who they are.

We would also like to acknowledge our gratitude to our own PhD supervisors, from whom we learned much, much more than we realized at the time. Our remaining sins are our own faults, not theirs. Finally, we would like to acknowledge the students who have, directly and indirectly, brought colour of one sort or another to our lives, and wealth to coffee manufacturers round the world . . . without them, this book would never have been written, and our lives would have been much less fun.

1 So you want to do a PhD?

You can't imagine, even from what you have read and what I've told you, the things I shall have to see and do. It's fiendish work, Carter, and I doubt if any man without ironclad sensibilities could ever see it through and come up alive and sane.

There are two classic ways of doing a PhD. One involves knowing just what you are doing; you will then go through a clearly defined path, suffer occasional fits of gloom and despair, emerge with a PhD, unless you do something remarkably silly or give up, and then proceed smoothly with the next stage of your career. The other way is the one followed by most PhD students, which involves stumbling in, wandering round in circles for several years, suffering frequent fits of gloom and despair, and probably but not necessarily emerging with a PhD, followed by wondering what to do next in career terms. This book is written for those who find themselves following the second path.

There are many good books out there for people wanting to do a PhD. If you're thinking of doing a PhD, you should read at least one of them. They give much good advice about what you need to do, and are a good start. We have spent a lot of time helping students who have read those books. The reason that we needed to help them was not because there was anything wrong with the content of the books; the problem was the things that the books didn't cover. One set of things involved the 'big picture' of doing a PhD; the other set involved low-level skills that the books typically didn't cover, probably on the grounds that their writers assumed these skills would be taught either by supervisors or by the training courses which most PhD students now undergo. This book is intended to fill at least some of that gap.

So, returning to your interest in doing a PhD, you will have various questions about the why and the how and the what of it all. Most of these are answered by the usual texts on doing a PhD, and/or by the procedural documentation of your intended institution. However, the answers may not mean very much to you at this stage. The next section therefore describes the outline of what a PhD is about.

The PhD: its nature and content

The books will tell you that the PhD is several things, including a professional qualification, a training in how to do research and an initiation rite. All of these things are true, but what does it all mean?

At a sordidly practical level, the PhD is a qualification which shows that you are good enough at research to be appointable in a university post. If you're thinking of working as an academic in a university, a PhD is highly advisable. It is also helpful if you want a career as a researcher in industry. A further practical point is that PhDs are recognized around the world, and tend to have pretty good quality control, so a PhD from one country will be recognized in another without too much snobbery. Still at the practical level, if you have a PhD, you usually go onto a higher pay scale.

At a professional level, a PhD involves you doing a decent sized chunk of research, writing it up and then discussing it with professional academics. This demonstrates your ability to do proper research without someone holding your hand. You have a supervisor to help and advise you, but in theory at least the PhD is something where you take the initiative.

A closely related issue is the PhD as initiation rite, where you undergo an ordeal and, if you come through the ordeal in a creditable manner, are admitted to membership of the academic clan. Continuing the analogy, having a PhD will not be enough to make you a clan elder, but it will mark the transition to full adulthood. You are treated differently if you have a PhD – there is a distinct feeling of having become 'one of us'. It's not just a snobbery thing; you will gradually start to notice a different way of thinking about things, especially when you start making administrative decisions in your subsequent career. A good example of this in many departments is under-graduate student projects, where staff with PhDs typically want to use the projects as a way of teaching the students how to conduct research, and staff without PhDs typically want to use the projects as a chance to give the students an industrial placement. The PhDs' view is that the students need to learn critical thinking as a valuable skill for later life; the other view is that this is unrealistic nonsense, and that we need to equip the students to find a job as soon as possible after graduation. Which is right? This is a good question, and one which would take us off on a lengthy diversion. The main point is that doing a PhD *does* change you.

So, that's the standard picture. What does it all mean? That's another good question. Here is how that picture unfolds.

Important section: the standard picture

Firstly, you choose a topic to research. You then find someone willing to be your supervisor. You get yourself through the procedures to sign up for a PhD at your supervisor's institution. You then research that topic for a year or two, at which point you are assessed to see whether you are doing well enough to continue to the end of the PhD. If that goes well, then you do another year or two of research. In the third or fourth year of the PhD, you write a large document (typically around 300 pages) about your research. This is read by a panel of experts who then ask you questions about it to check that your understanding of the topic is good enough. They will typically conclude that you need to make some changes to it. If you make these changes to their satisfaction within a specified period, then you will be awarded a PhD.

The realities behind the standard picture

That's the standard picture. It's pretty much true. There are, however, numerous things to note about it. One is the frequent use of words such as 'typically' in this book; an important thing to grasp about the academic world is that institutions, disciplines and departments vary widely in their norms and conventions. There are good reasons for this, but it doesn't make life any easier for would-be students, or for people trying to write books explaining academic life to would-be students. Another thing is the number of points at which you can fail; PhDs are academically rigorous. Another is the sheer size of the document you produce: the written PhD thesis. A lot of students have trouble coping with the prospect of writing something that big. (Writing it is not really that much of a problem once you know what you're doing, but that doesn't feel much of a consolation at this stage.)

There are also various things which are not elaborated in this picture. One thing which is seldom mentioned is what happens to you after you finish the PhD. A classic story is as follows. A student focuses clearly, submits the thesis and starts looking for a lecturing job, only to discover that they need two years of lecturing experience and preferably a journal publication as well if they are to be appointable for a job in a good department in their field. If they had known this two years previously, they could have started doing some part-time lecturing and submitted a paper or two to a journal. There are other things which look simple until you stop and think about them. For instance, how do you choose a topic, and how do you find a good supervisor? The standard books give quite a lot of good advice about this, but there will still be quite a lot of things that you aren't sure about.

So, what do you do about this? One good step is to read the rest of this book at this point. A lot of it won't have much real meaning to you yet, but that doesn't matter. The main thing is that it should give you a fair idea about which things matter, which things are well understood and which things are comparatively peripheral. For instance, we have a lot to say about academic writing as opposed to formal English (because most students are pretty bad at it) and about feeling lost (because most students have problems with this from the second year of their thesis onwards). Similarly, we don't say much about statistics and about experimental design, because these are comprehensively covered by numerous excellent texts and training courses, so you should have no problems getting access to them if they're needed for your research. Likewise, we don't say much about whether the Harvard referencing system is better than (for instance) the APA system, because your departmental PhD regulations will almost certainly specify the referencing system that you must use, so that question is pretty much an irrelevance unless you happen to be doing a PhD on referencing systems, within an information science department.

The next sections describe some concepts which we have found invaluable, but which don't usually appear in other books. These provide a useful structure for (a) what you are trying to do in a PhD and (b) understanding how things work in the big picture. The first of these is the cabinet-making metaphor; the second is the distinction between instrumental and expressive behaviour.

Cabinet-making – the PhD as a master piece

Doing a PhD has a lot in common with traditional cabinet-making. Back in The Past, an apprentice cabinet-maker would finish his apprenticeship (back in The Past, apprentice cabinet-makers were all 'he') by making a cabinet which demonstrated that he had all the skills needed to be a master cabinet-maker. This piece of furniture was known as the 'master piece'. A successfully defended PhD dissertation fulfils a similar role. It demonstrates that you have all the skills needed to be a researcher in your own right. The issue of *demonstration* is essential. The basis of the PhD examination is the dissertation, together with the subsequent *viva voce* examination. It doesn't matter how brilliant or well-informed you are – if the brilliance and erudition isn't visible in the dissertation, then you're going to fail.

You therefore need to know what the requisite skills are for your branch of academia (since different disciplines require different skills) and make sure that you demonstrate mastery of each of these somewhere in your thesis. If you're a methodical sort of person, you might go so far as to draw up a list of the skills required and tick off each one as it is represented in your thesis. For a cabinet-maker, the skills required would be things like making various complex joints, fitting hinges neatly, applying veneer, achieving a high polish and so forth. For an academic, the skills are things like mastery of formal academic language, familiarity with the relevant literature in the discipline, knowledge of the main data collection techniques, adherence to the standards of rigour and so on.

Things which do not normally appear on the list include personal interest in the area and the ethical importance of the topic. There is no point in going on about these at length in your thesis – you are awarded a PhD as an acknowledgement that you can make cabinets at master craftsman level, not an acknowledgement that you find cabinet-making fascinating, or that cabinets make the world a better place. In practice, few people would spend several years of their life doing a PhD on a topic which held no interest for them, so personal interest is usually taken for granted by examiners. Ethics is a more interesting question. One reason that examiners tend not to take account of claims about the ethical importance of a question (e.g. finding a cure for cancer) as a criterion for assessing a PhD is that bad research can actually impede the search for an answer to the problem by leading other researchers in the wrong direction. Bad research into a highly ethical question is still bad research. Back to the main theme.

Different disciplines have different required skills; most experienced researchers are so familiar with these that they take them for granted, and would be hard pressed to produce a list from memory over a physical or metaphorical cup of coffee. However, other experienced researchers (especially those who teach research methods courses) will be able to give you some answers; in addition, it is worth having a look at the contents section of research methods books in your discipline, which will cover most of the main topics. The PhD regulations for your institution should also help.

An illustrative list of typical skills is given below. It's illustrative rather than definitive – your discipline will almost certainly have a different list. However, many of the skills will be the same, and the list will give you the general idea.

Most of the skills below assume that your work will be located within a single discipline. There is a reason for this. Interdisciplinary PhDs can be extremely interesting and useful. However, they need to be handled with care, since otherwise there is the risk that they will fall between two stools. This can be a problem in terms of practicalia such as finding an external examiner, and in terms of theoretical issues such as deciding which approach to follow when the different disciplines involved have very different ways of doing things. It is usually much wiser to decide on a 'host' discipline, locate the interdisciplinary PhD within that, and then import the concepts from the other discipline into the host discipline.

Cabinet-making skills

Most disciplines require most of the following skills, though individual cases will vary.

Use of academic language

- Correct use of technical terms
- Attention to detail in punctuation, grammar, etc.
- Attention to use of typographic design (white space, layout, headings styles) to make the text accessible
- Ability to structure and convey a clear and coherent argument, including attention to the use of 'signposting' devices such as headings to make the structure accessible
- Writing in a suitable academic 'voice'

Knowledge of background literature

- Seminal texts correctly cited, with evidence that you have read them and evaluated them critically
- References accurately reflecting the growth of the literature from the seminal texts to the present day
- Identification of key recent texts on which your own PhD is based, showing both how these contribute to your thesis and how your thesis is different from them
- Relevant texts and concepts from other disciplines cited
- Organization of all of the cited literature into a coherent, critical structure, showing both that you can make sense of the literature – identifying conceptual relationships and themes, recognizing gaps – and that you understand what is important

Research methods

- Knowledge of the main research methods used in your discipline, including data collection, record-keeping and data analysis
- Knowledge of what constitutes 'evidence' in your discipline, and of what is acceptable as a knowledge claim

- Detailed knowledge – and competent application – of at least one method
- Critical analysis of one of the standard methods in your discipline, showing that you understand both its strengths and its limitations

Theory

- Understanding of key theoretical strands and theoretical concepts in your discipline
- Understanding how theory shapes your research question
- Ability to contribute something useful to the theoretical debate in your area

Miscellaneous

- Ability to do all the above yourself, rather than simply doing what your supervisor tells you
- Awareness of where your work fits in relation to the discipline, and what it contributes to the discipline
- Mature overview of the discipline

Necessary skills

Those readers who are familiar with *1066 and All That* will be pleased to know that skills are currently viewed as a Good Thing. This is especially the case with skills which can be described as 'transferable skills'. You can therefore treat them as a positive asset, to be added to your CV, rather than as another cheerless obligation. Your institutional training course will probably wax eloquent on skills of various sorts – transferable, generic, project-based, discipline-based (though readers with an interest in BDSM may be disappointed to hear that this does not normally involve whips and leather), and doubtless many others. Transferable skills are particularly favoured by The System because they are allegedly usable in areas other than just academia. They include (depending on whose versions you receive) writing, public speaking and coping with prejudice.

We will pay The System the graceful academic compliment of treating this ground as so thoroughly covered that it does not need to be covered again by us; the rest of this section describes skills which may not be included on your institution's training programme.

Tact and diplomacy

As a PhD student, you need to accept that you are not exactly at the top of the academic pecking order; as a new PhD student, you are also the new kid on the block. There is therefore a time for being right and a time for using the quiet word that gets you what you want. PhD students tend to do a lot of complaining about how The System treats them (often with some justice on their side), but tend to forget that they are in a system which dates back to the Dark Ages, and which has learnt a thing or two about dealing with complaints. An important skill is to learn when to let something pass and when to stand up (tactfully and politely, but firmly) for an issue. Otherwise, you are likely to find yourself winning the battles and losing the war. For instance, you will probably have complaints about the shortcomings of the library; PhD students almost everywhere have complaints about the library, usually ill-founded, so if you get stroppy about this issue, you are unlikely to get a huge amount of sympathy. ('The library doesn't have many books on my area of interest' usually translates into: 'I haven't learnt yet that I should be reading journal articles at this stage' – not the strongest position for winning an argument.) A second example: you may have grave reservations about the quality of the research methods training course that your institution puts on for PhD students. Bear in mind that PhD training courses are still in their early days, and that a tactless confrontation with the professor responsible for the course is unlikely to produce the result that you need; some suggestions, phrased in a face-saving manner, are more likely to achieve this. Remember also that most PhD students know what they *want*, not what they *need*; there is sometimes an enormous difference between the two. This leads on to another important skill.

Having the right cup of coffee

Probably the most important research tool you will encounter is the cup of coffee. Successful students know this; unsuccessful ones tend to wonder why we're wasting time with jokes, and then wonder why the world is so unfair to them. Knowledge is power; rare knowledge is greater power. The best way of finding out what you really need to know is usually to have a cup of coffee with the right person, and to ask their advice (tactfully and diplomatically). Who is the right person? Someone with the knowledge, which for most situations means someone who is not another PhD student – if they're still a student, then no matter how helpful and friendly they are, you can't be sure whether their advice is sincere and right, or sincere and mistaken, since they haven't yet got successfully through a PhD. There are a lot of folk myths in circulation among PhD students. Fellow students are a good source of social support, and of help with tasks like blind judging for data analysis, or with babysitting; they're not a good source of advice about what your thesis should look like, or where to find the equipment you need for your next bit of fieldwork. The right person is someone who has a successful track record in the relevant topic – for instance, supervisors whose students usually have happy endings, chief technicians with a reputation for producing the right bit of kit out of a cupboard when all hope seemed gone, librarians who have helped your friends to find obscure but essential references. Show them due appreciation and treat their advice as confidential unless they specify otherwise. The most useful knowledge is often the sort that people will not want to be quoted on – for instance, hints about good or bad people to ask for help.

Asking the right research question

Once you learn this skill, life becomes very different. We have an entire section on this elsewhere because it's so important; we mention it here because it's well worth mentioning twice.

Academic writing

Writing is indeed a transferable skill; you can transfer academic writing skills from one academic setting to another, and you can transfer business writing skills from one business setting to another. It is quite possible that there are areas where you can even transfer academic writing skills appropriately to industry or vice versa.

Table 1 Ten top tips for research students

Read, read, read	Seasoned researchers typically have an evolving 'reference set' of around 100–50 papers which forms the core of the relevant literature in their specialty, and with which they are conversant. Students need to read enough to form an initial reference set.
Write, write, write	• Writing is a skill that requires practice: the more you write, the easier it gets • You should aim to write up as you go; this will both make it easier at the end (when you rewrite it all) and give you something to show people who are interested in your work • Don't throw writing away; date it and store it in an 'out-takes' file; that material can be useful • Revising is often easier than writing new
Keep an annotated bibliography	This is the single most powerful research tool you can give yourself. It should be a personal tool, including all the usual bibliographic information, the date when you read the paper and notes on what *you* found interesting/seminal/infuriating/etc. about it.
Form an 'informal committee'	Try to find a small set of reliable, interested people who are willing to read for you, comment on ideas, bring literature to your attention, introduce you to other researchers and so on. They may be specialists who can provide expertise on which you can draw, or generalists who ask tough questions.

Expose your work	Make your work public in technical reports, research seminars and conference papers. The best way to get information is to share information; if people understand what your ideas are, they can respond to them. Making your work public exposes you to questions and criticism early (when it can do you some good), helps you to 'network' and gather leads and gives you practice articulating your reasoning.
So what? Learn to ask the other questions	Students often get a result and forget to take the next step. 'Look, I got a correlation!' '*So what?*' Learn to go beyond your initial question, learn to invert the question in order to expose other perspectives and learn to look for alternative explanations.
Never hide from your supervisor	'Hiding' is a pathological behaviour in which most research students indulge at some point. Communicating with your supervisor is a prerequisite to getting the most out of your supervisor.
Always make backups (and keep a set off-site)	More than one student has had to start writing from scratch or to repeat empirical work because he or she neglected this most basic of disciplines.
Read at least one completed dissertation cover to cover	Reading something that has 'passed' is an excellent way to reflect on dissertation structure, content, and style – and on 'what it takes'.
A doctorate is pass/fail	Part of the process is learning when 'enough is enough'.

Terminology: a brief digression

There are various types of research degree; what they have in common is that they involve research by the student as a core component. This is different from a taught degree where there may be a research project (for instance, an MSc project), but where this research project is only one component among many on the course.

Strictly speaking, a research degree involves a thesis, which is the argument that you propose as a result of your research. Again strictly speaking, the dissertation is the written document which describes your thesis. In common usage, the dissertation is often referred to as 'the thesis'. It's worth knowing about the distinction in case you have a particularly pedantic external examiner – it helps you get off to a better start.

Instrumental and expressive behaviour

In fairy tales, you sometimes encounter a magic book. This is usually a book which appears once, in time of need, and which contains the information needed to solve the crisis at the heart of the tale; when the hero or heroine returns afterwards to look for further wisdom, the book has vanished from the place where it was left, never to be seen again. In the tales, finding the book is something which happens once in a lifetime, when you most need it.

Real life isn't quite like that. As we can testify from personal experience, the book can appear more than once in a lifetime, and not always at the immediate point of need. On the first occasion, the book was an anthology of writings about new religious movements, which appeared at the time to be very interesting, but of no immediate relevance to anything that the author was doing. On the second occasion, the book was an extremely good encyclopaedia of psychology, which provided the key information needed for a successful large funding bid. The author neglected to note the full bibliographic reference for either book, and no amount of detailed searching of the relevant libraries (both on the shelves and in the online and printed catalogues) subsequently produced anything quite like those books. These experiences are (a) one of the reasons why we go on at such length about the need for proper bibliographic references for everything you read, and (b) the principal reason for the lack of a proper bibliographic reference for the concepts of instrumental and expressive behaviour which are discussed in this section. If you'd like to track down the original article, it's a chapter describing the de Leonist political movement in the United States, in an edited anthology of writings about new religious movements, which was in the University of Nottingham library sometime between 1986 and 1992 and, yes, we would be very grateful for the full reference if anyone happens to encounter the book somewhere on its travels . . .

The author of the said chapter was a sociologist who was studying the de Leonists. Some of their behaviour made little sense to him – for instance, they once spent a lot of time putting up posters around the city advertising a talk which had already happened. Eventually he realized that they were engaging in what he called expressive, rather than instrumental, behaviour. Instrumental behaviour consists of actions leading towards a stated goal; for instance, the goal of learning to drive a car might involve the instrumental behaviours of booking driving lessons, buying a copy of the *Highway Code* etc. Measured against this criterion, the de Leonists' behaviour appeared senseless. Expressive behaviour, on the other hand, consists of actions demonstrating to other people what sort of person you are; for instance, sitting in the front of a lecture theatre and taking copious notes in a very visible manner to show that you take your studies very seriously. Against this criterion, the de Leonists' behaviour made a lot more sense; much of it was intended to demonstrate group loyalty, and was intended for other members of the group to see. Sticking up large numbers of posters publicizing an event which had already happened could therefore be a good way of demonstrating that you were a committed member of the group and, in consequence, of increasing your standing within the group.

Instrumental behaviour and expressive behaviour are both important. In our experience, students are normally good at some types of instrumental behaviour and woefully bad at the sensible sorts of expressive behaviour, usually because nobody has explained to them which signals they need to send out.

An example of this is the use of bibliographic referencing. At an instrumental level this is important, because inadequate referencing can lead to your being unable to relocate a key text which you read earlier; it is also important for other people who might want to follow up one of your points, or to check one of your assertions (external examiners for PhDs, for instance, often want to do this . . .) At an expressive level, good referencing is also important: it sends out signals saying that you take core academic values seriously, that you are familiar with the core craft skills, that you are thorough and professional, and so forth.

More often, however, students engage in expressive behaviours which send out signals such as 'look how hard I'm trying' – for instance, spending all day every day in the library, regardless of whether what they are reading is particularly useful or not. The usual sequence of events is that the supervisor sooner or later notices that the student is not making any progress, and points this out; the student reacts by even more expressive behaviour sending out the same signal; the supervisor notices continuing lack of progress; and so on, until an ending occurs which is usually unhappy. What students in this situation need to realize is that the problem is not how hard they are trying, but what they are omitting to do. One large part of this book is about the instrumental skills which are needed to do a good PhD, and another large part is about the signals of skilled professionalism which you need to send out via the right sort of expressive behaviour. (There is also yet another large part which is about identifying the wrong sorts of expressive behaviour, and about what to do to rectify them.)

2   Procedures and milestones

Or, what will happen to you

. . . take this woman out of Bren-paidhi's way, or face administrative procedures.

When you do a PhD, you will encounter numerous procedures, milestones, deliverables and the like. These can appear a pointless waste of your time and can cause you much needless grief if you don't approach them in a sensible manner. This chapter discusses how and why you should do this.

In the case of procedures, you need to remember the literature on the theology of just wars. In case this has temporarily slipped your mind, one key conclusion was that there was no point in fighting a battle that you have no hope of winning. Your chances of persuading the institution to change its procedures within the duration of your PhD are somewhere between nil and zero, so what you need to do is to reach a mutually acceptable arrangement with The System. One way of doing this is by viewing the institution's procedures as useful practice for important skills in later academic life, such as applying for large research grants which will fund your trips to conferences in exotic locations, or buy you very large bits of equipment, or whatever else appeals to you. However you choose to view them, the procedures are designed to measure you against a set list of criteria, with imperious disregard for your opinion on the suitability of these criteria for recognizing your genius. What you need to do is to find out what the criteria are and then present the truth about yourself in the way best suited to those criteria. The procedures and The System are then satisfied, duty has been done, and everyone can get on with their lives.

There are several stages that you will undergo on the PhD, each with its own procedures, and each a hurdle which has to be crossed. These are listed below in reverse order, which will probably irritate you initially, since you are likely to be focused on the next stage in front of you, rather than your final destination; however, the whole process makes a lot more sense if you work backwards from the end point.

Procedural stages

Submission and viva

The PhD is a long process which results in one document and one discussion. The document is your written dissertation; the discussion is the *viva voce* examination, or viva, when you are asked penetrating questions by a panel of formidably bright and knowledgeable examiners. When the academic system decides whether or not you should have a PhD, it does this only by assessing your performance in the dissertation and the viva; all your other work is irrelevant. There are three main ways in which people tend to view this:

- you still need to concentrate on each stage and do each properly, because otherwise you won't get to the submission and viva stage;
- all that really matters is the dissertation and the viva, as long as you get through the previous stages somehow;
- all of this is preparation for what you do after you get through the PhD.

The first of these views is popular among administrators and among nervous students (who probably constitute the majority of PhD students), since it reduces the risk of people crashing into early hurdles because they didn't aim to jump high enough. The second is less popular, but is more accurate, though it's open to misinterpretation which can cause you needless grief (for instance, failing to realize that knowing how to deal with procedures is an important skill in later academic life). The third one is the least popular, but is actually the one which will stand you in best stead both for the PhD itself and for life afterwards. We will return to this topic repeatedly throughout this book.

That is the final stage; you may not enjoy it much at the time, but it's actually good for you, and has a reasonable proportion of fairness and sense involved. It is not, however, the only stage. In many institutions, you will have to go through other stages before you reach the viva.

The candidate declaration form

Before you can submit your dissertation, you will have to notify your institution formally that you are ready to do so, using a form called something like the 'candidate declaration form'. This form has two major purposes:

- it requires your supervisors to vouch for the quality of the work, because in signing the form they must declare both that they have read a complete draft and that the work is worthy of examination;
- it sets the machinery in motion to appoint your examiners, a process which may take some time, because it requires the provision of CVs, completion of forms and approval by relevant committees.

The annual report

Each year during your doctoral studies, most institutions require your faculty, department, postgraduate tutor or supervisors to submit an annual report outlining your progress during the year, assessing your continuing potential for PhD completion, and making a recommendation about whether or not to continue your registration. A sensible strategy is to dig out your report from the previous year and write your report for the current year in a way which makes it very clear that you have made progress – members of the relevant committees will probably be checking this year's report against last year's and playing 'spot the difference'.

Transfer

Before you undergo trial by thesis and viva, you go through a process called 'transfer', short for 'transfer of registration to PhD student', also sometimes known as 'passing probation'. This stage is academically as well as administratively important.

Contrary to pessimistic folklore among PhD students, institutions *do* care about whether their PhD students survive or fail, if only because a high incidence of failed PhDs reflects badly on the institution and can affect its funding. One simple and effective way of reducing the number of students who fail at the submission and viva stage is to reroute the problem cases before they reach that stage – if they don't reach it, then they can't fail it. The point at which this is traditionally done is known as the transfer stage. This is a point somewhere between the end of your first year and halfway through the PhD, when you should have done enough work for The System to have a fair idea of your ability. (If you haven't done enough work, or it doesn't give a fair idea of your ability, then this suggests that you are clueless, and should be rerouted on grounds of cluelessness above and beyond the call of duty.) The official way of presenting this is as the point where a decision is made about whether you should proceed to a PhD submission, or should follow another route to another qualification (note that there is nothing in this phrasing about 'failure'; the university system did not survive from the Dark Ages to the present day by being bad at phrasing). Proceeding to a PhD submission is phrased as an active step (hence 'transfer') rather than as the default option.

The transfer is therefore an important stage, which normally involves genuine academic assessment of how you are doing, rather than an administrative convenience. It normally involves you producing two things. One is a substantial document which shows (a) that you have done some decent work and (b) that you know the appropriate academic skills involved in describing and presenting that work. The other is some live performance, either a viva or a department seminar, at which you present your work and demonstrate many of the same things as with the document, except that the skills here involve *spoken* presentation. By an amazing coincidence, these two things can be viewed as useful practice for writing the thesis and undertaking the viva. The purpose of the document and the oral presentation is to demonstrate your competence – not to demonstrate perfection, nor to set your research plan in concrete.

Some students decide, around the transfer assessment, that doing a PhD is not for them. An honourable withdrawal, or an informed choice to undertake an MPhil, is actually a success for the student, the supervisors and The System. It's a much happier option for everyone than years of anxious and often unsuccessful toil.

The lesser transfer

Some institutions have a preliminary stage, a sort of demi-transfer, under a variety of names. Unfortunately, the names are not terribly enlightening or are used in different ways across institutions, so we have made up this term instead. It describes another 'quality control' step, typically 6 to 12 months into the course of study (note that they will probably use some such phrasing, to make it clear that you aren't a full PhD student yet). If it exists at your institution, you need to get through it by filling in the forms correctly and writing the right sort of document to support it, with the right sort of claims about what you are going to do in your research and how you are going to do it. Good strategies include correctly completed forms, neat presentation and spelling, plenty of worthy references to the right literature and a clear, practical-looking workplan. Bad strategies include asking what evidence there is that this stage actually has any value and asking whether they seriously think the workplan is anything more than evidence that you know how to do a workplan.

Signing on

This stage does not involve unemployment benefit; it is our term for the stage where you are accepted by the institution to start studying toward a PhD. It will be called by different names in different institutions, and at least some of these names can be confused with the 'lesser transfer' stage described above, which is why we have used this name.

Note the phrasing: you sign on as a prospective PhD student. The whole process is phrased in terms of your having to make active moves from one stage to another, rather than a default assumption that once you have started a PhD you will automatically end up being examined for one, unless you do something remarkably silly.

Because institutions worry about failure rates, they use procedures to filter applicants. These filters are fairly good at detecting some types of applicants who are disasters looking for somewhere to happen; they can also give the supervisor and the applicant a chance to decide whether they hate one another at first sight. Since the relationship between a supervisor and a student lasts as long as many marriages, and is about as close, this is an important issue. Just how good the filters are at identifying other types of problem student, and at predicting a given applicant's chances of success, is a very different question.

A bit about why procedures are like this

Back in The Past, one popular procedure for a PhD was something along the following lines. You sought out a potential supervisor, told them about your plans to study something and then, if they thought you were worth taking on, you would start a PhD with them, quite probably on a totally different topic from the one you originally intended. You would then potter around doing a PhD with whatever level of supervision your supervisor felt like providing, and be left pretty much in peace until you either submitted your dissertation (quite probably on a different topic both from your original idea and from the one you subsequently changed to) or gave up and did something else instead, like becoming a mushroom farmer in Devon. A second popular procedure was for the department to show a student into a closely packed office, shut the door, open it in three years and demand, 'Are you finished yet?'

Days long past; times long changed. Politicians started asking unpleasant questions about the amount of money being spent on funding PhDs which were never completed, and started making noises about quality and value for money. Funding bodies started insisting on 'best practice'. Motherhood and democracy were praised. Procedures were implemented which, to paraphrase the classic quote, gave the appearance of progress while producing other things.

The result is that you will probably have to go through procedures such as the ones described above. Our advice is to cooperate with them, however much or little sense they seem to make; if they don't seem to make much sense, cooperate with them all the same and save your energy for other battles. Fill in the forms neatly, hand them in before the deadline and, essentially, show the skills that you need to show.

Useful further material

Filling in forms

Some useful habits, in no particular order:

- read every form through to the end before starting to fill it in;
- if the form is important and you only have one copy, photocopy it, and fill in the copy as a practice run before filling in the final version;
- if you're not sure what a particular section means, then refer to the notes – most forms have accompanying notes which most people don't bother to read;
- if you find forms terrifying, ask someone to help you; if your fear is intense, then consider asking for help from someone who deals with phobias – the process is usually fast and surprisingly pleasant;
- photocopy every form that you fill in, after you have completed it, and keep the copies neatly filed – they can be useful reminders for how to fill in the forms, as well as a record of what you claimed last time.

Criteria for a PhD: some reassurance

PhD students often worry about whether their research will be good enough for a PhD. It's useful to remember the criteria which most universities have at the core of their PhD assessment: the PhD is normally described using phrases such as 'an original and significant contribution to knowledge'. By a fortunate coincidence, most successful contributions to journals and conferences are thought of in the same way. Therefore, you can provide evidence of 'significance', 'originality' and 'contribution to knowledge' in advance of submission of your thesis by publishing your work in refereed journals or conference papers. There is more on this at various places later in this book. You don't need to make a major discovery to get a PhD – you just need to show that you're able to do good enough research by yourself.

3   The system

It was here that he first came into conflict with the authorities, and was debarred from future experiments by no less a dignitary than the dean of the medical school himself . . .

This section describes some key features of the academic system. One of these is the academic pecking order – ranks, roles, positions, etc. Another is trouble, in the form of potential sources of trouble from within The System.

Ranks and stations

Academic titles, ranks and roles can trace their heritage back to the time of the Byzantine Empire and beyond. It shows. The account below should be treated as a general set of principles, rather than gospel. It starts with the most menial position, which ranks just above administrators and students on taught courses in the eyes of the research community, and works up to the most exalted. An important point to remember is that although the titles are known and used around the world, the same titles are frequently used in quite different ways in different institutions.

Research assistant

A research assistant is someone who is employed to carry out research for a member of academic staff. This research is usually, but not always, work on a research project, paid for out of a research grant obtained by the member of staff as a result of a successful research proposal to a funding body. This means that the research will probably have been planned in advance, quite possibly in considerable detail. This in turn means that the research assistant's role is mired in ambiguity from the start. The grant-holder will probably take the view that any glory arising from the work (including first authorship of papers) should go to the person who planned the work and obtained the grant which made it possible (namely themselves). The research assistant will probably take the view that the grant proposal consisted largely of a series of plausible claims which could not be translated into meaningful research without a lot of further detailed work, carried out by the research assistant, who should therefore have a fair share of any glory which arises (including first authorship of papers). A standard-issue research assistant who has just completed a first degree is not in a strong position to argue this case. The situation is somewhat different for postdoctoral research assistants, but usually not entirely different.

Postdoctoral research assistants

This title covers an interesting variety of sins and virtues. Postdoctoral research assistants have a PhD of their own, and may be anywhere on a spectrum from fresh young and newly qualified beginners embarking on a career, to massively experienced and often bloody-minded veterans who know at least as much about their area as the grant-holder. Postdoctoral research assistants are often given the title of 'research fellow', which is a fine source of potential confusion, since the same title is used in a very different sense in very old universities.

Lecturers

A lectureship is usually the first solid step on the way to a career. Research assistants normally live from one short-term contract to the next. Lectureships are usually permanent or indefinite in duration, and offer enough stability to let you get things done. There are also important things which you are not usually allowed to do until you are a permanent member of staff, such as applying for research grants from the main funding bodies, so the transition to lecturer is an important one. However, the position of lecturers (as opposed to senior lecturers, Readers, etc.) is demonstrated reasonably clearly by the entry below on cats, which features a true story (one of us knows the room and the armchairs well, though the cat had sadly died before our time there).

Cats

One of our colleagues, when a new lecturer at an old university, was in the senior common room for the first time, looking for somewhere to sit. The senior common room in question is in a country house with wooden panelling and old leather armchairs. The only old leather armchair without anyone sitting in it was occupied by a cat. Our colleague went to evict the cat and take the seat. He was nearly thrown out of the room in disgrace for not realizing that this was the cat's favourite armchair, and for having the temerity to wake it.

Senior lecturers

One grade up from lecturer (and cats), this is the point at which many (perhaps most) academics end up. It's respectable, and it's no disgrace to be at this grade. If you want a career, though, rather than a job, you will need to think about moving on from here, either to become a principal lecturer (PL), a Reader or a professor.

Principal lecturers (PLs)

This role is usually (but not always) treated as an administrative rather than a research role. It is usually (but not always) occupied by harassed, overworked, under-appreciated people who have gone prematurely grey. Few departments would last long without PLs. Most PLs deserve better out of life.

Readers

Spelled with a capital 'R' to make it clear that this is a role, not a simple indication of literacy. Usually a Readership is a stepping-stone to a chair on the research route (yes, we could more helpfully have specified that a 'chair' means a professorship, but that would have spoiled a vivid mixed metaphor); Readers typically move on from this role fairly swiftly, assuming that they are continuing to do the right things which earned them a Readership in the first place – papers out in good journals, research money in and indications of plenty more where that came from. Many people bypass this stage completely – some institutions favour Readerships as a sort of probationary stage, others don't bother with them. Some institutions treat Readerships as broadly equivalent to a proper research fellowship.

Proper research fellows

A full-time permanent research post, usually in a very eminent old university; much coveted, and highly prestigious, though the accommodation may be draughty.

Professors (also known as chairs)

There are several different formal types of professor. To understand this, it is necessary to remember the distinction between a title, a post and a person. Some people are professors because they are occupying a post which brings a chair with it – for instance, the post of Head of the Department of Difficult Concepts might be accompanied by a professorship. Some people are professors because they have successfully applied for a specific chair which has an identity of its own – for instance, the Disney Chair of Archaeology. Others again are professors because they are all-round good eggs (i.e. they have shown such academic merit that they are given their own personal title of 'professor'). Still others are given honorary professorships at other institutions – it is perfectly possible to be a principal lecturer (PL) in Stochastic Ethics at one institution and to be an honorary professor at another institution, both at the same time. Others again are given the title of professor in their own institution, but are employed as Readers. Yet others are emeritus professors because they have done too many worthy things to ignore. Confused? Be honest . . . The situation is worse at American universities, but we won't go into that. By the way, one of the titles in this paragraph is genuine, which just goes to show something, though we're not quite sure what.

How to become a professor is a rich topic; the ground rules will almost certainly have changed by the time most of our readers reach that exalted state, but it's too juicy a subject to ignore. Formally speaking, would-be professors nowadays usually have to submit their applications through a panel, and there are numerous regulations about what needs to be produced as supporting evidence, who can and cannot be on the panel and so forth. The central concept is that the applicant should have a body of work which forms a coherent whole, and which is of at least national significance. Things such as publication rates, income generation, PhD student completions, academic roles and so forth are involved. Formal academic qualifications are splendidly ignored in this process. In fact, many older professors don't have PhDs – the PhD was viewed by many within living memory as a rather dubious foreign innovation.

There is, however, more to the story than this. Anyone who reaches this stage on the slippery pole has to be either reasonably competent at *realpolitik*, or too much of an asset to lose, or both. The adroit applicant will usually have made very sure that they are a significant asset to the institution (or at least to the bit of it concerned with their potential chair). No institution wants to risk losing someone who is a significant asset, so any implicit risk of that person moving elsewhere in high dudgeon after being refused a chair is likely to be treated seriously. Various discreet manoeuvres are likely to be made by both parties at around this stage.

As you have probably guessed by now, the topic of academic ranks, roles and titles is a rich and wonderful world in its own right. Describing it in all its dubious glory would bring death to a large number of trees, so we will draw a discreet close at this point.

Potential sources of trouble: knowing your enemies

Your enemies are not only the wolf-pack (i.e. hostile audiences when you give a talk). Not all of them are people (enemies, that is, not colleagues). Some enemies are things; others are your own habits.

People

The kid in the baseball cap

Baseball caps are very useful to supervisors since they are usually a good indicator of a student whose dissertation should be supervised by somebody else (preferably a loathed colleague). The package which usually accompanies the baseball cap includes idleness, a belief that research is a sissy waste of time anyway, a tendency to search on the internet rather than do a proper literature search and a surprising fondness for badly designed surveys, preferably involving either even more badly designed questionnaires or alleged interviews for which no contemporaneous records were kept. Their theses usually start with some facile truisms about the spread of the internet (or whatever the hot topic is in their field), and then degenerate via bad spelling and appalling grammar into clip art and coloured pie charts in the vain hope that these will impress the examiner.

If you are reading this book, then you are unlikely to belong to this stereotype. However, you need to know about them, since one of their annoying byproducts is to make some topics potential minefields for good researchers.

An example of this is any research topic involving the internet. Since this is a favourite among kids in baseball caps, anyone doing serious research into this area has to make it extremely clear to the reader from the very first sentence that this thesis was not written by someone in a baseball cap. Here are some examples:

Example 1
Successful web page design can be fundamental to the success or failure of a venture on the internet.

Example 2
At the heart of software design is a seldom-acknowledged tension between on the one hand the desire for standards and conventions, and on the other the desire to avoid plagiarism and infringement of copyright.

Example 1 could equally easily have been written by an authority on web design or by someone with only superficial knowledge of the topic.

Example 2 could not have been written without (a) detailed and advanced knowledge of the topic under discussion and (b) some original thought about the topic.

Examples 1 and 2 were both written by the same person. Example 1 was the first draft; Example 2 was the second draft, rewritten with the explicit aim of making it clear that the thesis was not the work of someone in a baseball cap.

Fashions come and fashions go, but the wearers (and their bad habits and their spiritual descendants) will be there for the foreseeable future . . . anyone diligent and hard-working who genuinely likes baseball caps might draw consolation from the thought that someday the baseball cap may be a sign of an excellent student . . .

The informed layperson

Science starts where general knowledge ends. We do not give degrees to people for their store of general knowledge; we mark theses on the basis of how much they go beyond general knowledge.

You need to make it clear how your findings go beyond what an intelligent and well-informed layperson would be able to say from general knowledge. If you can't do this then you will probably fail, and rightly so. Before you even start your data collection, you need to know exactly why you are asking the research question at the heart of your work; if the answers are trivial, general knowledge answers, then there's something seriously wrong with your question. A good question has clear possible answers, each of which would tell you something useful, and preferably have practical as well as theoretical implications.

Advocates of common sense

It's not quite clear what common sense is, but it is widely advocated as an alternative to research. (Asking an advocate of common sense to define exactly what they mean by 'common sense' can be an interesting exercise, if you don't mind being shouted at . . .) The term usually means something involving general knowledge and reasoning from first principles. There are several problems with this. One is that general knowledge is general; it has nothing to say about (for instance) whether autism is a discrete condition or a continuum. The second is that reasoning is a fine thing, but needs to be checked against reality at each link in the chain of reasoning. What usually happens when you do this is that you find a mismatch between reality and prediction every couple of links or so. This is probably one of the reasons why research is widely disliked among the lay public: it is pretty uncomfortable to have your general knowledge and reasoning called into question, and research has an ugly habit of doing just that. A famous Victorian described the tragedy at the heart of science as the slaying of a beautiful theory by an ugly fact. (It doesn't stop researchers constructing more beautiful theories, though . . .) Anyway, that's moving onto a different topic. Back to your enemies.

The external examiner

There are two main types of external examiner. They are actually your friends, but hardly anyone manages to believe that deep down, so they are described here as enemies. They are the sort who either destroy you or make you stronger; Nietzsche would have approved.

If you are undergoing a PhD then you will be examined by your very own personal external examiner (or, more often, two external examiners: institutions vary in their customs). The external examiner will be an authority in the area of your thesis. Externals (to use the normal abbreviation) are frequently nit-picking pedants with a bad habit of reading every single line of your thesis, using a ruler or equivalent to mark their place so they don't miss a line. Their role is to make sure that your work is up to the standard expected of a PhD at any institution in the country. PhD students tend to worry a lot about external examiners, sometimes with good reason.

The regulations usually lay down conditions about who is or is not eligible to be an external. For instance, someone who has co-authored with you on your last three journal papers would normally be judged to have a potential conflict of interests through being too closely involved with your work. This might in extreme cases be a problem, if you are working in a very unusual area where there are very few potential externals. A shrewd supervisor might identify a couple of potential externals at the start of your PhD with the specific aim of ensuring that you keep enough professional distance from them to be able to use them as externals. A sensible supervisor will make sure that the externals have enough standing in the field to be credible, and that they are likely to treat you fairly (not necessarily gently, but fairly). Unfair externals tend not to be invited to many places; word gets around.

The external will be expecting your work to be of a sufficient quality for you to count as 'one of us'. You will need to demonstrate this in the thesis itself (the external will probably never have met you before, and will in any case be looking at the thesis alone, not at how nice a person you are or how hard you have worked). Your thesis needs to look like the work of a professional who pays attention to detail, particularly the details which matter. (Have you ever tried tracking down an article from an incomplete or incorrect reference? If so, you'll know why externals get particular about things like your bibliography.) You need to write like a professional academic writing for other professional academics, not in the simplified language of a textbook or a popular article.

If you are doing an MSc then you have to share your external examiners with everyone else on the course. These externals are chosen to ensure that academic standards are met on the course; they are usually respected figures from another academic institution or from industry.

Your supervisor

Your supervisor has a balancing act to perform. On the one hand, you are a potential source of publications, fame and support in the eternal struggle against chaos, darkness, rivals and suchlike. On the other hand, you require time, attention and energy, all of which are in short supply and could be poured into other things with more obvious short-term pay-offs, such as grant applications, journal papers and professional politics, not to mention doing DIY around the house and occasionally noticing the family.

Supervisors are human, and have remarkably varied approaches to supervision. These range from hiding in a cupboard when they hear you in the distance (allegedly true), to making Zen-like cryptic comments (true, as we can testify from personal experience), to giving detailed blueprints of what to do and how to do it (also true, but not always as much use as you might think). Some are good, and some are bad, but it's not always easy to tell the difference. Being told exactly how to do your particular PhD may feel good at the time, but what happens when you go into your first job and are expected to do things all by yourself, without your supervisor to guide you?

Other students

Other students can be a source of support and inspiration. They can also be a source of misinformation and depression, which is why they are listed here among enemies.

There are all sorts of legends floating round the research student population. One or two of them are probably true, but most are folk myths at best, and dangerously misleading at worst. If in doubt, ask a mentor about the legend, and ask them to explain why it is false (or true). The answers can be very enlightening.

A favourite occupation among research students is gloomily comparing progress ('I only managed to work for 16 hours yesterday. How are you getting on?') This sort of mind game is good for chocolate sales, but not much else. One effective way of getting out of this one is to lie ('Oh, things are great, thanks – lots of interesting results, and the writing up is going well'). This usually deters the doom-mongers pretty quickly and persuades them to leave you alone.

Things

Books

There are different types of book. Textbooks are for undergraduates. They are simplified accounts, made easy for the unenlightened. At postgraduate level you are expected to read the real thing, unsimplified, in all its messy and complex glory. You normally find this in journal articles and some specialist books. Books are only a minor source of cutting-edge information in most sciences;

they are useful reference sources, especially when they are classic texts that changed a field, but they are not usually anywhere near enough by themselves.

The reason for this involves resources. Books take a lot of time and effort to write; there's also no point in writing a book unless you have a bookful of things to say. Usually the findings from an individual piece of research are about enough to fill a chapter in a book, or, by a fascinating coincidence, a journal article. Also, the findings of most individual pieces of research are unlikely to be of sufficient interest to the world to sell more than a handful of books. For a career researcher, it's no contest: the same amount of effort can produce either several years' worth of good journal papers which will be read by most serious players in the field, or one book which will probably sell only a few copies. (Textbooks and reference books are different; they are written with the market in mind. However, they are not intended to be used as primary research tools.)

There are, however, books which are invaluable and often classic sources of information. For instance, the classic text on the shortcomings of human judgement and decision making is a book edited by Kahneman, Slovic and Tversky. Writing a book like this can make a great difference to a career, provided that you can find a topic which will repay the effort.

One useful thing you can do with books is to get an overview of an area when you are deciding whether or not to delve into it. A book chapter normally has about the right level of detail for this – for instance, if you were wondering whether or not to include something about game theory in your research, a book or journal article on the topic would probably overwhelm you, but a book chapter would be a lot more manageable. It would also give you the conceptual framework you need to make sense of the more detailed and advanced literature if you decide to follow that line.

Journals

Journals are your friend, but we've included them here so we can make some points again. You should read lots of journal articles, including ones outside your field, from time to time, as a source of interesting insights into other disciplines. You never know when these might come in useful. If you're in a science or related discipline, it's also useful to read *New Scientist*, *Science*, *Nature* and *Scientific American* as a way of keeping up to date with what's happening elsewhere. Whatever your discipline, you should know which the main journals are in your field and read them regularly.

If you are a PhD student, you should be aiming to publish in journals. It is not as hard as people believe, if you know what you are doing. Reading the section on getting articles published in journals (see p. 85) is a good start; so is reading the 'Notes to contributors' section of your target journal (a surprising number of people don't bother, and pay the price for their sloth).

The internet

The internet (or more precisely, in most cases, the worldwide web) is much loved by kids in baseball caps. It is useful for known-item searches, where you want a single answer to a clear question such as 'When was the battle of Wagram?' (You may not get a single answer, and if you do, it may be wrong, since the internet puts you at the mercy of every teenager in Idaho who can put up a web page full of unreliable facts, but usually you will get a decent answer.)

For anything else (e.g. 'Who really wrote the *Consolatio?*'), the web is a treacherous, unreliable and usually amateurish source of information, misinformation and downright lies. A search may happen to find a brilliant, relevant and up-to-date reference; however, as a source of overviews about what is going on in the field it is pretty much useless. What you find on the web reflects what has been put on the web (and also the quality of your search). A lot of the sites on the web were put there by people with very strange agendas (trying to find out anything about the pyramids via the web will tell you everything you ever wanted to know about extraterrestrial visitors and conspiracy theory, for instance . . .)

You have no way of knowing what sort of match there is between what is actually going on and what has been put on the web. For systematic information about research in your field, you need to use proper sources of information such as bibliographic databases, which will accurately reflect the work going on in the field. You should know what the main sources are for your area, and should be on friendly terms with the relevant librarians who can be invaluable allies. Learning how to do a proper search is also an invaluable help.

Habits

Learned helplessness

If you give animals electric shocks when they attempt escape, in a situation where they can't escape, eventually they stop trying to escape, even when the situation changes and escape is possible. (Like Milgram's conformity experiment, the research behind this finding would probably not get past an ethics committee today, but is invaluable as an insight into apparently unlikely behaviour.)

PhD students are particularly prone to this feeling, and usually go through at least one phase of feeling that they are getting nowhere and that there is no point in keeping going. If this is an accurate description of how you're feeling, then pull yourself together long enough to eat some chocolate and acquire a self-help book (e.g. *Feel the Fear and Do It Anyway*). Read the book, set yourself some manageable goals that are at least vaguely relevant and talk things through with someone who can give you sensible supportive advice. Also, get some exercise away from your usual haunts, to help acquire a sense of perspective. Once you've done this, you should be sufficiently clear of the immediate doldrums to be able to plan a sensible way forward for yourself.

One of the advantages of well-designed research is that you should know precisely what you are doing at each stage of the research, and what you will do in response to each eventuality that might come along. The bad news is that this might involve knowing in advance that you will go through a long phase of data crunching; the good news is that if you know this, you should know precisely how to crunch the data, and what to do with the results when you finally get them. If you don't know this in advance, then you need to rethink your research design.

Expressive behaviour

Expressive behaviour often accompanies learned helplessness. Instrumental behaviour is behaviour which moves you towards your goals. Expressive behaviour is behaviour intended to demonstrate to others what sort of person you are. A student sitting in the library wading through the six key texts for their area of research is engaging in instrumental behaviour. The student sitting at the next table reading the same page of an irrelevant paper over and over again in a state of nervous collapse is going in for expressive behaviour ('Look how hard I'm working! Please have mercy . . .') The student who produces a thesis containing all the features that their external examiners love is also engaging in expressive behaviour, but of a much more useful sort. Unfortunately for some, examiners mark what you produce, not what sort of person you are; the brilliant piece of work by someone who hacked it together in a couple of days will be better received than a mediocre piece of work produced by someone who laboured over it for months.

Taking ages to get nowhere

There are several quite different reasons for this, with different implications.

Reason 1: you are taking ages to get nowhere because you don't have the faintest idea what you are doing and where you are going. If you suspect this is the case, draw a diagram. It consists of an arrow going into a box. The arrow is your research question, the box is the data collection and analysis. Now draw arrows emerging from the box, with each arrow representing a different logically possible outcome from the data collection and analysis. For instance, the outcomes may be 'A is greater than B', 'A is smaller than B' and 'A and B are the same size'. You should be able to list all the possible outcomes and explain why each one tells you something useful and significant. You should also know exactly what form your data will take and how you are going to analyse it, right down to the level of what tables you will use to show your results. (You should not, however, have more than a shrewd suspicion which particular answer you will find, otherwise the research is probably too trivial to bother with.)

If you fail this test, then you are taking chances and may well end up getting nowhere. Redesigning your research is a good idea in such cases;

it doesn't mean that you have to use quantitative methods or whatever your personal bugbear is, or that you have to abandon your area of research. It simply means that you have to revise your question so that it's guaranteed to reduce the problem space (i.e. eliminate a set of possibilities which had previously seemed plausible), rather than being a bet on a particular finding. Gambling with several years of your life is not usually a wise idea, and undertaking research only if you are sure that the results will confirm your initial beliefs is a very dodgy undertaking – what would you do if the data disagreed with your initial beliefs? Fiddle the data or face the prospect of changing your opinions?

Reason 2: (in no particular order) you are taking ages to get nowhere simply because you are in the middle of a PhD or an MSc project. If you pass the diagram test and are more than a third of the way through your planned time, then this is likely to be the explanation. The 'second-year blues' are a fairly normal part of doing a PhD.

Reason 3: you are engaged in an *invisible support activity*. These are essential to good research, but by definition involve effort with no visible output. Examples range from stocking up your stationery, to checking whether anyone has done any previous work similar to your next intended piece of research, to doing general background reading (as opposed to focused reading). You have to do these things. Stationery is essential, as is background checking.

General reading is highly advisable, since a lot of the best work comes from applying work from one area to another area. (One of us once supervised an undergraduate dissertation which took a nineteenth-century researcher's formalisms for describing the structure of Russian folk tales and applied them to the plots of computer games . . . excellent and highly entertaining work, with a lot of implications for the computer games industry, but not exactly the sort of thing which is likely to emerge from focused reading.) The trouble is that you can never tell in advance when something will be useful or where; the Russian folk tale idea derived from reading about the topic some 20 years previously. The good news is that when you do encounter a relevant area for this sort of cross-fertilization you can produce brilliant work for very little apparent effort. This is one area where keeping your ideas to yourself until you're ready to publish might be advisable, since the important issue is the concept of applying one particular body of work to another area, rather than the actual findings.

Other assorted bad habits

There are numerous other bad habits which afflict researchers, such as bad time management, procrastination and not bothering to become familiar with the tools of the trade. If you are to sort yourself out properly, you need to learn how to identify and correct bad habits. That doesn't mean you have to proceed to correcting them. Many habits, such as following an interest regardless of whether it looks like a good career move, are personal choices and you might decide that the positive side of the habit is well worth the price. Others, though, such as refusing to accept that you are wrong, are bad for you. You won't improve without change; you won't undergo change without pain. Learn to accept the pain as a friend and your life will be transformed.

Those of you who are worried about the long-term consequences of close familiarity with pain might be reassured to learn that there are ways of tackling research which involve a minimum risk of having to admit that you are wrong. Phrasing the research question in such a way that you have not committed yourself to any of the possible outcomes is a good example of this: whatever happens (short of a total shambles) you will have proof of your brilliance in identifying the right question in the first place. This is probably a good place to end this chapter, before uneasy images of BDSM and leather start to creep into the darker corners of your subconscious . . .

4   Supervision

Or, PhDs, marriage and desert islands

Could that fellow have me whipped?

When you become a PhD student, you embark on what is likely to be an intense relationship, both personally and professionally, with your supervisor. It's likely to be different from your previous academic relationships, because as a research student you'll take up much more of your supervisor's attention and time. You can't hide among the other students the way you could on a taught course if you wanted to keep a low profile for whatever reason; you're a visible individual as a PhD student.

Similarly, your supervisor is going to be a lot more important to you than your undergraduate project supervisor, who was only one member of staff among many.

A good relationship between student and supervisor needs work by both parties. It isn't your supervisor's responsibility to make everything all right; it's up to both of you to work together. Many doctoral students encounter unnecessary problems because they make classic mistakes in dealing with their supervisors. Unfortunately, our experience is that most students don't think this relationship through, and that most supervision problems are predictable and preventable. So, it's time to start thinking things through ... If you've already thought these things through, then you will be much more likely to be viewed as an asset to your supervisor and the department, and to finish with a happy ending.

Most PhD horror stories have their origins in the supervisory relationship rather than in the research topic or the external examiner. The most common cause is that the student didn't take the supervisor's advice. Less common, though not unknown, is horror due to an incompetent supervisor. The current trend is for PhDs to be supervised by more than one supervisor, which reduces the risk of your having a rogue incompetent supervising you; in addition, departments normally pay keen attention to students' performance at stages such as the transfer seminar, where incompetence is usually spotted and subsequently investigated.

The relationship between student and supervisor is about as close as many marriages, and lasts as long as many marriages. It's a fairly good analogy in several ways. One important issue is compatibility. Nobody in their right mind would expect to have a happy marriage if they married the first single person they met; similarly, you can't expect that your relationship will be equally straightforward with every potential supervisor you might meet. Likewise, it's not your supervisor's job to put up with every unpleasant idiosyncrasy of every idiot who wants to do a PhD with them. As a student, you are an apprentice, not a customer who is always right.

Also on the subject of rightness, there isn't a single type of 'right' student or 'right' supervisor, any more than there is a single type of 'right' partner. There are various types of supervisor, and various types of student; each type of supervisor will be well suited to some types of student, and less well suited to other types of student. At this point, the marriage analogy starts to become somewhat strained. In the old days, a high proportion of students signed up to do a PhD with a specific supervisor; now it's increasingly common for students to sign up with a department, and then to be issued with a supervisor or, more often, a supervisory team. A closer analogy for this situation is two or three survivors shipwrecked on a desert island and having to learn not just to get along with each other but also to work constructively together, regardless of whether they would have chosen each other as companions if they had had a choice. Sitting on the beach complaining that the other survivors aren't perfect human beings isn't going to get a fire lit; similarly, sitting at your desk expecting your supervisor to be perfect isn't going to get your dissertation written. You have to make the most of what you've got, unless the situation is completely pathological (discussed in more detail below). Note that this is an active process, not a passive one; you don't simply put up with the situation that you first encounter, but instead you identify the resources you've got and then put them to the best use you can. With this in mind, it's a good idea to assess yourself in relation to your personality and your needs as a student, so that you can assess what you would like from your supervisor and how to set about obtaining those things in a way which suits you both. Relevant factors usually include your need for technical support; your need for emotional support; your need for guidance and structure in planning the work; your ability to handle criticism; and your ability to deliver on time, to the agreed standard.

It's also a good idea to ask yourself which of your characteristics (a) will make you awkward for anyone to supervise and (b) are likely to lead to problems with a particular type of supervisor. You should then think about which of these things you are willing to improve and what the implications are for how you approach your supervisor and your PhD.

The role of the supervisor

Another fruitful area for misunderstanding involves what services supervisors are supposed to provide. Students seldom think much about this.

One common misconception is that the supervisor is a purely technical resource, there to provide expertise in (for instance) the obscure area of Unix programming that you are studying for your PhD. Students with this misconception typically encounter problems when their supervisor doesn't have the answer to an obscure technical question; such students typically complain loudly that the supervisor is incompetent, and then wonder why they receive so little sympathy from the department. The purpose of the PhD is to demonstrate that you can operate as an independent researcher and uncover new knowledge; if you expect your supervisor to know more than you about every aspect of your PhD, then you have missed the whole point.

There are many different ways to supervise a PhD, and many different roles which a supervisor can have; each student is different and will require different support. At one extreme is the student who can be pretty much left to get on with it, with supervisory meetings being something that both parties enjoy, and where each party learns from the other. This is rare, but it does happen. Such students don't always have brilliant academic grades from their first degree; what they tend to have in common is a willingness to learn for themselves and good judgement about when to stop and ask for feedback. At the other extreme is the student who doesn't take the initiative about anything, who needs constant feedback, active encouragement and who appears to expect a worrying degree of spoonfeeding. For students at the first end of the spectrum, supervisors will often be very busy behind the scenes, trying to find funding for the student after they graduate; for students at the other end of the spectrum, the supervisor may have different priorities.

The minimum supervisory role involves filling in the relevant forms as you progress through The System, writing annual reports, liaising with the organization where you are doing your fieldwork etc. Beyond that, there are numerous possible roles, which may or may not be relevant to your case, and which will probably be invisible to you.

Other roles include:

- **Specific technical support:** for instance, skills training in using the library or specialist software; pointers to relevant literature; providing contacts with other researchers; guidance on structuring the thesis; training in critical reading.
- **Broader intellectual support:** for instance, helping the student develop skills in discussion and critical thinking; providing high-level knowledge about the field and about research issues in the field; providing specialist expertise in conducting studies in the field.

- **Administrative support:** for instance, finding funds; finding other resources; protecting you from political and administrative difficulties within the institution; publicizing your work.
- **Management:** for instance, providing a structure (meetings, deadlines, goals); deadline creation and enforcement.
- **Personal support:** for instance, career advice, emotional support and counselling.

If you're feeling cynical about this, it's worth remembering that the student's performance reflects on the supervisor who has to undergo, among other things, institutional procedures and reports (including scrutiny of PhD failure rates); supervisors' meetings; peer scrutiny at transfer seminars; research assessment exercises; and scrutiny from funding bodies.

Why do people become supervisors? It's certainly not for the money as supervision is almost never remunerated. And it's not for release from other tasks, since workload planning almost always underestimates the time supervision takes. There are many reasons, ranging from a direct order from the head of department, via a feeling of duty, on through mercenary self-interest (such as using the students to further the supervisor's career), to idealism and a love of working with students.

Whatever the supervisor's motivation, it's in both your interests to get along. Whatever the moral rights and wrongs of a particular issue, it's very much in your interests to make the relationship work; failing your PhD is much more of a disaster for you than it is for your supervisor, so expecting your supervisor to do all the running in your relationship is not an advisable strategy. It is, as usual, a good idea to try seeing things from their perspective. If you were asked to supervise an undergraduate project, what sort of student would you want to supervise and what sort would you not want to supervise at any cost? Once you've thought about that for a while, try looking long and hard at your own behaviour from that point of view: how often have you missed a meeting, turned up late, turned up unprepared, expected your supervisor to do all the thinking and so forth?

You are ultimately responsible for your work; your supervisor is not. Taking your share of responsibility in the supervisory relationship is good practice for the dissertation and viva, where the burden is on the student to communicate – if the thesis is unclear to the examiner, it's the student's problem, not the examiner's. So practise on your supervisor. Decide what you want from the PhD and from the individual meetings, and communicate this to your supervisor.

As with marriage, it's worth putting the effort in, because the relationship is likely to last at least three years, and a good supervisory relationship will benefit you for the rest of your career. Also as with marriages, it can be useful at times to remember that supervisors are human too – they'll have bad days and human failings. Be realistic and forgiving in your expectations and the chances of a happy ending for you both are much better.

Practical ways of establishing a good relationship with your supervisor

As usual, try looking at it from the other person's point of view – most of the answers will then become pretty obvious. Supervisors are research-active academics and research-active academics are hideously overworked. PhD students take up time, which is the supervisor's scarcest resource, and are in that sense a liability. A sensible student will reduce their liability rating; a good student will find ways of being a positive asset.

Reducing the liability rating mainly involves basic professional courtesies. It's your PhD, not the supervisor's; if you can't be bothered to work on making it happen, why should they? Making it happen includes making supervision meetings work: you should take the initiative in setting up the meetings, circulating relevant information in advance, drafting an agenda and coming with a clear set of things to report and questions to ask. Something which is easily overlooked is that you should also minute the meeting, recording decisions and actions, and circulate those minutes afterwards, then check that the actions are in fact done. A related issue in many organizations is keeping logs of meetings for The System.

Running meetings properly is a rare skill, so we've summarized the key points here – this particular skill is valuable in most walks of life.

Several days before the meeting, the organizer of the meeting should:

- circulate the agenda;
- check that the venue is still available, if it isn't the supervisor's office;
- remind people of the time and place of the meeting;
- circulate any briefing material, including minutes of the last meeting.

During the meeting, the chair of the meeting should:

- record the date and the parties present;
- check that everyone agrees with the minutes of the last meeting;
- check that actions from the last meeting have all been done;
- record any decisions made, including milestones and deliverables (and check that everyone agrees with this record);
- record any actions agreed (and check that everyone agrees with this record);
- fix the time and place of the next meeting.

After the meeting:

- the organizer should write up the minutes and distribute them;
- everyone should do what they have agreed to do.

There are different types of meeting, suitable for different purposes. The description above relates to formal meetings, but PhDs also require informal meetings when you explore ideas or discuss your longer term career plans, or work through a problem which is bothering you. These usually take place over the legendary cup of coffee.

Some classic irritating habits which students often show in relation to meetings include the following:

- failing to take deadlines seriously;
- failing to respect the supervisor's time pressures (you are but one demand among many);
- dumping demands on the supervisor at the last minute instead of allowing them time for reading, thinking, enquiring etc.;
- expecting the supervisor to read every draft, usually by the next day;
- expecting the supervisor to organize everything;
- organizing things without consulting the supervisor (independence is good up to a point, but you need to check you're being independent in the right way).

Dealing with your supervisor

There are various strategies which students can use to make life better for all parties in the PhD, but which are not as widely used as they should be. These include:

- exchanging favours, such as tracking down an obscure reference for your supervisor in exchange for some advice about a job application (but make sure that the exchange is agreed explicitly, so you both know where you stand);
- showing explicitly that you value your supervisor's knowledge and experience;
- trying to do something the supervisor's way, but setting criteria and a date for evaluation of the success of it (especially if you're reluctant);
- not just refusing to do something you don't like, but offering an alternative instead;
- being scrupulous about giving credit where credit is due (e.g. when you publish papers);
- finding out about your supervisor's research – surprisingly few students do this, even though their supervisor's research is probably one of the most valuable resources available;
- allowing your supervisor to be human – tolerating human weaknesses, and making the most of your supervisor's strengths.

What to put in

The supervisory relationship is a two-way one; you are supposed to be actively learning, not passively waiting to be told all the answers.

At the most academic level, you should be actively finding things out and actively generating ideas. One sign that you're doing a proper PhD is that you are finding out things which are new to your supervisor; another is that your supervisor finds at least one of your ideas sufficiently interesting to merit genuine engagement and discussion. It's useful as well as courteous to give your supervisor a précis of what you've found, and to offer full copies of any material that the supervisor would like to read in more detail.

At the implementation level, you should be generating ideas about specific research questions to ask and specific research methods to investigate them. You should be doing this increasingly as the PhD progresses and you learn more. Your supervisor will probably advise against most of these ideas; what you need to do is to assess the reasons for this advice, rather than going into a corner and sulking. One thing which most students never consider is that a good supervisor will be generating ideas about their own research all the time, and discarding the vast majority of them on various grounds. If you expect to have a higher hit rate than your supervisor while you're still an apprentice, then you're being a bit silly.

What to ask for

There are various things that you should ask for, with appropriate courtesy, at various stages of your PhD.

From an early stage, you should ask for appropriate training, both in research methods relevant to your research and also in other areas which will help you – for instance, many students would benefit from assertiveness training and relaxation training, as well as time management and numerous other ancillary skills. You should ask specifically for skills advice if you need it (e.g. what is the form of a conference paper; how does one read a paper and make notes about it?) It's particularly helpful if the supervisor can work through an example with you, rather than just telling you how to do it. A lot of students are embarrassed to ask for this sort of advice on the grounds that they think they should already know it. That's a faulty assumption. The point of the PhD is that it's about learning these skills; if you had them already, there wouldn't be much point in doing the PhD.

When you are at a later stage and have some findings to discuss, you can ask your supervisor to recommend (or introduce you to) other experts who might help. This needs to be done with discretion. Your supervisor will probably not introduce you to someone who will steal and publish your ideas (a frequent source of generally unfounded nightmares for PhD students), but you do need to have enough knowledge of academic etiquette to handle such encounters properly.

What to tell your supervisor

You should keep your supervisor informed:

- about the state of your work;
- about what interests you and what concerns you;
- about outside opinion: report feedback from talks and papers accurately and promptly; be specific about both compliments and criticisms;
- about decisions and turning points (the supervisor can often provide helpful insight and forestall hasty misjudgements);
- about life circumstances: let your supervisor know about personal or practical matters that are affecting your work, preferably before they turn into a major issue.

Things you can do for yourself

There are also various things you can do for yourself. You should keep your supervisor briefed about all of these, in advance. This is partly common courtesy and partly practical self-interest (so that the supervisor can stop you if you're about to do something remarkably stupid on your own initiative).

Another thing worth doing is to assemble an informal 'committee' of people (both staff and students, both in the department and external) who are able and willing to help with your PhD. The key thing to remember is that this is to complement your supervisor, not as an alternative to your supervisor. The informal committee can be helpful for things ranging from low-level logistics (e.g. babysitting) and low-level practical skills (e.g. learning how to use your computer properly) up to general emotional support and specific academic advice on topics complementing your supervisor's advice (e.g. help translating foreign language articles about your area of research).

Another thing you can do is to give seminars and/or circulate draft papers. This both gives you experience and provides you with feedback.

In brief, there are a few cardinal rules about dealing with your supervisor which are subtly different from the three golden rules of public presentation described elsewhere in this book. When dealing with your supervisor, you should:

- be honest;
- be articulate (say what you mean and what you need);
- be informative (keep the supervisor informed);
- be respectful;
- be adult (i.e. responsible for yourself).

Supervisor caricatures

Although every supervisor is different, there are, to paraphrase Evingolis, patterns which fall within a frame and we have categorized some classic types of supervisor below. The descriptions contain a fair amount of caricature, but also enough accuracy to be worth noting. We have divided them into generally bad, tolerable and good, though this interacts with personality types – a particular student might get along well with a supervisor whom every other student in the department finds intolerable.

The generally bad

The catatonic: does nothing unless asked; apparently without emotion; supervision is wholly reactive, as they wait for the student to run the meetings, make suggestions etc.

The sexist/racist/general bigot: 'Women/Welsh people/arts graduates just don't have the thrust and drive for research'.

The slave driver: makes all the decisions; treats student like a lackey; publishes student's results and forgets to include student's name on the authorship list.

The generally tolerable

The assembly line manager: ('crank 'em out') produces PhDs to a formula; directs students into topics (often subsidiary to one of the supervisor's funded projects) over which the supervisor has control; usually runs an empire. Will probably see you through a PhD efficiently but impersonally; will probably drop you if you become a liability; will not be very interested in whether the PhD topic you do is the right one for your future plans.

The good buddy: tries to run supervisions in the pub; spends lots of energy on discussing interesting but extraneous topics; knows all about your personal life. This may sound fun, but such supervisors may not be able to provide the structure you need and may make you feel uncomfortable about the degree of their intrusion into your life.

The formal traditionalist: stiff, formal, plays strictly by the rules; may be good for teaching you the formally correct way of doing things. On the negative side, often expects their name on all papers regardless of amount of personal input; usually does not welcome any discussions outside research; often has condescending assumptions about students.

The absentee: usually over-committed, but sometimes actively hiding. If faced by this, you need to find out which category they are in. Over-committed people can sometimes be excellent supervisors if you can catch them (they are often over-committed because they're so good that they're dragged into all sorts of responsibilities); actively hiding supervisors are unlikely to be of much help to you.

The schoolmaster: sets assignments, guides with a firm hand, has strong ideas about how things should be (may provide necessary structure in the first year, but may not give you enough room for growth in subsequent years).

The novice: you may be your supervisor's first student. This doesn't mean that you won't pass, or that the supervisor won't be useful. Usually these days novice supervisors are part of a team for their first student, so you're unlikely to end up with a novice as your sole supervisor. Novices can be very conscientious and keen, because they're keen to get it right, but they will probably not know as much about *realpolitik* and the field as someone more experienced.

The lightweight: neither a profound researcher nor a deep thinker, but may well be a conscientious supervisor; lack of innovative flair may not impede their ability to recognize good ideas or nurture a good student. If your supervisor is of this sort, then make use of what skills they *do* have.

The boffin: loves technical detail and gadgetry; phenomenally knowledgeable but loses sight of the big picture (don't get lost in technical detail – look elsewhere for strategic advice).

The bumbler: well-meaning, knowledgeable and committed, but slightly inept, absent-minded or insensitive (ignore the presentation and concentrate on the substance).

The Zen master: gives cryptic advice, often via anecdotes, parables and obscure references; may give little help with structure or detail, but may work well with a strong student who can handle independence and who can appreciate the insights behind the inscrutability.

The generally good

There is only one type of generally good supervisor:

The idealized academic: respected researcher; experienced supervisor; approachable; reasonable; balances guidance with license and specific support with spoonfeeding. If you have one of these, you should show appreciation via visible professionalism, and learn as much as you can from them.

Most supervisors are combinations of two or more of these types, and play different roles at different times. A supervisor who's perfect in the first two years may not be able to support you through dissertation writing. Recognize and use your supervisor's strengths. Recognize others who can shore up your supervisor's weaknesses. Recognize the difference between a normal, imperfect supervisor and a supervisor gone wrong.

Strategies for when things go wrong

When, not *if*: in something which lasts as long as a PhD, and which involves learning new skills and engaging in a long-term relationship with a fallible human being, something *will* go wrong. The key questions are what that thing will be and what you are going to do about it.

Most difficulties in the supervisory relationship are 'cock-ups' rather than 'conspiracies'. Always start from the assumption that all parties are acting in good faith. As is often the case, prevention is the best cure: if you have good work habits (e.g. networking effectively, keeping good records, letting other people know what you're working on, publishing internal and external reports promptly, communicating clearly and promptly), then many difficulties can be avoided altogether. Good habits will also make early diagnosis easier. Good communication can usually sort problems out before they become serious.

A classic example is dealing with the supervisor who is never available. Make friends with your supervisor's secretary; get to know your supervisor's schedule; and make sure your supervision meetings are on that schedule. Discuss the problem with your supervisor. Explain your needs. You may not be able to reduce the travel schedule of an international expert, but you can probably work out means for remote communication, so you can still get advice when your supervisor is away. Use your informal committee to fill in when your supervisor is otherwise occupied – and keep your supervisor informed about developments.

If you are convinced that you have the wrong supervisor and you can articulate *exactly* what quality or problem is irredeemably fatal to the supervisory relationship then you'll need to find a new supervisor. It's crucial that you find the replacement before rocking the boat, otherwise you'll destroy the relationship you have, and you'll have ruined your reputation with everyone else. The point is to find a better match, not to throw verbal rocks at your present supervisor. So find positive reasons for the change (different research specialism, better personality fit). The more diplomatically you handle the transition, the better it will be for you and for everyone else involved.

There are some classic problems that are usually fatal to the supervisory relationship, sometimes immediately, sometimes late in the PhD, when change is most difficult. These are in a different league to the inevitable misunderstandings, arguments, disagreements and suchlike that occur in any PhD.

The really serious problems include the following:

- **'isms:** sexism, racism, anti-Semitism, etc. Most institutions have procedures for dealing with this. Whether or not you want to become embroiled in formal procedures, you should find a new supervisor.
- **Intellectual property issues:** 'absorption' or theft of work, obstruction of research, suppression of results. Good habits (like letting people know what you're working on, writing up results promptly) can help here, but sometimes they are not enough.
- **Non-communication:** when no matter what you try, you can't get through.
- **Harassment:** sexual harassment, bullying, damaging insensitivity. Again, most institutions have procedures for dealing with this, or at least a trained person to help you deal with it.

If you find yourself in any of the above situations, you must proceed with extreme care and diplomacy. You will need to:

1 Find out exactly how supervision is coordinated in your department; there will be a procedure for changing supervisor. The bottom line is that, once it has accepted you, the university has an obligation to find someone to supervise you. There may be a bullying and harassment policy which is applicable. Go about this investigation discreetly.
2 Establish the paper trail: write things down, keep all emails etc. Write down the facts, with dates and details, as dispassionately as you can. If there really is a problem, the facts will speak for themselves.
3 Consult a third party, confidentially. There is often a designated third party, a 'third-party monitor' (whose job it is to review the progress of the supervisory relationship), a postgraduate tutor (who oversees all research student supervision), a professor or director of research, an equal opportunities officer, a research dean. Sometimes there is an accessible Wise Person in the department, often one of the professors, someone who has been around and knows the ropes and who is kindly and sympathetic. Sometimes it will be easier to speak to someone outside your department. In any case, choose an academic who is experienced and respected as well as compassionate. Speak as calmly and dispassionately as you can, bring along your documentation, ask for advice and listen.
4 Call in a third party (not necessarily the same one that you consult for advice). It may be appropriate to ask someone – usually someone senior – to act on your behalf. This person can sit in on your supervision, in order to see what's going on, can intervene with your supervisor, or can help you through the procedures. Choose your third party carefully and listen to the advice this person gives you.

It's usually better not to get into this situation in the first place; a cup of coffee in a tactful way can make an enormous amount of difference (for instance, a cup of coffee with someone discreet who can give you some hints about your potential supervisory team). Assertiveness training can also help prevent some situations arising.

A simple scheme for effective supervision meetings

- **Provide a discussion document:** send something to your supervisors a week before the meeting (this can be a progress report, a study plan, a critique of the literature you've been reading, an annotated bibliography, data, a draft conference paper – whatever represents what you're working on). Having something concrete to discuss always helps, and preparing something can be a good way to focus your thinking. Bring copies of the discussion document to the meeting.

- **Provide key publications:** send copies of papers you consider to be seminal to your supervisors in advance of the meeting, particularly if you wish to discuss them. Make sure the full citation is marked on the copy. Providing papers is a courtesy you can do your supervisor, and having them on hand can facilitate discussion.
- **Show up on time:** if you're late, bring sin-offerings, such as chocolate biscuits.
- **Write down your objectives:** know what you want to get out of the meeting, whether it's technical, administrative or emotional. Give yourself a prioritized checklist in advance. It helps to have something interesting to discuss when you enter the meeting – if you don't have ideas, then prepare questions.
- **Check the agenda with your supervisors:** find out what your supervisors want to get out of the meeting. Agree an agenda.
- **Behave well:** listen and consider before you speak. Be prepared to give a candid account of your progress. Ask the obvious questions – they may seem stupid to you, but they rarely are. It's horribly easy to overlook the obvious. Focus on ideas, not emotions. Trust your supervisor and don't take things personally. Make counter-proposals if you don't like what your supervisors are advising – this can help expose discrepancies in your thinking and help you understand the rationale for your supervisor's guidance.
- **Take notes.**
- **Book the next meeting:** set a date for your next meeting before you leave. Set a preliminary agenda.
- **After the meeting, email an action-item summary:** immediately after the meeting, write a list of agreed action items (both yours and your supervisor's), with deadlines if possible, and email it to all concerned, asking for confirmation that you've summarized correctly. Include the date of the next meeting.

Some classic ways to undermine your relationship with your supervisor

- Hiding (yourself, or real or imagined problems)
- Ignoring (advice you don't understand; advice you don't like)
- Mixing (business with pleasure or with personal issues)
- Gossiping (about your supervisor or colleagues)
- Denigrating (your supervisor, department or institution)
- Bypassing (your supervisor, by making decisions without due consultation)

- Assuming (what something meant; what you're entitled to do)
- Sinning (illegal or unethical acts – these are in a different league from the failings listed above)

If in doubt, ask. This is particularly important in relation to assuming and sinning. Students often don't check that they really understand something that they're not quite sure about, and then end up with serious misunderstandings and serious problems. Similarly, students often have mistaken understandings of what is considered reasonable; for instance, is it reasonable or not to phone your supervisor at home without explicit prior agreement? Illegal acts are usually fairly easy to identify, but unethical ones may require much more knowledge. For instance, thanking respondents by name in the acknowledgements section may be intended as a sign of genuine appreciation, but may breach their anonymity and lead to significant professional and legal problems. Commercial sensitivity is another problematic area, as is publication of draft material. If in doubt, ask . . .

5   Networks

The first horrible incident of our acquaintance was the greatest shock I ever experienced, and it is only with reluctance that I repeat it.

Contrary to a widespread belief among the general public and among depressed second-year PhD students, you don't complete a PhD in gloomy isolation. There are lots of people who help you, not just through your doctoral research, but also throughout your subsequent career; there are more who can help you, if you find them. This network won't be confined to eminent academics who are noted experts. It will more usefully also include lesser mortals whom you find good for conversations, who are good readers and commentators, who may have insight into theories, literatures and methodologies with which you are less familiar, who themselves have good networks and are happy to introduce you to useful people, who understand The System and so on. Some students have good networks; others don't. This chapter describes networks and how to create a good one for yourself.

One common misconception is that networks involve cliques of people doing morally dubious favours for each other, at the expense of more virtuous but less well-connected ordinary people. That's only one type of network. We're using the term in the different sense of normal, ethical support networks and normal, ethical professional networks – people you know and can turn to for advice.

Building a network

Networks don't just happen; they're something you build, whether consciously or without thinking about it. Even if you're normally good at building networks without conscious effort, PhD networks will by definition be new to you, so it's worth knowing about a network structure which most students find useful.

At the heart of your network, of course, are your supervisors.

A second important component of your network is your informal 'committee', (i.e. people who will help you to ensure that your research is of good quality). For this, you need a small set of reliable, interested academics who are willing to do some work for you, to read, to comment, to advise, to critique, to provide pointers, to introduce you to other researchers and so on. They may be specialists who can provide particular expertise, or they may be generalists who can ask incisive questions.

A third main component is your personal support network (i.e. people who give you encouragement and moral support, who help you manage your work, keep life in perspective and bring you pizza when you're in the throes of inspiration). They may be family, or fellow students, or old friends. They may be academics in your department who are good at bringing you to your senses.

In addition, you need people who can be called on occasionally for specialist help, or whom you can visit once or twice to pick their brains. They may be leading researchers in your specialist field, or they may be technical experts who know about things like laboratory instruments, running databases and formatting documents.

Targeting

Most networking is opportunistic: if you meet someone that you happen to like, or find a useful contact, then you stay in touch with them. Sometimes, however, you need to find particular kinds of help or expertise, and for that you need a strategy. Three particularly useful starting points are:

- the writers of particularly relevant papers;
- people you saw or met at a conference who had pertinent and interesting things to say;
- people recommended by someone reliable (e.g. your supervisor, or a member of your informal committee).

Once you've identified some possible leads, you need to do some initial work and then make contact. The initial work consists of some homework. There's a reason why you've identified this person as someone to contact, but don't forget to find out what else you can about the person before you make contact, since there may be other ways in which they can help you. It also makes the contact easier if you know something about the person you're contacting. Some things you can do are to:

- check their website;
- ask people who know them;
- check with the person's secretary about when would be a good time to call, and whether the person is in the country.

Another useful bit of preparation is to consider what it is that you want to ask them. It's not enough to say that you're working in the same area as they are – they might justifiably react to this news by thinking, 'So what?' You need to say whether you want to clarify something about their work, or want a chance to discuss ideas, or want them to review your work. The more focused and informed the question you ask, the better the chances of things going well. Remember that anyone with enough stature to be worth approaching is probably also approached by other students. A surprising number of these students will ask vague, lazy questions which amount to, 'Can you tell me everything I need for my literature review, to save me the effort of finding it out for myself?' This is why we stress the need for tact and courtesy when asking someone for an overview of something over a cup of coffee – there's a world of difference between a cup of coffee with a well-read, hard-working student and a cup of coffee with an ignorant, idle one.

Tools for networking

Two of the main time-honoured tools for networking are shameless flattery and bribery. Shameless flattery usually takes the form of shameless flattery; bribery usually takes the form of coffee, chocolate biscuits and practical favours such as unearthing obscure references. (Just in case of mis-understanding, real bribery via monetary or sexual favours is unethical and illegal, and we emphatically disapprove of it.)

Flattery

The secret of effective flattery is that it is barefaced, precise, economical and accurate. That is, it has to flow easily and openly from the flatterer, it has to relate specifically and accurately to the flatteree, you mustn't overdo it, and it must bear some relation to reality. One well-informed, well-placed compliment on a recent publication will do more good than ten vague generalities. It also reduces the risk of your compliment being mistaken for the opening line in a seduction attempt – attractive women researchers at conferences apparently have more than enough unwanted attention of this sort.

Coffee

Eminent people are human too, and at venues such as conferences they can be very glad of a break and a decent cup of coffee paid for by someone else. Coffee can be used in various ways. One is as the setting for unofficial advice of one sort or another – career prospects, organizational politics, the future of a research field. Another is as a chance to unwind a bit at a gruelling conference or similar occasion. Treating someone to a cup of decent coffee as a break from a long admin session can be a real act of kindness, especially if you behave with tact and consideration during the coffee (for instance, by not talking about work, if your guest wants to get away from it for a while).

Chocolate biscuits

These are a surprisingly useful incentive. If you offer someone some cash to be a subject in your experiment, it might motivate them to some extent. If you offer them an upmarket chocolate biscuit and real coffee, then this is likely to motivate them considerably more, and make them more cooperative and friendly into the bargain. There is a literature on the reasons for this (it involves 'currencies', 'strokes', and 'judgement and decision making', if you feel inclined to follow it up, not to mention 'cognitive dissonance').

Not many people believe in the efficacy of chocolate biscuits, which is probably just as well, because if everyone adopted this approach then it would devalue the currency, and the shrewd researcher would need to find a different incentive (which would be a double annoyance to those researchers who happen to like upmarket chocolate biscuits).

Trading favours

People are busy. Interesting people are often very busy. One way to borrow some of their precious time is to offer them an exchange – to do something of value for them which allows them to free some time for you. For example, you could offer to do some administrative work or library searching in exchange for half an hour of discussion over coffee (you still buy the coffee).

First contact – people in your institution

It's usually easier to make contact with someone local, because it's feasible to 'just drop by' their office and take them to coffee. Just because they're local, that doesn't guarantee that they're available or friendly; you still have to do the homework first.

First contact – cold calls

'Cold calls' (contacting someone who doesn't know you) outside your own institution can be awkward both for the caller and the person being called.

It's hard to establish the basis for a conversation in a sentence or two, but you can make it easier if you prepare in advance. Cold calls can succeed if you can establish quickly that the exchange can be of mutual benefit. So think through in advance what you want, and what you have to offer in exchange.

Your best chance is to establish an immediate connection with the person you're contacting (e.g. through an introduction by a mutual acquaintance such as your supervisor or through reference to that person's publications). Having made that link, you need to say who you are and what you want.

Smart researchers like students with interesting ideas, and so they generally respond well to them, especially ones who have potential as named candidates on future grant applications. But sometimes active researchers already have as much work as they can handle, so you shouldn't assume that they'll have time for you – or that a lack of response necessarily means a lack of interest.

Be prepared to follow up your initial contact with some substance, for example a good, one-page précis of your research, or a well-constructed conference paper reporting some of your early findings. Make sure what you send represents you well: ensure that it is clearly written, free of major and minor errors and clear it with your supervisors and other experienced readers first.

Via phone

Phoning works best if you have a 'hook' for the person you're calling, for example if you've been referred to them by someone they know, or if you've already emailed them and suggested that you will call. You need to establish quickly who you are and why you're calling, and then you need to ask if this is a convenient time for, say, a five-minute conversation. Often, it won't be – be prepared to call back at another time. Also be prepared to follow up via email or post.

Via email or post

Published researchers, especially well-known ones, are inundated with requests from random research students wanting favours. Requests that run 'Dear Professor Haagen, I am a graduate student in Budapest researching ice cream and I wonder if you could offer me any advice about a choice of research topic' are tediously uninformative and suggest that the student, being incompetent, is not worth the bother of answering. On the other hand, concise requests that give substantive information about the student's research and ask specific questions are far more interesting and usually attract a response, though perhaps not an immediate one. It might well take the researcher six months to find time to read your message, decide to think about it, lose it in the crush of work, and eventually find it again and reply. Maybe the researcher won't reply but will remember a good message when you meet at a conference and introduce yourself. Think about it from their point of view:

if you had 50 emails about a research bid with a budget of several million pounds, and a deadline next Tuesday, would you defer answering them until you'd read every word of an email from a PhD student you'd never heard of before? If anything, it's surprising how many positive responses you can get to a well-constructed cold call.

If the researcher does reply to your message, be sure to send a thank you message immediately. If you have a good summary of your research, or of a piece of it, then you might attach it to the follow-up message.

We have deliberately not included examples of good cold call emails, since we don't particularly want to be lynched by eminent colleagues who receive large numbers of identically worded requests for help in the weeks following publication of this book, but some things to think about include the following:

- Did you get their name and title right?
- Does your question show that you've done some homework?
- Does your mentor/supervisor think that your question looks interesting?
- How long would it take a reasonable human being to write a reply to your question? (If it's more than ten minutes, then consider rephrasing the question.)
- Is your message so long that it scrolls off the page when the addressee opens it? (If so, shorten it.)
- Does the message show you in a good light, as someone who can spell, write clearly, think and generate interesting questions?
- Does the message offer them anything (e.g. access to data), and if so, can you deliver on that promise?

At a meeting or conference

Have something interesting and relevant ready to say. A compliment is handy, but be prepared to follow it up with a question, otherwise the conversation will die. (Even the most eminent researchers can be embarrassed by compliments, especially if they're too gratuitous.) It's best to have a question prepared that requires a multi-word response: for instance, 'Professor Katz, I was intrigued by your paper in *Nature* on semi-stochastic systems. I wondered whether you had tried applying that approach to trade networks?'

Use the opportunities that the meeting provides. If your person asks a good question during a session, you might catch them after the session and remark on the question and its implications. If you see your person talking to someone you know, you might ask the person you know to introduce you. If you see your person in a loosely arranged group, you might stand visibly on the periphery until you get a chance to make a contribution (a short question or a joke is good) or ask if you may join the group. A good time to catch people is as a session breaks up, before they've found their way to coffee or lunch. But don't keep them from refreshment – offer to walk with them.

Have a business card to hand, and perhaps a copy of a summary of your research (previously read and approved by your supervisor).

Don't assume that you are beneath notice, or, worse, beneath interest. Here are some home truths about Great Researchers to help you put them in perspective:

- they are usually great because they love ideas and asking questions – so they usually have an appetite for nifty ideas and good questions;
- they are usually just as susceptible to deft flattery as the rest of us;
- they were once research students and many of them still remember that.

People you should remember to include in your network

Most of the section above refers to contacting researchers about research. There are other categories of very useful people that it's easy to overlook, so we've included a short section about them here.

Mentors

Mentors are Wise People who take an interest in your personal, professional and intellectual development. They're the people who teach you the 'unwritten rules' and who can see the 'bigger picture'. In theory, your supervisor should be a mentor, but it doesn't always work out that way. A mentor is a more experienced researcher who will show you the ropes from this perspective of success and informedness. A mentor can show you the things you don't know how to look for. This is particularly useful for the things that you don't *know* that you need to look for or do, such as getting the right things on your CV as early as possible – a friend won't always know what the right things are, and some of the right things are counter-intuitive. Other students are often good at identifying things actively wrong with your institution, but bad at identifying things which are passively wrong (i.e. things not being done which ought to be done). Mentors are useful for this, among many other things.

Secretaries and other support staff

Always treat support staff – secretaries, technical support, custodians of facilities – with respect. *Never* underestimate their value. *Never* confuse salary level with worth. Support staff are the keepers and collators of useful information – they are the ones holding together the department, they are the providers of services and assistance, they are often the gatekeepers to things you need. Consider: if you really wanted to know the inside story about government policy, would you ask the prime minister, or the civil service? Journalists know all about this, and successful journalists always get on well with the secretaries of the people they investigate.

Wonderful People

One invaluable resource is Wonderful People. There are a few people who have invaluable skills such as improbably excellent social or professional contacts, or encyclopaedic knowledge of one or more literatures, and who are helpful and pleasant. Such people should be cherished and appreciated. As a new researcher you will probably not know any people fitting this description (or more probably, not realize that you know them). When you do start meeting them, treat them well; they should be declared living national treasures. Librarians and secretaries are also often wonderful, and friendships with them are almost always well worth cultivating.

6 Reading

. . . those frightful parts of the Pnakotic Manuscripts which were too ancient to be read.

During a PhD, you have to do a lot of reading. That reading needs to be the right reading, and you need to make correct use of it. This chapter covers these topics.

The chapter overlaps considerably with the chapter on writing. This is for various reasons. One is that you are doing the reading so that you have the information required for writing (for instance, writing your thesis). Another is that if you know about the concepts and structures used in writing by experienced academics, then you will be able to make much better use of what you read.

We have included a fair amount of detail about online searching, as opposed to internet searching. If you're going to be a good professional researcher, you need to be aware of the differences, and able to use the tools of your trade efficiently and well. Few students are strong in this area; few students do outstanding work.

We have also included a fair amount about different types of papers and about different types of research. If you understand these concepts then a lot of things about the literature start to make more sense. It's also worth reading this part if you're thinking about writing a paper, or about planning some research with a view to publication outside the dissertation – if you know what you're aiming for, then you can plan and conduct your research much more efficiently.

Finding the right references

You have to convey the right message when you are writing, and that involves some hard work beforehand reading what you need to read (the first golden principle: *don't lie*, in this case by pretending to have read things which you haven't read). However, there is no point in overkill. One of our usual examples of strong academic writing contains eight references in one paragraph on the first page. Do you think that page 24 of that thesis contains the same number of references per paragraph? It doesn't, because it doesn't need to – the writer has by then already cited practically all the references he or she needs to. How do you know what references you need to cite?

The easiest solution is to ask your supervisor, politely, where to start. If your supervisor doesn't know, ask someone else, politely, and keep your supervisor informed, in case you start blundering in where angels fear to tread. You need to send out the signal that you're a hard-working individual who will make good use of the advice, rather than an idle brute who can't be bothered to do their own research (mentioning what you've already read and asking where you should go next is a good start). Your supervisor can be invaluable here.

If you are lucky and virtuous, your supervisor might say something along the lines of, 'The person to talk to about this is X; I've emailed them, and they're happy to give you some guidance. Here's their email address'. This is an encouraging sign, and is academic shorthand for the following things:

- here is something which will save you a lot of effort;
- here is a chance to make contact with a major player in this area;
- I trust you to enough to let you speak to important players in this area by yourself.

(It does *not* mean, 'I am too ignorant or idle to provide guidance on this by myself'.) If your supervisor offers you this opportunity, then grab it with both hands.

The researcher's core literature

Most good researchers carry around in their memories a good, accessible database of relevant papers. That means, out of all the reading they do, they maintain a working knowledge of about 100–50 papers. As they continue to read, the core adjusts, shifting to follow developments in the discipline or to follow their changing interests. But some of that core will persist for years. Interestingly, the lower limit for a good bibliography on a dissertation tends to be around 100 citations. One of the things a good doctoral student will accomplish is to amass a first 'core' literature. (Of course, there's huge variation, but the numbers don't really matter – the idea of keeping a selection of pertinent literature accessible in memory does.)

So, where is a good place to start looking for references? Your supervisor is likely to remind you about literature reviews in the papers you've already read, and also about review articles. You may also be pointed towards some online searching, with keywords either supplied by your long-suffering supervisor, or included in the articles which you have already found. The following sections cover these topics in more detail. We've included some discussion of how papers as a whole are put together, not just literature reviews, to save duplicating this in the section on writing.

After that, you have the problem of evaluating the quality of what you're reading. This is not always easy for the average student. If you find a paper impossible to understand, is it because the paper is far too brilliant for you to understand, or because it's a pile of pretentious, obfuscatory garbage? A later section of this chapter describes some ways of reading between the lines of academic writing, so that you are in a better position (a) to evaluate what you're reading and (b) to improve the quality of what you're writing.

Literature reviews

Academic papers and dissertations normally begin with a literature review. There are good reasons for this.

The ostensible reason for a literature review is to set the scene for the work described in the paper – explaining what has been done previously by other researchers etc. This is done via standard referencing conventions, so that interested or sceptical readers can locate the original sources and read them to check the alleged facts in the literature review, if they so wish. The second, and equally important, reason for a literature review is to demonstrate that you have done your homework thoroughly, so that readers are assured that they will not be wasting time wading through the rest of what you have written.

The literature review needs to have a structure, since even the best academic prose is pretty hard reading at the best of times. The structure is also a way of demonstrating that you have a clear understanding of what you are doing and why you are doing it. It is your responsibility to make your work understandable; it is not the reader's responsibility to make sense of a pile of references indiscriminately grabbed from the internet and then tacked together with semi-coherent prose.

The usual structure, and one with which we have no quarrel, is one which begins with the earliest work in this area and proceeds via the most important past work up to the present. Your references will therefore usually begin with old seminal references, then continue with more recent key references and assorted examples of less important references, and end with very recent foundational references. Some readers may notice the similarity to the Whig view of history; this is probably a suitable subject for a paper which would be viewed as quite amusing by at least four readers . . .

One widespread source of confusion is the link between literature reviews and introductions. Institutions and people differ. Some favour a completely separate literature review and introduction; others favour a complete integration of the two. The best advice is to find out whether there is a specified formalism for your venue (including PhD regulations). If there is, follow it; if there isn't, use whichever approach you prefer. There's no point in getting into a war on this topic.

At the heart of your literature review is a good plot. The story should start with a problem of some sort (for instance, a dragon laying waste the land, in a good legend, or a problem in the domain, in research). The literature review and/or introduction then follow the steps taken by previous work in an attempt to resolve the problem. The literature review and/or introduction end at the point where you, the hero or heroine, enter the scene, armed with your enchanted sword/improved research methodology. The rest of the paper/dissertation follows your adventures, to the point where you emerge triumphant. If you do not emerge triumphant, then you should have got your experimental design right before you started, and it is your problem. (Interested readers might wish to try reading Propp's work on formalisms in Russian folk tales, or Campbell's examination of archetypes, or a good book on experimental design, depending on their precise problem.) This strand is known by various names, such as 'plot', 'red thread' and 'narrative spine', and is viewed as extremely important by most experienced and able writers.

Novices usually have a lot of trouble with narrative spine. The situation normally improves with practice, if you deliberately work at it, but will not automatically improve otherwise. There are various ways of helping yourself with this issue. One simple way is to use top-down decomposition. This involves starting with a very short list of key points in the story – half a dozen brief sentences at most. For example:

Elicitation of software metrics via card sorts

- Choice of metrics for software is difficult
- Card sorts should have advantages over previous methods for choosing metrics
- What happens if you use card sorts in this area?
- Card sorts do have advantages over previous methods

Once you are happy with this top-level structure, you then break down each part of it into smaller parts, and keep on repeating the process as necessary.

You should end up with a set of section headings, subsection headings etc. which will give you the main structure.

In practice, readers tend to get lost quite easily, even in a well-structured paper, because of the sheer volume of information which should be in there. (If there isn't much information, this is usually a danger sign.) The wise writer therefore uses bridging text and signposts. Bridging text is used to join two sections of a paper or other document. It usually consists of a closing paragraph or two at the end of a section, summarizing that section, telling the reader what will be in the next section and explaining how the previous section leads on to the next section. A signpost is a piece of text flagging (i.e. indicating) something which will be mentioned later.

At this level, you should be making extensive use of journals as your main source of information. Although textbooks and the internet are useful starting places, they are usually not appropriate as main sources of information because they tend to present simplified accounts.

Cynical supervisors have been known to give students explicit advice about which sources to read, but not quote, as a source of an initial overview so that they understand the area. Alleged examples range from *How to Lie with Statistics* (almost certainly true) to *The Ladybird Book of Computers* (surprisingly, perhaps true to some extent).

Online searching

Although literature reviews are a useful way into the literature, they are not infallible, and were not written with your particular needs at the forefront of their writers' minds. You therefore need to do your own trawls through the literature, to see what's out there and find bits of the literature that are relevant to you.

Supervisors and externals are not allowed to kill students who include in their literature reviews a sentence starting, 'A search on the internet found no previous work on this topic'. They are, however, allowed to fail students, and to write elegant, cutting comments on the offending page, which goes some way towards remedying this shortcoming in the legal system.

Why do supervisors and externals get so worked up about that sentence? Answer: because it's equivalent to writing in large letters, 'I am either ignorant or lazy or both'. That is not a signal that you want to send out to the reader.

Sending out the right signals

If you want to be treated as a professional, you need to send out the signals that show that you are a professional. Professionals know the tools of their trade – for instance, a brain surgeon should know about surgical instruments and about other relevant issues such as the physiology of the brain. If someone claimed to be a leading brain surgeon and then appeared to be unsure of the difference between a clamp and a retractor, that would not be an encouraging sign.

Anyone in the academic system ought to know the tools of the academic trade. The amount of detail required will vary with the academic level – for instance, undergraduates will not normally be expected to know as much as PhD students, who in turn will not be expected to know as much as leading professional researchers in the area. However, if you know more than you are expected to, this is usually viewed as a very encouraging sign.

Academics deal with knowledge and information, and should know how to find, interpret and present knowledge and information. An important part of this is finding the best possible sources so that your assessment of the problem in question is based on the best information and knowledge available. The academic literature has a pecking order, ranging from publications which are accepted on sufferance through to publications which are treated with considerable respect. Some of this pecking order is quite possibly based on snobbery, but most of it is based on the quality control that the publication uses. The more rigorous the quality control that a publication uses, the more prestigious the publication is. It's a simple and sensible concept, and it makes life a lot simpler and more reliable for everyone involved. If you are about to spend months or years of your life, and perhaps sizeable amounts of money researching a topic, then it's very reassuring to know that your initial assumptions are as solidly based as they can be.

At the top end of the pecking order come encyclopaedia articles and the top journals. Encyclopaedias usually choose the leading international experts in an area to write their articles – it is a considerable compliment to be asked to write one. Anything submitted to a top-quality academic journal for publication will normally be checked in detail by several leading international authorities on the topic before being accepted for publication. Anything which is not of suitable quality will be rejected.

Further down the pecking order come the middle-range journals, which also use refereeing, but which normally use less eminent referees. Towards the bottom of the scale come specialist newsletters and professional trade magazines, where articles may be reviewed by the editor rather than specialist referees.

The precise status of a publication will be affected by individual factors – for instance, some specialist newsletters will be edited by very eminent authorities, have very high-level contributions and be higher on the pecking order than some journals. Books are also very variable in their status. As a fair rule of thumb, textbooks are low on the pecking order, because they usually present simplified accounts for students. Specialist books may be extremely prestigious.

The observant reader will by now have noticed that this description of the pecking order contains absolutely no mention of the internet, of newspapers or of popular magazines. There is a good reason for this. The internet has absolutely no quality control as regards the content of the sites accessible through it. If you find an interesting-looking site relating to your chosen area, it may possibly have been written by a major authority on the area, but it could just as easily have been put together by someone who believes that they are being controlled by devices put in their brain by aliens, and who has a degree from a college based above Joe's Pizza Shack in Peoria. Newspapers and popular magazines at least have some quality control, but if you think that reading a newspaper sends out the signal that you are a professional with considerable expertise, then you might be better advised to transfer your registration to that college based above Joe's Pizza Shack. Remember that 'online' includes things like using library databases and CD-ROM indexes: you don't have to be on the internet to be online.

Online searching: overview

One of the main reasons for performing an online search is to find out what has been done before, so that you don't reinvent the wheel and make it square. If something has been done, then you need to get a clear overview of that previous work. If you can't find any sign that anything has been done previously, then you need to be pretty sure of your ground before saying, 'No previous work has been done in this area'. At best, you might look a bit silly if there is a major literature which has been missed; at worst, you might be accused of academic malpractice in claiming priority over a previous researcher in this area (not too likely if you are a final year undergraduate, but more of a worry if you are a PhD student aiming for a career in academia). For this reason, saying, 'No previous work has been done in this area' is simply asking for trouble, and most sensible professionals use expressions such as, 'This area appears to have received little or no attention in the past', which allows them to wriggle out with some face saved if a previous literature does exist.

So, how do you set about finding out what has been done previously? There are three main things you need to think about: sources, strategy and tactics. 'Sources' involves where to look; 'strategy' involves ways of structuring the search process; 'tactics' involves things such as the search engine features that you use.

Sources

The amount of information in the world is enormous. For instance, the number of physics journals alone is so huge that reading the physics journals which are published each year would take more than a year of non-stop reading – you simply couldn't keep up with the current publications, let alone the previous issues stretching back to the nineteenth century.

To make life simpler for everyone, librarians and professional indexing bodies thoughtfully index the contents of journals (and other sources of information too, for that matter). This means that you can look up a term in an index of this type and find out when and where something about it was previously published. For obvious reasons, indexes usually cover journals relevant to the index topic, so physics journals will be indexed together in one index, chemistry journals in another and so on. The old indexes were printed; more recent ones are on CD-ROM or accessible on specialist sites, usually password-protected (librarians will have passwords to many relevant sites, though some sites will charge you for searches).

This means that if you want to find out what has been done previously in a particular area, then your friendly campus librarian will probably be able to direct you towards an appropriate index covering the relevant topic. This in turn means that (a) you will have a good chance of finding anything worth mentioning on the topic, and (b) that if nothing turns up in your search, then this probably indicates that nothing has been published previously – an important consideration if you're doing something like a PhD where originality is important. (It might also mean that you've mis-typed a keyword, which is why the next two topics below are important too.) An added advantage of the indexing process is that there is a certain amount of quality control – only reputable sources are usually indexed. If you find a fact or a claim via an index of this type, then it will probably be sound.

Strategy

Once you have found the right index, you need to have a strategy for searching it. The usual novice strategy is to type in two or three keywords and see what happens; the usual system response to this is to say either that no records have been found, or that 231,768 records have been found. A more sophisticated strategy offers some advantages over this.

There are various good articles about conducting effective searches, and time spent reading them is time well spent. This section is just an introduction to the topic and you would be well advised to read some of the specialist articles.

One useful strategy is to plan in advance what you are going to do during the search. Another is to keep a written record of the things you have done, so that you don't end up going round in circles.

There are different types of search. The standard information science literature has the useful concept of the 'known item' search, where you are looking for one specific item or fact – for instance, trying to locate a copy of J.R. Hartley's *Fly Fishing*, or to find out its date of publication, when you already know that the book exists. For this type of search, as soon as you have found the answer, you can stop.

With other types of search, however, you will not always know when to stop. If you are trying to get an overview of the main previous work in an area, for instance, you will need to do a fair bit of searching and you will almost certainly encounter problems with the system either claiming that there are no relevant records or claiming that there are millions. You therefore need strategies for improving your hit rate.

One simple but effective strategy is to use a keyword search and then wade through the list until you find a relevant record. You can then look through the relevant record for other potential keywords to use in your next search. Authors' names are well worth considering for this (unless they are extremely common ones such as Smith) – someone who has published one relevant article on a topic will probably have published more, and you can then start adding their co-authors' names to your list. The same is true of technical terms, where you might find different names for the same concept, or more specialist names (if the number of hits was previously too large), or broader terms (if the number of hits was previously too small).

Tactics and commands

Different search engines operate in different ways: it is an instructive experience to type in the same keyword to different search engines on the internet and see what results you obtain from each. Underlying them all, though, are a few basic concepts, and understanding these can make your searching a lot more productive and efficient.

Two key concepts are weighting and Boolean search.

Weighting

Weighting involves assigning different weights (in the sense of e.g. importance or relevance ratings) to something – in this context, usually keywords or records. This allows the search engine to list in a systematic order the records which you find. One popular way of doing this is to use 'inverse frequency weighting' – the rarer a term is, the more weighting it is given, on the assumption that it will be more specific and information-rich. So, for instance, a search on 'low entropy systems' would result in low weightings for 'low' and 'systems' on the grounds that there would be millions of records containing these terms, and a much higher weighting for 'entropy', which is a much rarer term.

It is worth bearing this in mind when choosing your keywords: more specific terms usually produce lower numbers of hits, but a higher proportion of relevant hits.

Boolean searching

Boolean searching involves using the operators 'AND', 'OR' and 'NOT' on the keywords which you enter. So, for instance, 'repertory' AND 'grid' would find only records which contained both the words 'repertory' and 'grid'. A search for 'repertory' OR 'grid' would find records which contained either 'repertory' or 'grid' or (usually) both. A search for 'repertory' NOT 'grid' would find records which contained 'repertory' but which did not also contain 'grid'. This approach can be very useful when you are trying to exclude records on a topic with a similar name – for instance, if you are trying to find out about repertory theatre, but keep finding records about repertory grid technique.

Most online search engines on the internet use Boolean 'OR' searches as the norm, but offer 'AND' and 'NOT' in the 'advanced search' option. The same is true of most library online search systems.

In addition, 'advanced search' usually offers other features, such as being able to treat two or more words as a phrase (for instance, by enclosing them in inverted commas). In the case of repertory theatre, for instance, you might be able to search using the key phrase 'repertory theatre' in inverted commas, which would then ignore the phrase 'repertory grid'.

It is highly advisable to learn to use advanced search. Librarians are usually supportive if you ask for help with this – they have a hard time from many users, so it is a welcome change for them to encounter someone who wants to learn how to do it right.

Other sources of information

As usual, a cup of coffee with a friendly expert can save you an enormous amount of effort.

It is also a good idea to get an overview from a textbook, which will list relevant articles in its bibliography, and an even better idea to get an overview from a review paper or from a recent encyclopaedia. Review papers and encyclopaedias are usually good things to quote in your bibliography; textbooks are usually not a good thing to quote in your bibliography, since they are saying to the reader: 'I've read the simplified account for beginners, not the professional account'.

It is also worth being pleasant to librarians – they have a wealth of information which they are usually happy to share with polite, appreciative people.

How a seasoned referee reads a paper

The most interesting things in a paper are usually written between the lines. In the stereotyped picture of the good old days, this was something which your supervisor would teach you over a glass of sherry (and a very pleasant way of operating it was too for both parties, as we can testify from personal experience). Nowadays you usually have to pick this up the hard way.

This section describes some of the things that an experienced professional (such as your external examiner) will be looking at.

One point worth mentioning at the outset is that it is not a safe strategy to hope that the reader won't notice mistakes if they're tucked away late in the text. There really are readers out there, particularly external examiners, who actually do read every single line of a thesis – for instance, by moving a ruler down the page a line at a time to make sure they don't miss anything, and noting every mistake, question or comment that they want to draw to your attention. It's also worth mentioning that experienced professionals can skim-read and spot errors at speeds you might find hard to believe.

The sections below are arranged in roughly the sequence in which a seasoned professional might look at them. This is not the same as the sequence in which they would appear in a paper, which is different again from the order in which you would write them.

References

Seasoned professionals often turn straight to the references before even looking at the main text. References tell us a lot. Usually failure to do the right thing in the references is reflected in shoddy work in the main text. Things the professionals will be looking at include the following.

Mandatory

- Are your references laid out correctly down to the last comma?
- Have you cited all the seminal and core references?
- Have you cited a good spread of sources, ranging from the seminal texts to something within the last year?
- Are your references all from respectable journals rather than textbooks or the internet? (At this stage you should be using journal papers as the norm, with textbooks and the internet being the exception.)

Desirable extras

- Have you cited work which is little known except to people doing advanced work in the area?
- Have you cited anything which is in press? (This implies you are sufficiently part of the research community to be given pre-prints by researchers.)
- If you have cited something in press, is the author a major figure in the field?
- Have you cited a discreet number of your own papers, in respectable journals, preferably co-authored with an authority in the field?

Appendices (for theses, not papers)

Seasoned professionals also tend to turn to the appendices before reading the main text. The appendix contains copies of things such as the briefing sheet which you gave to research subjects. If these are badly designed or presented, then the data which you have collected are likely to be garbage.

Good signs

- Complete 'cradle to grave' examples of each stage of the process from data collection to final tables
- Materials that were seen by respondents which look neat and professional

Bad signs

- All the raw data are in the appendix, making the appendix longer than everything else
- Scruffy, tatty, poorly presented materials seen by respondents

Title pages and acknowledgements

A seasoned professional reading a student's thesis will look at these to check for spelling mistakes and the like. A seasoned professional is quite likely to find some. A favourite mistake is to misspell the supervisor's name and/or to get their title wrong. By PhD level you will probably have learned the nuances, but at MSc level a significant proportion of students, particularly those from industry, will not bother to check, or will not understand the rules. If in doubt, check the staff list, or ask. Getting titles wrong is a good way of irritating people, in industry as well as in academia, and is a sign that you still have a lot to learn.

Acknowledgements are usually a source of harmless amusement before grappling with the abstract and the main text. Sometimes they are useful – for instance, an acknowledgement to a leading authority in the area for help given is a sign that this student has probably been doing some interesting work.

The choice of title for the thesis is itself interesting – is it pompous, vague, full of empty buzzwords, impenetrably technical, boring or forgettable? A good title is informative, short and memorable (so that it will stick in the mind of the reader and increase your prospects of fortune and glory). One device which often works well is the two-part title, with the first part being memorable and eye-catching, and the second part, after the colon, explaining what the first part is about. Our own titles include a range such as: 'laddering' and 'knowing the unknowable: the causes and nature of changing require-ments'. The first is a brutally short minimalist title for a brutally short minimalist paper; the second is a deliberately eye-catching title, which did attract quite a bit of attention.

Bear in mind that people searching for relevant documents about a topic will often search on titles, so a whimsical title with no relevant keywords in it will probably be doomed to oblivion (unless it's so good that word of mouth makes people aware of the title), whereas a title like 'laddering', though brutal, is a fair guarantee that a search for 'laddering' will come up with a hit. If you use a two-part title, the second part is usually the one which contains the keywords (but doesn't have to be).

One plausible story is that some seasoned researchers include in the acknowledgements anyone that they don't want to have as a referee for a paper being submitted to a refereed venue. The rationale for this is that the editor will not use as a referee anyone mentioned in the acknowledgements, because of potential conflict of interest problems. So, if you have fallen out with someone in your field who might relish the prospect of refereeing one of your papers, you use a form of words such as 'we would like to thank X for various discussions about this topic' and reduce the risk of unwanted trouble.

Abstracts

Writing abstracts is an art form in its own right and needs practice. You need to say (preferably on one side of A4 for a thesis or in one paragraph for a paper) what you did, why you did it, what you found and why it is significant work in terms of both theory and practice. If you can't guarantee from the outset that you can achieve all of this, then you need to replan your research design, but that's another story.

The best advice is to practise a lot and to get feedback from experts. The next best advice is to look at the abstracts of papers that are generally viewed as significant in your area.

Good signs

- Appropriate use of specialist language
- Clear
- Significant findings and implications
- Immaculate spelling and punctuation (this is the first page of text, after all, and the one which makes the first impression, so you should make a lot of effort to get this one right)

Bad signs

- Inappropriate style
- Buzzwords
- Sales pitch
- Content-free
- Unclear

The contents page (for theses, not papers)

There should be a contents page.

Good signs

- Layout and structure of the thesis follow standard conventions for the domain (if there are standard conventions)
- Neat
- Clear
- Informative
- Appropriate number of tables for the domain
- Appropriate number of figures for the domain

Bad signs

- Non-standard layout and structure for no obvious reason
- Tatty and scruffy
- Inappropriate number of tables and figures for the domain
- Page numbers do not correspond with those in the text

Domains differ. Some like tables and figures, some don't. If you're using figures from other people's work, watch out for copyright.

Every table should be there for a reason; there should be as many as necessary, but no more. Beware of presenting the same information more than once in different formats – for instance, once as a histogram and once as a pie chart. This looks like gratuitous padding and makes the reader wonder what you're trying to divert attention *from*. There are some situations where it is necessary to use different formats, but these are rare and should be preceded by a clear explanation of your reasons.

Favourite methods of padding a weak piece of work include:

- Humour (second golden rule: don't try to be funny)
- Clip art
- Excessive reworking of the same material into different tables
- Gratuitous use of colour in tables and figures
- Excessive quantities of appendices

If any of these are visible in your contents pages (or anywhere else) you are looking for trouble.

The first page

This normally forms part of the introduction (though some writers have eccentric styles and domains differ). It is an important page, because it is here that most referees and other assessors will form their first impression of whether your work is excellent, acceptable, borderline or dreadful. Once they've formed that impression, it's pretty hard to change it. Here are two examples of text from first pages of published papers.

Example 1

Laddering is a technique initially developed by Hinkle (1965). Like repertory grids (e.g. Shaw, 1981), laddering originated in clinical psychology and personality theory, specifically in Kelly's (1955) Personal Construct Theory (PCT). However, similar techniques appear to have arisen independently in cognitive psychology (e.g. Graesser, 1978; Graesser, Robertson, Lovelace & Swinehart, 1980), and in occupational psychology, in the form of hierarchical task analysis (e.g. Annett & Duncan, 1967; Hodgkinson & Crawshaw, 1985). It should, though, be noted that although the output from the latter is similar to that from laddering, the elicitation method used to generate it appears generally to consist of unstructured interviews (see Hodgkinson, *op. cit*).

Example 2

The basic idea behind the sorting techniques is simply to ask respondents to sort things into groups. The things may be *objects*, such as different types of mouse, or *pictures*, such as screen dumps of various screen layouts, or may be *cards*, with the names of objects or situations on the cards, such as the names of different editors. The groups may be ones chosen by the questioner, or ones chosen by the respondent, or a mixture of both. The sorting techniques are a useful way of eliciting respondents' groups, and of finding out how much agreement and disagreement there is between respondents about the categories.

The first example is tersely written and includes the seminal texts, as well as references to relevant approaches in two other literatures. This shows that the authors have done their homework and more. There is also a note about differences between approaches, which shows that the authors have read the other texts in detail and understood them. The language is formal and the authors use specialist academic forms of abbreviation such as '*op. cit.*' This was clearly not a paper written by someone making it up from general knowledge supplemented with secondary sources from the internet.

The second example is written in a much less formal style, with no references, and with unsupported assertions. The authors clearly have practical experience of what they are talking about, but the paper gives little clue about whether they are from academia or industry, or whether they are expert or novice.

The first example is user-hostile at first glance, but sends out a clear set of positive signals to the academic reader – it is solid, heavyweight and written by professionals who know what they are doing. Although it is heavy reading, it is not vague or packed with buzzwords. A journal referee or an external examiner's reaction to this text would be to think: 'Well, we're not looking at a rejection/fail here if the rest is like this'.

The second example looks user-friendly, but would set a referee or external examiner's alarm bells ringing because of the lack of visible evidence of academic weight (as opposed to practical experience of the technique). Their reaction would probably be to flick rapidly through the next few pages to see whether there was any improvement later; if not, there would be a real risk of a rejection or fail.

One of the interesting things about these two examples is that they were written by the same authors, on closely related topics, but for very different venues. The first example was from a journal paper submitted to a journal through the normal channels; it had to be heavyweight enough to convince the referees that it was well worth publishing. The second example was from an encyclopaedia article, where the encyclopaedia invited the authors to write the paper for a non-specialist audience. This meant a quite different set of possibilities and constraints from the journal paper – there was no need to use a terse, condensed style for instance.

Good signs in a first page

- Clear
- Appropriate writing style (formal, erring on the side of being dry and terse)
- Right references
- Good research question

Bad signs in a first page

- No evidence of academic content
- Unclear
- Poor or missing research question
- Pleas for mercy and other indications of blood in the water

The next thing the critical reader usually turns to is either the method section or the results section (not always, but often – they will return to the second page later).

Method section

The method section is there for a reason. The reason is that if anyone wants to replicate your work, or to build on it, then they need to know exactly what you did, how and to whom. A second reason is that the reader needs to be able to make an informed judgement of the quality of what you did. If, for instance, the reader discovers that you recruited all the subjects for your study of hobbies in the high street on a Saturday afternoon, then the reader may have just cause for suspecting that hobbies such as mountain climbing might be seriously under-represented.

In some disciplines, such as psychology, the methods section is usually so formulaic that it is (a) extremely terse and (b) more or less incomprehensible to a layperson. Using such formulae can be a useful way of sending out the right signals to the reader. For instance, if you see something along the lines of 'a counterbalanced within-subject design was used' then this implies that the writer is a professional who knows just what they are on about.

The method section is a feature of experimental research and will not usually be present in papers following a different approach.

Results section

Domains differ. In experimental domains, the usual preference is for the results to be given as baldly as possible, preferably with no comment or discussion. Explanation or clarification is usually acceptable, especially if space constraints mean that you have to use short names for column headings etc.

Good signs

- Enough tables
- Clear rationale for each table and its position in the sequence
- Tables well laid out
- Numbers add up correctly

Bad signs

- Too few or too many tables
- No clear rationale for why each table is where it is, or why it is included in the first place
- Poorly laid out; tatty and scruffy
- Numbers don't add up

Discussion

For some reason, discussion sections are less rich grounds for hunting signs of expertise and weakness. It may be that desperation spurs even inexperienced researchers to generate eloquent and plausible stories to explain what they have found.

As usual, appropriate use of technical terms and of references to the literature are a good sign; buzzwords, general knowledge and irrelevant references to outdated textbooks (more likely to occur in theses than papers) are a bad sign. An elegantly constructed experimental thesis will often have a discussion section whose structure mirrors the introduction and the results sections, with a series of questions being asked in the introduction, answered in the tables in the results section, and then discussed in the discussion section.

Conclusion

The conclusion section often also includes a section on 'further work'. The conclusion should provide a clear set of answers to the questions raised in the introduction. These should be supported by the evidence in the results section (if it is an experimental piece of work) and in the discussion section (whatever type of work it is).

The further work section is a useful place to stake a claim and establish priority in an area. An experienced researcher will often include here a brief description of something which they are planning to do; an experienced reader will know that by the time the paper has appeared the writer will already have spent at least a year on the topic described in the further work, so there is no point in rushing into that area.

Critical reflections section

Some people favour a critical reflections section in which the writer reflects on what they have learned during the research process, and on what they would do differently knowing what they know now. Other people believe that this is pretentious navel-gazing at best, and gratuitous pouring of blood into the water at worst, not to mention a gross breach of the third golden rule (don't panic and blurt out the truth). We can appreciate the arguments on both sides.

Sometimes a critical reflections section is a requirement for MSc theses. If you are an MSc student reading this book with an eye to the future, and this is the case for you in your MSc, then you don't have a lot of choice about omitting the critical reflections section completely. All is not lost, however, if you are in this situation. Here are two examples.

Bad example

I realize now that my questionnaire was poorly constructed, and would pay more attention to constructing it better if I started again.
(Subtext: I am a raw amateur, ignorant and low in self-worth; there is no good in me.)

Good example

It would be interesting to compare the rough set theoretic analysis used here against Rosch's concept of prototypical set membership with fuzzy boundaries.
(Subtext: I analysed my respondents' categories using a state-of-the-art mathematical approach which few people have even heard of, instead of boring old standard content analysis. I am also familiar with a completely different approach from a completely different discipline, which not

many people have heard of. I am not the sort of person who pours blood into the water at any time, and I certainly don't plan to start doing it now.)

As might be apparent from the closing sentence of the allegedly good example, there are potential dangers in sending out too strong a signal of this sort, so this approach needs to be used with discretion.

Reading a lot

You need to read a lot. You need to read a lot in your own discipline (so that you have a thorough grasp of what it is all about) and in other disciplines, both apparently relevant and apparently irrelevant. Much of the best work comes from cross-fertilization between apparently unconnected fields.

In your own field, you should read in depth and in breadth and in *time* – you should have a detailed knowledge of the relevant literature in your chosen area, and a general knowledge of the main work in related areas, and of previous work in your area for as far back as possible. For your own area, you should be reading everything up to and including the most specialized journal articles. For other areas, you might find book chapters a more appropriate level (though be careful about the level of the book – don't even think about popular books for the lay public, and be wary of textbooks unless they are prestigious ones).

Reading habits of lifelong readers

- Steady consumption. The idea is not so much to read voraciously as to read regularly. Use a tortoise strategy, rather than a hare.
- Always carry reading with you – use the ten minutes on the train platform, or while you're waiting for your supervisor, or between seminars, or while dinner is cooking.
- Leave papers in the loo.
- Keep an annotated bibliography – and keep it up to date.
- Find a regular reading time, about an hour a day. For many, this is first thing in the morning. Don't go straight to your office; go to the library first for your hour.
- Read books as well as papers.
- Most great readers are a little obsessive and like to get a sense of 'completeness' when they're reading on a new subject. Many 'map' the key writers.
- Make sure all your photocopies of papers have full citations on them, down to the ISSN or ISBN and page numbers.
- Most great readers maintain more than one reading strand – so morning time may be technical reading, but bedtime is philosophy reading.

- Read a chapter every night before you sleep, no matter how tired you are.
- At conferences, carry the proceedings to the sessions with you and annotate the paper with your notes during the talk.
- Even when you find a paper uninteresting, cast your eye over the remainder, so that you have a portrait of the contents.
- Use your network to filter your reading, hence increasing the interest level of what you pick up.
- Join (or form) a reading group, or find a reading buddy.
- From Feynman (as recalled by Michael Jackson): when reading something difficult, if you get stuck reading something, start again from the beginning (this allows you to rehearse the early sections, correct misunderstandings that accumulate and benefit from elapsed time).
- Elapsed time can help: skim-read the material, then set it aside briefly before coming back to read it thoroughly.

Using material from the literature

You will never lose by giving credit. Indeed, you are likely to gain respect and trust by doing so fastidiously.

Plagiarism

The interpretation of what constitutes plagiarism is subject to cultural variation, but it's the British academic interpretation that applies to your work, and the British academic interpretation is strict: plagiarism is using someone else's ideas, words or material – directly or indirectly – without giving them credit.

The rules are very clear:

- Any time you use ideas, words or material of any sort that relates to a specific source, you must attribute it to that source. Paraphrasing (restating) still requires attribution.
- Any time you use someone else's works verbatim, you must put them in quotation marks and attribute them to that person.

Let's be absolutely clear. Plagiarism is academic suicide. In British academia, plagiarism is a 'mortal sin'. If your dissertation plagiarizes, *you will fail*. If you submit work for publication that plagiarizes, your work will be rejected and *you will be blacklisted*. So, if in doubt, attribute.

Uses of citation

Authors convey many things through their use of the literature. Some of what they 'say' is about the content of the paper (instrumental use). But some is about themselves (expressive use):

- establishing your authority;
- siting your work in existing knowledge;
- coverage – showing that you know the conventions, what is expected;
- depth – showing you've come to grips with esoteric aspects of the literature;
- excluding areas you don't want to cover, while indicating that you do so informedly;
- showing respect for your referees;
- establishing a justification for your research question;
- establishing a justification for your methodology;
- establishing a justification for your analysis;
- providing a theoretical context or perspective;
- corroborating your findings.

Consider the following:

- If you cite a philosophical text from 1925, what are you saying?
- If your bibliography contains mainly books, what are you saying?
- If your bibliography includes the three key players in the field, what are you saying?
- If your bibliography includes only papers published in the last two years, what are you saying?
- If half of your bibliography is self-reference, what are you saying?
- If your citations appear in clumps (e.g. Sponge 1982; Bloogs 1998; Gloomer 2002), what are you saying?

Now try the following:

- Look at the first page of a few published research papers.
- How many citations are there?
- How are they grouped?
- Where does the first citation arise?
- What sorts of paper are cited? Are the titles general, or specific?
- When were they published? Who are the authors?
- Look at the discussion/conclusion portion of the papers.
- How many citations are there?
- How are they used?
- Are they the same citations that appeared in the background/introduction, or are they different?

Incomplete or non-existent references: why they are sinful

So there you are in the library, two long weary years into a PhD on critiques of Marxism, browsing a book on something totally unrelated as a displacement activity, when you come across the following lines:

A critical flaw in classic Marxist theory, identified clearly in Mackay's classic work on the topic, is that Marx was not only writing before system theory, but also before even deterministic game theory. Mackay's recasting the Marxist enterprise in terms of system optimization versus subsystem optimization via multi-goal stochastic game theory, brilliantly synthesized with a version of possibility theory which incorporates schemata usage in implicit behaviour and provides a firm grounding for political thought in what might be termed the mathematics of virtue.

After some frenzied work with an encyclopaedia and the internet to discover what the technical terms mean, you realize that you have stumbled across a fleeting allusion to what appears not only to be a coherent, solidly based critique of Marx, but also a solid, coherently based model for a viable neo-Marxism, with enormous implications for politics and economics. This looks like something which could devastate your thesis, so you turn to the references to find out more about Mackay's classic work. And you find that there's no mention of it in the references. Nor is there any mention of any Mackay in any of the co-authored works in the references. Nor is there any mention of Mackay anywhere else in the text. A quick despairing search session in the library confirms your suspicion that there are a lot of Mackays in the world, but none of them appears to have written the text in question. You find yourself wishing that you could slowly torture the perpetrator of that missing reference to death. In desperation, you try to contact the perpetrator to ask them for more information, only to find that they died some years ago (perhaps at the hands of someone else who encountered the same missing reference).

You are now faced with a hard set of decisions. Do you continue with your thesis knowing that there might be a fatal flaw at the heart of it? Do you spend years trying to track down the missing reference? Do you abandon your approach because it looks fatally flawed? Do you give way to the dark side, use Mackay's approach, pretend that it was your own bright idea, and wake every night screaming from a dream in which your supervisor introduces you at your viva to your external examiner, one Dr MacKay, who has apparently taken considerable interest in your work?

An extreme scenario, perhaps, but many – perhaps most – researchers have had the experience of stumbling quite by chance across a piece of work in an unrelated discipline which has enormous implications for their own work. That has happened to us. It is enormously frustrating to have to spend months or years trying to track down the relevant article because the person who mentioned it does not give an adequate reference. That has also happened to us.

And this is why references are taken so seriously by professional researchers.

What's the difference between a literature survey and a literature review?

Students' use of the literature usually matures and focuses during the course of their research in a way that corresponds to the development of their research question. The development goes through several phases, as shown in Table 2.

So, the difference between a literature survey and a literature review is the difference between report and critique. Ideally, the completing student should have developed a 'critical voice'. The literature review in the dissertation should 'make sense' of the literature in terms of the thesis. If the literature review is well-structured and appropriately critical, then, ultimately, the research question 'emerges' as an 'inevitable' conclusion of the literature review.

Keeping an annotated bibliography

The core literature repertoire

One of the things that established researchers have is a working knowledge of the relevant literature. Most established researchers have a core repertoire of some 100–150 works on which they can draw readily. These are a useful selection from the hundreds or thousands of articles and books the researcher has digested over time. The repertoire gives a researcher a context in which to place ideas: the collection characterizes the major strands of thinking in the field, identifies the major researchers, and provides research models and examples. Of course the repertoire evolves and must be updated.

Part of doctoral study is acquiring one's own core repertoire. The annotated bibliography is an effective mechanism for facilitating this acquisition – and for keeping a record of the majority of papers that fall outside the core. The annotated bibliography is a powerful research tool. It should be a personal tool, keying into the way you think about and classify things.

Table 2 Development of students' use of literature

Entering student	Later student	Still later student	Completing student
Knows which research area	Knows which research topic	Knows what research question	Knows what research evidence
Reads to find what's already known			Reads to know what isn't already known
Surveys, collects, reports	Organizes information	Selects information relevant to research question	Judges information (quality and gaps)
Wonders how to organize sources	Wonders how to identify problem	Wonders what has been already said about the problem	Wonders what has not been said about the problem

What the annotated bibliography should include

It should include, as a minimum:

* the usual bibliographic information (i.e. everything you might need to cite the work and find it again);
* the date when you read the work;
* notes on what *you* found interesting/seminal/infuriating/etc. about it. (The notes should not just be a copy of the abstract; they should reflect your own critical thinking about your reading. They can be informal, ungrammatical, even inflammatory, as long as they retain meaning about your reading. If you read a paper more than once and get different things from it, then add to the notes – but do keep the original notes, which can prove useful even if you've changed perspective or opinion.)

It can include many other useful things, such as:

* where the physical copy of the work is (e.g. photocopied paper, book borrowed from the library, book in one's own collection);
* keywords, possibly different categories of keyword;
* further references to follow up;
* how you found the work (e.g. who recommended it, who cited it);
* pointers to other work to which it relates;
* the author's abstract.

The discipline

Keeping an annotated bibliography is a discipline. It is easiest to establish a discipline of writing notes about papers as soon as you read them and not going on to the next paper until you have done so. It's *much harder* to go back and try to catch up. Because keeping the bibliography is an 'overhead', and because the point is to maintain access to material, it's best to keep entries to under a page per paper.

Never delete things from the bibliography. 'Discards' can be re-categorized or filed away separately, but one year's 'junk' may be another year's 'gem' (and vice versa). There is also genuine value in keeping track of the changes in categorization: one way is to keep a list of working category 'definitions'. Don't discard the old scheme after a revamp; rather, file it as part of the record.

The discipline is to keep up a continual, accumulating record of your reading and thinking.

Other ways the bibliography can help

* It can help you to 'backtrack' on your own thinking
* It will reflect the evolution of your reading, of what you found important over time, and of your writing about what you read

- When you find a reference and can't remember the paper's particular perspective, the notes can give you the key
- When you reread a paper just before your viva and say: 'Oh no, it doesn't say that at all, what could I have been thinking?' then the notes will be invaluable

The bibliography can help you to manage your reading effectively and keep accessible much more information than you can remember without aid. Always remember:

- keeping a bibliography allows you to use a 'flat', unambiguous physical filing system (e.g. alphabetical by author) while being able to categorize, re-categorize and search fluidly;
- the bibliography can help you avoid rereading papers that are useless and forgettable but have interesting titles;
- the bibliography can help you keep track of the physical form and location of materials.

Mechanisms

There are different ways to keep a bibliography. The most common forms are card catalogues and electronic databases.

Card system examples (from Sally Fincher)

- Kenneth O. May (1973) *Bibliography and Research Manual of the History of Mathematics*. University of Toronto Press. (particularly pp. 2–27).

- Robert M. Pirsig (1991) *Lila: An Inquiry into Morals*. Bantam Press (particularly pp. 22–9).

Bibliographic software packages
Papyrus: http://www.rsd.com/
ProCite: http://www.risinc.com/
EndNote: http://www.niles.com/

Many people don't use specialist packages, preferring to adapt database, spreadsheet or word-processor usage. Many effective bibliographies are simply kept as very long text files.

7   Paper types

Alien it indeed was to all art and literature which sane and balanced readers know . . .

There are different ways of categorizing papers. These ways are seldom described in writing; they are usually treated as craft skills, and also as a matter of personal choice. The categorization described here is a fairly standard one, and some of the paper types in it are recognized fairly formally (for instance, journals have an explicit category of 'review article'). Others, such as 'method-mongering paper' are less formal.

Data-driven papers

This is what most people tend to think of when thinking about papers. The data-driven paper concentrates on describing and discussing the data reported in the paper (as opposed to the methods used to gather the data, for instance). Classic examples include papers reporting the results of surveys or of formal experiments.

Data-driven papers are important for several reasons, and the astute researcher using the 'cabinet-making apprentice' model of research will take care to have at least one data-driven study in their portfolio, if only to demonstrate that they know how to do them.

If the central focus of your paper is the data, as is the case in this type of paper, then the data need to be good. This means (a) solid and also (b) interesting.

'Solid' means that the sample size, quality, representativeness etc. need to be at a level where nobody sensible will even think of questioning them. Novice (and, often, less novice) researchers tend to spend a lot of time worrying about their sample size, on the grounds that more must be better. They also spend quite a lot of time worrying about representativeness, because representativeness is something they feel comfortable speculating about – anyone with an armchair and reasonable general knowledge can usually find several reasons for querying the representativeness of a sample without much effort. These scruples tend to be slaughtered on the altar of expediency the moment that the questionnaires go into the post (questionnaires are a favourite method for collecting large and dubious data sets). If you're doing this sort of work, you need to know about statistics.

The need for interesting data somehow tends to receive less attention among novices, though experts are well aware of it. This is probably because novices do not usually give much thought to what will be in their data until the questionnaires arrive in the post (again, questionnaires are a favoured tool for bad research in this area), and then fade out of public view when the full banality of their results becomes apparent. A more experienced researcher will probably take the view that the best way of conducting a fishing expedition is shooting the fish in a barrel (i.e. only doing a large data-gathering exercise when there is an extremely good chance that the data will produce an eye-catching result).

What catches attention is normally a surprising and useful finding, based on a sample so solid that the data can be treated as a safe foundation for further work. An example of this from computer science is the 'five-thousand year fault' – i.e. the bug which might only be expected to materialize once every five thousand user-years of use. The classic paper on this topic used a very large data set to show what proportion of bugs could be expected to surface with what frequency, and showed that a surprisingly high proportion might only appear once every few thousand years. This has profound implications for the software industry, in areas such as debugging and the development of ultrasafe systems for safety-critical areas such as software for controlling nuclear power plants. An added attraction for the researcher who publishes such work is that it will be quoted in just about every subsequent paper on the topic, thereby boosting the researcher's reputation considerably.

How do you know when you are dealing with fish in a barrel (and therefore a suitable area for a big study) as opposed to an empty pond? This is where a good understanding of theory is useful, because it can lead you to predict a counter-intuitive finding. Another useful approach which complements theory is keeping an eye open for interesting effects while carrying out other research.

A classic data-driven paper can make a reputation. Most data-driven papers, however, do not break new ground; you need to have solid, interesting data to make a reputation from this type of publication.

Tutorial papers

Tutorial papers describe a method and explain how to use it. They are invaluable, but journals are not fond of publishing them, on the grounds that they do not normally involve original research, which is what journals are all about. However, if you do manage to publish the classic tutorial paper for a method, then people will quote it for years to come.

Method-mongering papers

These papers describe a method, usually with the aim of suggesting that it should be more widely used. The method may be original (i.e. developed by the authors) or may be an established method from another field which has not received sufficient attention in the field where it is now being described.

These papers overlap with tutorial papers, but it is possible for a paper to be a method-mongering paper without being a tutorial paper. A common example of this is a paper which shows how a method can be applied to problems in the researcher's field, but which does not describe the method itself in great detail – instead, the author typically refers the reader to a suitable tutorial paper or textbook.

One advantage of method-mongering papers is that if you are already familiar with a suitable method from another field, then you can put together a method-mongering paper fairly easily; all you will need are some nice examples of your method cracking problems, traditionally viewed as difficult in the new field of application. You don't normally need a large sample size, since the point is made just as effectively with a small sample (or even a single example, if it's a good one).

Consciousness-raising papers

These are less psychedelic than they sound. They are intended to raise awareness of issues which have not previously received sufficient attention in a field of research; these issues often involve application of methods or concepts which are standard in another field, but not well known in the field where the consciousness-raising paper is written.

Good consciousness-raising papers can attract a lot of attention, and can change the viewpoint of an entire field. Bad ones can give the author a reputation as a pompous windbag. As usual in research, one of the touchstones is whether you are giving the reader some really interesting new tools to play with. Saying that (for instance) the methods of hard sciences are not always directly applicable to the softer sciences may well be true, but it doesn't really get us anywhere. Saying that (for instance) game theory can be used to provide a mathematical grounding for evolutionary ecology is the research equivalent of giving a small child the keys to a toy warehouse, and made John Maynard Smith the revered founding father of an entire new field of research.

First-year students are fond of complaining that their field neglects various important issues. They are usually less fond of checking whether this is a standard complaint of first-year students, and whether there is a good reason for these issues being neglected. Experienced researchers (a) have heard a lot of first-year students talking and (b) have reliable chums who can be used to see whether a promising idea will pass the giggle test or not, before going any further with it.

Theoretical papers

Theoretical papers have a lot of kudos. They discuss theoretical issues such as the inherent limitations of symbolic reasoning, and can be highly influential. The published papers of this type are typically written by authorities in the area, and actually have quite a large component of review and methodology in them (it's difficult to tackle advanced theory properly without considerable reference to the literature and to the methods used in the area). The unpublished papers of this type are typically written by inexperienced new researchers who have not bothered to do the research equivalent of reading the FAQs first. It's advisable not to try writing theoretical papers until you're sure you're ready for the task and have evidence to support this belief.

Review papers

Thucydides would have approved of review papers. Every ten years or so, someone in a given field will decide that the time is right for a paper surveying the key research in that field since the last review paper was written. They will then survey all the main papers, and many of the minor papers, written over that period. This is a very substantial undertaking and can easily involve reading and assessing hundreds of papers and books, in addition to identifying and summarizing the main themes within that work.

Review papers are invaluable for ordinary mortals, since they provide an excellent way into a body of research, complete with overviews and key readings.

Review papers are typically written by people so utterly familiar with a field that they will have read all the relevant papers anyway (and will probably have written quite a few of them as well). However, there is one useful exception to this generalization: if you have done the literature review for your PhD properly, then it should (pretty much by definition) be publishable as a review paper. In practice, most people by this stage of their PhD are so sick of the topic and/or scared of being told that they've missed something vital that they find reasons not to go down the review paper road.

Demonstration of concept papers

The demonstration of concept papers overlaps with various other types, particularly method-mongering papers. It involves demonstrating that a particular concept (usually a method, but not always – it may, for instance, be a conceptual framework) is feasible, useful and interesting. This is a handy precursor to applying for funding.

If you know what you are doing, you can get away with a single set of data from a single subject for a demonstration of concept paper. The tricky bit is finding a suitable concept in the first place . . .

Research methods with which these papers overlap

- Formal experiment
- Field experiment
- Case study
- Action research
- Survey

8 Writing

He wrote in a complicated style, overloaded and lacking in charm. Not that he was indifferent to language and its nuances; on the contrary, correct use of language was for him a moral question, its debasement a symptom of moral breakdown.

If you're an experienced academic and someone is trying to persuade you to take on someone you've never heard of as a PhD student, then one of the first things you ask is whether they can write. This is shorthand for 'write good academic English, preferably in various styles to suit different needs, ranging from journal articles to plausible opening letters to potential funders'. If the answer is 'no' then you are in a strong bargaining position if the other person really wants you to take this student on, since nobody in their senses is keen to take on a student who can't write. A point worth noting is that this refers to good academic English, which is not the same as formal grammar – there are plenty of cases of students who write very good academic English, even though they are not native speakers of English and their formal grammar is wobbly in places. Conversely, there are many native speakers of English whose understanding of academic writing is woeful.

So, what do we mean by 'good academic English' and why is it not the same as formal English grammar? That is the topic of this chapter. We discuss how to structure what you write; how to send out the right signals between the lines of what you write; and what to do when you encounter problems such as writer's block.

This chapter overlaps considerably with the chapter on reading, so if you're about to write something, then it would be a good idea to reread Chapter 6.

That concludes this introduction, which by an elegant example of poetic justice turned out to be more tricky to write than the rest of the sections on writing, even though it's much the shortest. However, it's finished now, so we don't care (another line which it would be wiser not to include at the end of your PhD thesis . . .)

Journal papers

This section focuses on journal papers, but much the same principles apply to conference papers and other forms of publication such as book chapters. We have gone for journal papers rather than the other types on the grounds that publishing a journal paper is usually viewed as a sign that you are a fully-fledged academic – there is a general assumption that the other publication venues are variable in their selectivity and quality control, but that journals are exclusive and discerning. This is far from invariably true, but it's a useful rule of thumb, especially if you are aiming for an academic career and want to get some useful things on your CV.

Supervisors differ in their opinions of students writing journal papers. Some think it is a Good Thing, and encourage it; some think it is a Bad Thing, and discourage it; others again think that it is a Good Thing in some circumstances, but not in others (e.g. if it is likely to be used as a displacement activity by a student who ought to be spending every last second finishing their write-up because the deadline is next Tuesday).

So, the first thing to do regarding writing a journal paper is to check with your supervisor about the wisdom of this scheme in relation to your particular situation. If they say no, with good reason, then take their advice; if they give you their blessing and send you off to get started, then you need to think about what to do next.

Where to publish

The first question is venue (i.e. where to publish). This involves consideration of the prestige of the journal, the readership of the journal, the degree of match between your chosen topic and the focus of the journal, and the acceptance rates of the journal. The usual strategy is to go for the most prestigious journal that you have a reasonable chance of being published in, which then raises questions of how to assess your chances. A cup of coffee with someone knowledgeable is a good idea at this point.

These things having been done, you need to do some basic homework, which is neglected by a surprising proportion of aspiring researchers. The first thing is to read the guidelines for contributors to your chosen journal. These are usually printed in the journal, or available on its website, or (as a last resort) from its editor. The guidelines will tell you the word limits for articles, the procedures for handling tables and figures, the number of copies to submit etc. All these guidelines are there for a good reason. If you follow them, then the editor will be more likely to think positively about you. It is inadvisable to antagonize editors needlessly. The following sections say a bit about each of the main topics in the guidelines, to explain their purpose and to suggest ways of improving your chances of success.

The focus of the journal is important. Journals have to focus, because of the sheer volume of research being published – even very specialist journals have to reject a high proportion of good papers because of space limitations. (Journal editors work to a page budget each year, which limits how much they can publish.) You therefore need to make sure that your article is relevant to the journal you are submitting to. If in doubt, contact the editor (politely) and ask. Journal editors are normally serious players in their research field, unlike commercial editors, so the editor will be the person who makes the decision about how relevant your paper is. If you are skilful and/or lucky, the editor may like the idea behind your paper and may give you some suggestions on how to present it (e.g. which themes to stress and which to play down). This advice is important, and should be treated seriously (though remember that following it does not guarantee acceptance).

What your submission should look like

Your submission should contain a covering letter, the relevant number of hard copies of your article, a soft copy if required and anything else specified in the guidelines to contributors. The letter should be polite and brief; it should make it clear which author is handling the correspondence (if there is more than one) and should give full contact details for that author. The article itself should follow the guidelines for contributors. The next few paragraphs describe the guidelines and explain why they matter.

The word length issue is important because of the page budget. The editor may have to choose between publishing one longish article and squeezing in two short articles, and will certainly be keeping an eye on the page budget. Tricks like using a small font or wide margins will not be well received. The page budget in the journal will be calculated from the number of words in your article (including tables and figures), not from the number of pages in your manuscript, so small fonts or wide margins won't deceive the editor for long.

Once your article has got through this initial check, the editor will send out copies to reviewers, who will give their opinion on it. Procedures vary between journals. Most prefer to send hard copies to the reviewers, since reviewers like to scribble on hard copies and don't like having to print off papers from soft copy which may be in an inscrutable format or font. Editors will therefore ask contributors to send enough hard copies for each reviewer, plus one for the editor's files. If there are two reviewers, you will be asked to send three hard copies; one journal which we know used to ask for *eight* hard copies. If you send too few hard copies, then the editorial team will have to make some copies themselves. Editorial teams have better things to do with their time than photocopying your manuscript, so it is a good idea to send the right number of copies. Some journals ask for electronic submission. The editorial team of these journals are unlikely to take kindly to your submitting a soft copy written in Grunt2004 or some other format which their system has never heard of, and will probably not be interested in your assertion that this is a technically superior format to what everyone else uses. Similarly, if you submit soft copy to a journal which asks for hard copy submissions, then the editorial team are unlikely to add you to their Christmas card list – soft copy submissions are a wonderful idea in principle, but reality is rather different.

Some journals use double-blind reviewing; others don't. In double-blind reviewing, the reviewers don't know who you are and you don't know who the reviewers are. For this purpose, the submission guidelines may ask you to put your name and contact details on a separate sheet from the rest of the paper, so they can be detached before the papers are sent to the reviewers. Editors of such journals will not want to spend part of their morning applying correction fluid over extraneous authors' names.

Reviewers may or may not scribble on your manuscript; copy-editors certainly will. A small proportion of contributors submit copy so clean (i.e. manuscripts so free of errors) that they are remembered by the editorial team for this fact alone. Most, however, require a noticeable amount of copy-editing, often involving mistakes with references (e.g. a paper described in the main text as having been published in one year, and described in the references as having been published in a different year). For this purpose, copy-editors and reviewers need double-spaced text so they can note what needs doing. Submitting a single-spaced manuscript is a sign that you are an amateur and probably clueless.

The guidelines will specify that the article has not been submitted for publication elsewhere. If you submit the same article to two or more journals simultaneously and are caught doing it (you probably will be, because the number of available reviewers for a given area is usually small), then you will be blackballed from the relevant journals (i.e. banned from publishing in them). This is because multiple submissions waste the time of everyone involved, and because there are legal implications involving copyright if two editors publish the same article. Editors are no keener on legal hassles than anyone else. Submitting different papers, describing different aspects of the same topic is usually admissible, but you need to be careful about the degree of similarity – if the two papers are very similar, the relevant editors are likely to take a dim view.

What happens next

After you have submitted the article, you will receive a letter of acknowledgement from the editor at some point. Editors are busy people, and the acknowledgement may take a few weeks. The paper will then go out to review and be reviewed/sat on/lost by reviewers for weeks or months. At some point after this, the editor will make a decision about what to do with your paper. If you are lucky, the editor will accept it subject to neatly specified changes. If you are unlucky, it will be accepted subject to satisfying the requirements of the reviewers, which will be enclosed with the editor's letter, and will contain confused, vague, verbose and mutually contradictory requirements. If you are moderately unlucky, your paper will be rejected. You should aim to have a reasonable proportion of your papers rejected; if they are all accepted, you are probably aiming too low and should go for a more prestigious venue. (Increasing your rejection rate by writing worse papers is not a good strategy . . .)

The wise thing to do with corrections is to take the initiative. Draw up a list of the required changes, work through them systematically and write a covering letter listing the changes and saying clearly and specifically how you have made them and where. This makes life much easier for the editor, who may well give you the benefit of the doubt and accept the revisions without passing them back to the reviewers. If you're unlucky, you may need to go through another round of slugging it out with the reviewers. Taking advice from experienced and wise colleagues is a good idea at this point.

The process of publication

Acceptance

When and if you get through to this stage, you will receive a letter or email from the editor informing you that your paper has been accepted for publication in the *Journal of Nude Mice Studies*, or whatever the venue is called. You may be asked to send some more hard copies and/or soft copies of the accepted version of your paper.

Copy-editing

At some point after this, you will hear from the copy-editor, who is sublimely unconcerned with the academic content of your work but who is very interested indeed in its presentation. The copy-editor's job is to ensure that your article is presented with proper spelling, grammar, punctuation etc. and also to ensure that things like dates and figures are internally consistent. The copy-editor will find inconsistent references, missing references, inconsistent numbers between text and tables and so forth, and will send you a list of questions to answer. A typical question will be along the lines of: 'Page 8, line 7 refers to Smith 1999, but the references show Smith 1998. Which is correct?' You then have the rewarding task of trying to track down the original article again, so you can find out what the answer is. Skilled and experienced researchers will generally reply with a complete list of answers on the same working day, and be much appreciated by the copy-editor;

novices will generally not manage this, and will realize why their supervisors have placed so much emphasis on getting references exactly right. If the corrections require an excessive amount of copy-editor's time, then you may be required to pay for that time (and copy-editors are not cheap), so there are also financial implications in getting it right.

Tables and figures

One frequent source of annoyance to all parties is tables and figures, lumped together here because the implications are pretty similar for both of them. Many printers, for obscure technical reasons, handle tables and figures separately from text, and insert them into the text after it has been sorted out. Others don't. The guidelines to authors will specify what you need to do with tables and figures. For many journals, you have to put each table and figure on a separate page at the end of your manuscript, and indicate in the text where each one should go (usually via a blank line, and then a line saying 'TABLE 1 ABOUT HERE' at the appropriate point in the text). If you include your tables and figures in the text when you have been told not to, then the usual outcomes are either that you are asked to rewrite the article in the right form, or that the printers produce beautiful text, accompanied by figures and tables which look as if they have been dragged through mud, and which stand in hideous contrast to the crisp, professional-looking tables and figures in the other articles of that issue. You can, if you wish to make a few enemies, tell the editorial team that in an age of electronic publishing the most technically excellent solution is to work from the soft copy with embedded tables and figures; it might, however, be a good idea to ask yourself whether the editorial team are using their current procedure out of uninformed stupidity, or whether there might possibly be other factors involved which they know about and which you don't.

Proofs

The next main stage involves the proofs. These are the printer's pre-final version of what your article will look like when it appears in the journal. For technical and logistical reasons, proofs appear at the last moment, and are usually sent to authors with instructions to check them for accuracy, and to reply within a specified and extremely short period, normally between 24 hours and three days. You might want to think about the implications of that, such as what happens if you are on holiday when the proofs arrive, and the proofs contain a disastrous misprint which makes you look like an idiot or a charlatan. You might also want to think about how much you know about copy-editing, and how you would indicate a misprint in a way which didn't end in tears (for instance, with your helpful comment of 'this should read "24" you idiot!' reproduced in full in the published version). The proofs arrive with helpful guidelines on how to correct them, but it's useful to practise proof-correcting in a safe environment before this stage (as usual, a cup of coffee with an experienced colleague is useful here – they will probably be able to tell you which secretaries have been concealing their expertise in copy-editing and proof-reading from you). It's also a good idea to line up a colleague to keep an eye open for proofs if you are away at the critical time.

Miscellaneous points

A couple of miscellaneous points: firstly, make sure that the soft copy you send with the final version of the manuscript is the version from which the manuscript was prepared. It is incredibly irritating to the editorial team to discover that you have helpfully changed the text, so that the soft copy does not correspond to the hard copy. Secondly, don't try to change the content of the manuscript at proof stage – only correct errors introduced by the printers. Adding a couple of words can have a knock-on effect that extends to later pages and adds considerably to printing costs. Editors have a correction budget as well as a page budget, and will not love you if you do bad things to either of these.

It's worth mentioning at this point that copy-editors are usually more human than they appear from their lists of questions, so if you're lost and confused, try phoning or emailing them and discussing the situation constructively with them. (They are usually working to tight deadlines, so contacting them quickly via phone is more helpful to them than belated letters in the post.) Faxes can be a very useful way of handling some parts of the corrections – you can annotate the relevant page and fax it through to the copy-editor.

Once you've got through this stage, you can add the article to your CV and wait for (a) the copies of the journal to arrive in the post and (b) the journal to appear on the library shelves. Some journals send you offprints (i.e. copies of your article in splendid isolation); others send you a smaller number of copies of the entire issue of the journal where your article appears. Be miserly with these; it's tempting to give them proudly to everyone in sight, but they'll need to last you a long time. Most departments will want a copy of the article for their records, to be used when the next research assessment exercise (RAE) or equivalent comes along; it's a good idea to give them an offprint rather than a hard copy of your own accepted draft, because when the time of the Great Annual Departmental Report comes along, they will need to include things like the ISBN and page number details for your article, which will not appear on your own draft but which will definitely appear in the journal, and probably appear in the offprint.

A closing point: most journals ask you to sign a copyright waiver as a condition of publication. The Society of Authors is conducting one of its quiet, polite and very efficient campaigns over this issue, and some journals are already changing their policy as a result. In the meantime, there's no need to be paranoid if you receive a copyright waiver form, but you might want to contact the Society of Authors as well as the usual experienced colleague if you have questions about this. The Society is helpful about all sorts of things and offers a fascinating range of services to members (including free legal advice on publishers' contracts); anyone who has had a book published, or a serious offer of publication for a book, is eligible for membership, and the Society's rates are very reasonable. It is also an affiliated trade union, which led at one point to the situation where Prince Charles (a long-standing member) had Terry Pratchett as his union boss.

Anyway, back to the closing paragraph. The main things to remember about journal articles are:

- most articles are rejected;
- leading researchers have developed thick skins, failed researchers haven't;
- reviewers are only human, so don't take it personally if they're rude and contradict each other;
- leading researchers are leading researchers because they learn from their experiences;
- even leading researchers had to start somewhere.

That's the end of this bit, apart from wishing you good luck.

Papers from theses

These guidelines are the ones that *we* use. We don't claim that they are perfect, or that they are the only truth. You might, however, find them useful as a starting point. The guidelines are intended for use with undergraduate and taught MSc dissertations as well as for PhD students; institutions vary about policy in this area, so don't be surprised if the system in your institution is different.

Before starting

- If you or your supervisor think that the work might possibly be publishable, then agree ground rules for publication as early as possible – preferably before you have committed to a particular project. If you can't agree at this stage, then you won't agree later. If it looks too acrimonious, then think about doing a different project, maybe with someone else. This is also particularly important in relation to intellectual property rights if the concept might bring in money.
- Agree venue – where you will submit the paper.
- Agree what you will do if the paper is rejected. You do not want to have all the team independently submitting revamped versions of the paper to

other journals without your name on them. One sensible option is to agree who will take on the lead role if the paper is to be submitted to another journal; that person will normally then become the first author. This can be repeated until success or exhaustion.

Authorship

- Authorship should be agreed at the outset with all parties – normally the student and supervisor(s), with the student as first author. If you can't agree, then forget about writing the paper.
- If the work is a compilation of several projects, then the compilation writer should be first author.
- Authors should have made a substantial contribution to the work. A single advisory session (e.g. from another member of staff) will not normally constitute a sufficiently substantial contribution. If you want to take advice from other members of staff about some part of your work, then check first with your supervisor to avoid inadvertently causing bad feeling.

Submission and revisions

- All authors and co-authors should agree to the final version before the paper is submitted.
- Don't submit to more than one journal at a time. Journals blacklist people who do it (i.e. they never publish anything by that author again). There are sound reasons for this – multiple submissions of this sort can lead to an editor inadvertently breaking the law via breach of copyright. It also wastes the time of the editors and referees, who are usually overworked and who do not like having their time wasted.
- If the paper is accepted subject to revision, then all authors and co-authors should have a reasonable opportunity to comment on the revised draft before it is submitted (e.g. by being sent a copy, with a request for any comments within two weeks).
- All authors and co-authors should be kept informed of any developments within a reasonable time of their occurrence (e.g. a verdict from the venue).

After publication

- Each author and co-author should receive at least one offprint of the paper.
- All authors and co-authors should receive at least one copy of any publicity about the work.

In case of disputes

- Seek advice from relevant people in the first instance, before matters become too unpleasant.

- Where possible, keep a written record of agreements at each stage – for instance, agree authorship via email.

Paper checklist

Content

- Do you have a clear question?
- Have you demonstrated why the question is interesting?
- Have you demonstrated why the question is non-trivial?
- Have you demonstrated why the answer is non-obvious?
- Is your 'red thread' evident; do you have a clear and coherent argument?

Setting your paper in context

- Have you located your work with respect to the existing literature?
- Is it clear what theory informs your work and how your work contributes to theory?
- Have you discussed the assumptions, antecedents and limitations of your work?
- Have you discussed how your work leads forward to future work?

Evidence

- Is your evidence clearly presented, according to the standards of your discipline?
- Is your interpretation distinguished from your data?
- Do your conclusions follow from your evidence?
- Can someone repeat or replicate your work based on the description given in the paper?

Due credit

- Have you agreed on authorship and on the order in which authors are listed?
- Have you acknowledged the people who should be acknowledged?
- Are the citations accurate and complete?

Use of literature

- Have you cited the seminal text(s)?
- Have you cited the classic texts?

- Have you cited the foundational text(s)?
- Do you have at least five references on the first page?
- Do your references span the period from the seminal paper to last year?
- Have you included a reference which shows you know the literature which goes beyond the standard references for a particular topic?

Venue

- Have you decided on the venue?
- Have you checked for deadlines (if applicable)?
- Have you read and followed the guidelines for authors?

Presentation

- Have you followed the guidelines for authors?
- Are figures and references in house style?
- Have you spell-checked the paper?
- Have you used appropriate national spellings (British or American)?
- Do the headings provide useful and sufficient signposting?
- Does your presentation conform to the conventions in your discipline?

9 Writing structure

Still, it gave the facts – some of them – and apart from being dated 'off Barcelona' in the customary way, whereas it was really being written in Port Mahon the day after his arrival, it contained no falsehood . . .

One sobering thought for most PhD students is the sheer size of the written thesis which they will have to produce. It will probably be the largest single piece of written work that they produce in their life. Most students are understandably intimidated by this. The reality is not so bad, once you understand how to break down the problem into manageably small chunks, which is what this chapter is about. The written thesis consists of a series of chunks, in the form of chapters; each chapter in turn consists of chunks, in the form of standard chapter sections. By the time you're down to that level, you're dealing with a few pages at a time, which is far more manageable. This chapter is about structure in writing: structure generally, and structure specifically for the written thesis.

Within each discipline, there are usually several well-established types of publication, each with its own standard structure. Chapter 7, on paper types, discusses this; so does Chapter 6, on reading. You should know what these types are for your discipline, be familiar with the structures and use these structures in your own writing until you are experienced enough to know when you can depart from them.

A useful structure for a paper or thesis describing empirical work is to have a series of clearly defined questions in the introduction, and then have corresponding tables of results in the results section and corresponding sections of discussion in the discussion section. This provides the reader (and yourself) with a clear idea of where you are going and why. So, for instance, you might have three main questions in the introduction, mirrored by three corresponding main sections in the results section, and then three corresponding main sections in the discussion, so that each question is clearly addressed and clearly answered.

Within each of these sections, you start by telling your readers what you're going to describe and discuss. Then describe and discuss it. End by telling the reader what you've just done. End on a clear, positive note.

Writing up

One day, if all goes well, you will have to produce the final written thesis derived from your research. Most people have strong feelings about this point. These feelings include dread, confusion, despair and being utterly sick of the whole topic. If you are in this state, then be reassured: these feelings are completely normal and are fixable. So, what do you do about it?

Good advice

Work backwards from where you want to end up. You want to end up with the examiners looking pleased and relieved as they finish reading your thesis and settle down to watch the latest episode of *Buffy the Vampire Slayer* or whatever examiners do in the evening. You do not want to end up with the examiners looking worried or angry. How do you do this?

A good way to start is to look at things from the examiners' point of view, particularly the external examiner's. If you're eminent enough and a safe enough pair of hands to be asked to examine, you'll also have acquired a depressingly large set of other responsibilities and a bloody-minded attitude towards having your time wasted. You'll therefore be torn between a desire to see standards maintained and a desire to get the whole business over with as soon as possible. The result of this is that you will want to see a thesis which is a clear, unequivocal pass. The thing you will least want to see is something which might just about scrape through with major revisions: this will entail weeks of further hassle for you if the wretched candidate ends up sending allegedly improved revisions to you for approval. So, what makes you as an external decide that something is a clear pass rather than a thing of horror?

The basic issue is whether the thesis is an original contribution to knowledge at an appropriate level for a doctorate. If these three boxes can be unhesitatingly ticked, then everyone is happy and can get on with their lives. You as a candidate can tackle the first couple of boxes ('original' and 'contribution to knowledge') by some judicious phrasing. If you use phrases such as 'this extends the classic work in this area by Smith and Jones (2002) by applying rough set theory' then the 'originality' bit is pretty clear: your original bit is the extension of Smith and Jones' work. If you use phrasing such as 'these findings have significant implications for research in this field, which has typically viewed this topic as of comparatively minor importance' then the 'contribution to knowledge' bit is also pretty clear. Judicious phrasing by itself is not enough; you need to have done good research as well. However, good research needs to be clearly presented or there is the risk that the examiners will miss the needle of your original contribution in the haystack of your unstructured prose. (Yes, we know that haystacks actually are structured, but why waste a vivid metaphor?) A good structure is useful for supporting the judicious phrasing; there should be clearly demarcated subsections which deal specifically with the originality and the contribution to knowledge of the topic you're investigating and/or of the method you're using. (These will have suitably tactful titles: entitling them 'original contribution to knowledge' is generally viewed as a bit tacky.)

The third box ('appropriate level for a doctorate') is not so easy to point to at a specific place in the text; like the lettering in a stick of rock, it runs all the way through. The tip about getting a couple of journal articles published to show you're working at the right level is quite a useful one, but if you have to resort to that as an argument in the viva, then you're in trouble – it's best viewed as a nice extra and/or as a last resort, not as a main component of your case. The chapters on reading and writing are particularly relevant here: the examiners will be reading between the lines of your thesis, and if you have written the right things between the lines then everyone will be happy. Most of this will consist of numerous small things, minor by themselves, but major when taken together. If you've been developing a taxonomy of social inclusion problems in secondary education, then showing that you have read some of the literature on taxonomic theory is likely to send out the right signals to the examiners, but will not by itself be enough to demonstrate doctoral-level research – you'll also need to use the right language and technical terms throughout, to refer to the right literature, to discuss the findings at the right level of abstraction and so forth. If you get into the habit early on of reading and writing between the lines, then you will do this automatically when you write-up, and significantly improve your chances of a straight pass.

Standard (but still good) advice

The first thing is to do some positive things to improve your mood. The standard self-help books are good on this. Most of the things they recommend are feasible even for impoverished PhD students with little spare time, and many of them are fun. For instance, 15 minutes of exercise will improve your mood, improve your health and will also help you to regain perspective. The exercise can include things like dusting those obscure areas of your house/flat/room/garret that you keep putting off till another day. Such tasks will either leave you with nicer surroundings or give you renewed enthusiasm for writing up, so you benefit either way.

The *other* first thing to do (you can do them in parallel) is to stop thinking about the thesis as a vast monolithic *thing*, and start thinking about it as a document composed of various bits, each there for a reason and each in turn composed of other, smaller bits. You can write each of those bits, so it's just a case of writing a manageable number of manageable-sized bits, rather than a case of taking on a massive single task. You might find it useful to write down the chapter headings of your thesis and then write the subheadings for each chapter. You can do a plan of which bits you will write when, remembering to allow plenty of time for the tables, references and appendices. All this sort of thing is in the standard-issue books on doing a PhD, and it's both true and useful.

What you need to remember, and what isn't always covered explicitly in the standard-issue books, is to get your cabinet-making skills visibly onto the pages. Your references are an obvious example. Do you have the key references neatly on display in your bibliography? Do you have the right spread of dates? Do you have references showing independent reading outside the standard stuff? Do you have references showing that you're a nit-picking perfectionist who has done thorough background reading? And so forth. Another obvious example is the types of study you have conducted. If you are working in a discipline where cabinet-making includes doing big surveys with heavy stats, and in-depth case studies without stats, then you need to make sure that your studies are clearly (but subtly) presented in a way which fits neatly into that framework.

You should have already written up a fair amount by the time you reach this stage. Some bits, like the bibliography, you should have been conscientiously building up as you went along. Others, like the 'method' section if you're doing an experimental PhD, can be written up as you do each study and are unlikely to change significantly.

What will change most are your introductory and discussion sections for each chapter (including your initial chapter with the main literature review). Over the course of the last few years you will almost certainly have realized that the real issues in the topic you're studying aren't the ones that you expected at the start, so the literature review you write in year three will be very different from the literature review that you wrote in year one. This is completely normal and healthy; it would be worrying if you studied a topic for several years and concluded that your initial hunches were as accurate a set of insights as those obtained by several years of study. It's highly likely that this is what happened to Thucydides, who stopped writing his great work in mid-sentence and then almost certainly returned to rewriting his opening chapters, to identify themes whose importance he had missed originally. By this stage, you will probably feel remarkably little sympathy for a humourless pedant who died centuries before Christ was born, but if a genius of his stature encountered this problem, then there's no shame in your encountering it too.

So, what is the implication for you? The implication is that you will, if you have any sense, seriously consider writing your introductory and discussion sections again, from scratch, at this stage. This will allow you to make sure that your narrative spine is good, with each section leading neatly into the next, rather than looking like a collection of random things strung together more in hope than expectation. You can, for instance, pose a neat set of questions in the introduction, make sure that each set of tables in the results relates clearly to one of these questions, and then discuss the answers to the questions one by one in your discussion section, with all the potential loose ends neatly tied off.

Using the cabinet-making analogy again, you need to polish the final work. Make sure that the first pages the examiners read are all pages which display your skills – good references, evidence of expertise, good presentation etc. Allow plenty of time for this. Fixing minor punctuation errors in your references is not conceptually taxing, but it takes a lot of time if you have made a lot of minor errors.

The rest of this chapter covers some of the questions whose answers you may be keen to know, but which you are too embarrassed to ask anyone. It also covers some of the questions to which you should know the answers, but which you may never have thought of. As always, the final word on this should come from your supervisor; we are describing general principles, but your particular thesis may be non-standard in ways which require different treatment.

Some classic mistakes, and how to avoid them

- Don't leave it all till the last minute. Plan ahead, and allow plenty of contingency time, including time for the binding of the finished article.
- Don't waffle. It's your responsibility to be clear, not the examiners' responsibility to divine your meaning.
- Don't try to evade an issue by vague or ambiguous wording – examiners are very good at spotting this and will grill you mercilessly about it in the viva.
- Don't simplify. Write for fellow professionals, or you'll come across as not understanding the full complexities of your area.
- Don't use big words if you aren't absolutely sure of your meaning. A big word, wrongly used, will make you look like an idiot. Examiners will almost certainly know bigger and more esoteric words than you do, and will not be impressed by your ability to misuse a thesaurus.
- Don't follow the conventions of another discipline or country in the style of your write-up. If you don't know the conventions of your discipline, find them out. If you disagree with them, then do so *after* you've got your PhD, not in your write-up.

- Finally, and most important, don't forget the three golden principles: don't lie; don't try to be funny; but above all, don't panic and blurt out the truth . . .

Dissertation structure: core concepts

What is the dissertation's *organizing principle?* Many are evident in existing work, for example:

- identification of gaps, *leading to* gap filling;
- unfolding of evidence (one study leading to another);
- theoretical motivation *leading to* hypothesis-driven investigation *leading to* refinement of theory;
- refinement or iterative development (iteration on a model; iterative development of an application);
- practice-based (historical progression, with reflection);
- problem *leading to* empirical research *leading to* emergent theory.

Although many first drafts are organized chronologically (in terms of how the ideas developed and the research was conducted), this is rarely the most appropriate structure. The archetypal empirically-based *dissertation structure* is:

- introduction;
- literature survey;
- methodology/research approach;
- presentation of empirical study/implementation;
- results/discussion;
- conclusions and further work, where the methodology/study/results sequence may be repeated for additional studies or iterations.

Some *familiar problems* with structure are:

- conclusions not foreshadowed;
- methodology entangled with data and discussion;
- evidence too dispersed;
- results not distinguished from interpretation and discussion;
- two topics whose relationship is not established;
- failure to 'close the loop' (i.e. failure to link back to theory, to show how the question/problem was addressed or to relate the outcomes to the objectives).

The dissertation: some common questions, some checklists and some questions to ask yourself

Length

How many chapters, and how long?

A maximum dissertation length (typically around 100,000 words) is specified by most institutions. Sometimes you can use appendices to extend the limit. However, it's worth remembering that the examiner has to read it all. The number of chapters should be determined by the structure of what you have done (usually one chapter per discrete chunk of work), and the length should be *as much as is needed* to give a proper scholarly account of what you have done, *and no more.*

Structure

This topic recurs throughout this book. A brief set of questions to ask yourself is:

- Is the argument clear and strong?
- Is everything that was included necessary to the argument?
- Conversely, is everything included that was necessary to the argument?
- Does the text flow, or does it read like a shopping list?

Headings

Headings are the 'signposts' to the argument: they should reveal the structure and suggest the content of the thesis. Headings should therefore be descriptive (and should be long enough to be so). Good headings are clear and informative. A good test is to look over the table of contents to see how much you can anticipate about the research just by scanning the headings. In Avic's words, when describing 'elegant' headings: 'Just looking at that I could tell what I could expect'.

Some useful questions to ask yourself about the headings in the table of contents are:

- Where is the problem stated? Can you tell what the problem is?
- Where is the methodology described? Can you tell what was actually done in the research?
- Where is the evidence presented? Can you tell what kind of evidence it is?
- What is the approach or stance adopted for the work?
- Is a new model or theory presented?
- What is important about this research?
- What are the conclusions?

The research question

This is the central part of your thesis; it is horribly easy to forget to state the research question explicitly, precisely because you are so familiar with it that you cannot imagine anyone else not knowing it. Some things to ask yourself are:

- Where does the statement of the specific research question occur in the introductory chapter? (i.e. how long does the reader have to wait to discover what the particular focus of the dissertation will be?) Is there a one-sentence or a one-paragraph statement of the thesis?
- Is the statement of the research question clear and concise?
- Is the statement of the research question phrased as aims, objectives, questions, goal, problems to be solved, challenges to be addressed, or in some other form?

Theory and evidence

Theoretical context provides the rationale for your work; evidence underpins your claim to have made an original contribution to knowledge. You might want to ask yourself the following questions:

- How is theory presented in the dissertation?
- How is theory used in the argument?
- Is it clear what theory the research relates to?
- How well is the design of the research related to theoretical underpinnings?
- Is it clear how the research contributes to theory in the domain?
- What are the proportions of theory and evidence?
- Is the evidence presented objectively?
- Are the premises stated?
- Are the methods described in a way that allows replication/repetition?
- Is the interpretation distinguished from the data?
- Does the interpretation-as-evidence follow from the data?
- Do the conclusions follow from the evidence?

Introduction

This is where you should (a) create a good first impression and (b) show your reader that there is a good reason for your spending several years of your life researching this topic. Typical ingredients of an introduction are:

- statement of problem/question;
- broad rationale for problem/question;
- explanation of language and terminology (if needed);
- aims, goals, objectives;

- general statement of contribution;
- indication of research approach;
- plan for the remainder of the dissertation: overview of argument.

Final chapter(s)

Your goals here reflect those in the introduction: you use the final chapter(s) to show the reader that you have achieved something worthwhile over the last few years, and to create a good closing impression. Typical ingredients of the final chapter are:

- summary of results (may be compared explicitly against objectives stated in the introduction);
- discussion about how the results generalize;
- discussion of limitations (phrased positively);
- statement of contribution to knowledge;
- future work (phrased strongly and positively);
- speculation (in moderation).

Literature review

This reviews the literature, as opposed to simply reporting it. Where should the literature review appear? The answer is in another question: what is the literature review for? The answers to that question are:

- to frame the research (setting it in the context of existing theory and prior research, showing how it is motivated and showing why it is needed and significant);
- to distinguish this research from other work;
- to establish authority.

Given that the literature review should frame the research, it makes sense that it should be presented at the *beginning* of the dissertation. Many dissertations add additional, specific references throughout the work – for example, elaborating a technique or providing corroboration or contrast within a discussion section. Some distribute the literature review throughout the dissertation on an 'as needed' basis, in effect providing an introduction and literature review for each major part of the research – this can be effective, but is also risky. It is unusual and inadvisable to leave the literature review to the end (such a dissertation would not normally be considered to be well written).

The review should contain:

- an arguably comprehensive/representative collection of literature;
- seminal papers;
- selective papers relating strictly to the focus of the thesis.

The range of literature needed is discussed throughout this book, as is the desirable number of citations. The required range of publication dates is also discussed throughout this book.

Citations should take the following forms:

- a methodical, 'objective' summary of a given paper;
- single-sentence statements;
- direct quotations;
- collective paraphrasing – grouping papers as members of a line of thinking;
- editorial paraphrasing – choosing to report what serves the argument (i.e. reporting what the paper has to contribute to the argument, not what the paper is about in its own terms).

The report of the paper should be distinguished from its interpretation.

You should ask yourself whether the literature is just reported or whether there is analysis and sense-making.

The key to the literature review is establishing a well-founded base of 50–150 papers on which you can draw reliably.

Tables

How are tables used? What are they used for? Some uses are:

- summary (e.g. of results, statistical analysis, literature);
- comparison (e.g. a comparison of research methods and outcomes across a number of studies);
- providing context and assisting navigation (e.g. through a line of argument, through the dissertation);
- establishing categories and establishing what those categories include;
- providing a framework (e.g. for ideas and their relationships or for techniques and their applications).

Tables can't just stand in isolation – they must be described in the narrative and *relate to it*. Remember to check that the tables are labelled in the required format, and that they are labelled consistently.

Illustrations

How are illustrations used, and what are they used for? Illustrations are used:

- to emphasize key points;
- to illustrate (i.e. show pictures of things described in the text);
- to provide an alternative representation (i.e. alternative to text, tables, etc.);
- to summarize;
- to contrast two things;

- to clarify;
- as part of a sinful attempt, usually futile, to cover up for bad writing;
- to provide a conceptual map (a navigation aid through ideas, arguments or processes);
- as comic relief (usually inadvisable – remember the second golden rule about not trying to be funny).

Appendices

What sorts of things go into appendices? Answer: supporting material that doesn't need to appear in the focal argument, such as:

- data;
- detailed statistical analyses;
- instruments (e.g. questionnaires);
- examples;
- code (if the PhD involved writing software);
- glossary of terms.

Remember: examiners read appendices. Kind examiners read them to find reasons to spare you; unkind examiners read them to find evidence of sin.

Perspectives on writing

- Writing is difficult, and it takes time. Do the calculation: how many useful sentences can you write in five minutes? If you extrapolate how long it will take you to write the article, chapter or whatever you are writing, you can then plan your writing schedule more realistically.
- Writing is about getting the ideas straight, where 'straight' is the operative word (see our discussion of narrative spine, or 'red thread' on pp. 120).
- Writing imposes certain demands: substance (something meaningful to say); linearity (a clear sequence of reasoning and evidence); and completeness (no gaps in the story).
- Dodgy material (sloppy thinking, poor mapping to theory, dodgy results) makes writing difficult.
- Trouble with writing may indicate problem areas in your research rather than problems in your attitude – if you encounter trouble with writing, then look closely at what you are trying to do and the materials you are using.
- Organize the ideas/concepts/material before you start to write.
- Be precise.

What's 'enough' writing?

- A reasonably complete, analytic literature review. (Its authority derives from selecting the literature appropriately, putting the literature into a sensible conceptual structure that points toward your thesis and balancing recognition of gaps and limitations with synthesis of ideas and identification of patterns in the literature.)
- Progress on objectives, manifested as new insight supported by evidence.
- Answering the 'so what?' question. Articulation of the significance of the research findings, and of the contributions to knowledge. Understanding both their generalizability and their limitations.

Dissertation FAQS

Q: Do I need to include everything I've done?
A: No. If you decide that a subset of data, or an entire study, does not contribute to the overall composition of the thesis, you don't need to include it. Note, however, that this does not apply to the situation where one study shows that your initial hunch was clearly wrong: in this case you have to include the study. If you do research sensibly, then you will be phrasing your questions as a series of reductions of the problem space, rather than a search for confirmatory evidence, so this issue should not be a problem for you.

Q: Do I need to include the raw data?
A: That depends on the conventions of your discipline; check with your supervisor and your institutional regulations about PhDs. The usual principle is that the appendices should include examples of what you used at each stage, starting with instructions to respondents, continuing with examples of any data collection instruments that you used, and also showing one or two examples of completed response sheets or whatever it was that you used. This allows the examiners to check what you did at each step, and to satisfy themselves that you did it right.

Q: How long does the thesis have to be?
A: The real answer is that it is as long as it needs to be to do its job, and no longer. The full significance of this answer won't make much sense to you until you've supervised undergraduate projects and taught research methods for a while, so the more immediately helpful answer is to check the regulations and ask your supervisor. The lesser answer is: within the maximum page or word limit set by your institution.

Q: I've just discovered a mistake in my analysis of the data, two days before I'm due to hand in. What do I do?
A: Good question. Whatever you do, *don't lie*. Get in touch with your supervisor immediately and ask for advice about how to handle the corrections. If it's a major mistake, you'll need to redo the analysis, for all sorts of practical and ethical reasons. If the mistake is comparatively trivial and you are about to run out of time on your thesis, your supervisor may be able to suggest ways of buying time within The System so that the deadline is not an issue. Another possibility might be a rewrite which simply cuts out that part of the analysis from your write-up completely, if the mistake only applies to a manageably small subset of the write-up.

Q: I'm writing up, and I've just discovered that someone else has published something almost identical. What do I do?
A: Don't panic. It's usually possible to present the same material from at least two different viewpoints, if you know what you're doing. Talk to your supervisor about this. You should be able to rephrase your work to take the other person's work into account, and to differentiate yourself clearly from it. For instance, they might have studied a different social group from the one you studied; if so, you can put more emphasis on the social group aspect of your work, and less on the methodological novelty. You might well be able to get some benefit from comparing and contrasting your results and the other person's.

Q: I've developed writer's block. What can I do about it?
A: The standard-issue books have plenty of ideas, and there are some in the chapters on writing in this book. Examples include deliberately doing something completely unrelated to writing up; writing something deliberately inaccurate, so that your subconscious rebels and makes you start writing the truth; rewarding yourself with treats; setting yourself small, manageable goals; and getting a friend to help motivate you.

Q: Can I write-up in the same style that you use in this book?
A: You must be joking. This is the style we use over a cup of coffee; the style we use in our academic articles is very, very different (and a lot less fun, both to read and to write . . .)

10 Writing style

*Its tone of semi-literate, official, righteous dullness never varied . . .
and it never deviated into human prose . . .*

Writing is like dressing. You use different styles for different purposes. If you are
going swimming, you wear swimming gear; if you're about to do some welding,
you wear welding gear. Style, in this sense, is about function, as opposed
to 'style' in the sense of transient fashion. Unfortunately, many PhD students
are somewhere between adequate and dreadful when it comes to academic
writing; even those who are good still have to add many writing skills to their
repertoire if they're to perform at a good PhD level. That's what this chapter is
about. It should help you to understand how writing functions as a professional tool, and also to know about how to use appropriate styles of writing for
the different things you will be doing as a PhD student. This overlaps with
presentation skills, so we have included some coverage of that topic as well.

One important point to understand early is that this is not about using
traditional grammar, or about slick presentation – it's about *language as a tool*.
Another important point for students who are not native speakers of English is
that you don't need to speak perfect English to be able to write well. Good
academic writing is about structure and form, not just about grammar.

The first part of this chapter talks about the cabinet-making skills of writing:
how to avoid looking like an idiot, and how to look like a skilled professional.
This includes some detailed worked examples from different disciplines.
Remember that the signs of good cabinet-making can differ across disciplines,
so you'll need to find out the signs for your area, rather than assuming that
they're the same as the ones we describe here. The next part then tackles the
issue from a different angle.

Finally, there are various lists and tips, including a list of FAQs about academic writing in general and writing up the thesis in particular (see also pp. 101 ff).

Blood in the water

Swimming in shark-infested waters is a bad idea if there is blood in the water. It is an especially bad idea if the blood is yours. Much the same principle applies to writing. Critical readers can detect blood in the water a long way off, and will come cruising in at speed looking for a kill. Sometimes they go for a quick kill, but on other occasions they decide to play with their victim for a while first. It's not a pretty sight.

Another analogy for the same problem, which is less eye-catching but more directly applicable, is the wolf-pack. Wolf-packs will run near potential prey, sizing it up for signs of weakness. If an animal looks healthy and capable of looking after itself, they ignore it instantly. If an animal looks ill or weak, they go for the kill. If your writing (or presentation, if you're giving a seminar or conference presentation) looks healthy and professional, then you will probably be left alone. If there are signs of weakness, then the wolves start closing in fast. Begging a metaphorical wolf-pack for mercy has about the same chance of success as begging a real wolf-pack for mercy if you're a plump caribou in the middle of a long, cold, hungry winter.

So, what do you do about it?

Step 1: stay indoors until you're ready

The first and most simple step is not to go into predator territory if you have open wounds. If your work isn't good enough, then don't present it; go back and get it right, instead of presenting inadequate work and making apologies for it. Here is a good example (from a seminar by a colleague): 'We found the following results . . . however, feedback from the subjects afterwards indicated that our initial instructions had been ambiguous. When we replicated the initial experiment with revised instructions and a new set of subjects, the results were as follows . . .'

The subtext here is: 'I take it utterly for granted that you redo an experiment without hesitation if you have to, regardless of the time and trouble – trying to plead for mercy and present inadequate data isn't even on the agenda for me.' The key aspect of the presentation here is that the second sentence follows immediately from the first one, without hesitation, and plunges straight into the results without making a big thing out of the fact that the researchers took the trouble to redo the experiment. Somebody who treats this level of professionalism as taken for granted will probably have been meticulous about everything else in their study too, so the predators know there's not much point in trying their luck.

One thing which novices usually get wrong involves sample sizes and amount of data. Here is another good example, from an MSc thesis: 'There were three groups of respondents, each with four subjects . . .' (followed by description of subject groups). That works out as 12 subjects. Twelve. Not a couple of thousand, or even a couple of hundred. The average novice would at this point start making apologies for the small sample size, with blood gushing into the water at a rate which would have every shark in the neighbourhood abandoning its previous plans and heading inwards for an unscheduled easy meal. This thesis simply described the subject groups and moved on to the next section.

The subtext in this example was: 'This thesis is about a test of concept. For what I'm doing, I don't need a large sample size, and I know it. Now, let's move on to the next thing, which also shows that I know what I'm doing.'

Sample size and amount of data are important; however, the figures required will vary dramatically depending on whether you are doing data-driven work, test of concept or method-mongering. Not many novices know this. Even fewer know that excessively large sample sizes are often an indication of poor experimental design and inadequate knowledge of inferential statistics, both rich sources of blood in the water. If the previous paragraphs have left you with an uneasy feeling, then you might want to consider reading about types of paper, experimental design and inferential statistics.

Step 2: send out the right signals once you are ready

Show you're a professional: use the language and conventions of professionals in the discipline. If you don't know what these are, then you need to learn them. Reading this book, and other texts on this topic, is a good start. Make your language and non-verbal signals as different as possible from those of the clueless beginner.

What are conventions for?

Every discipline has its standards for presentation. Some are highly formalized, others are tacit. You discover the standards by looking analytically at the literature. Conventions are there to:

- embody standards in the discipline;
- make work accessible;
- make methods accessible, comparable and replicable/repeatable;
- make work comparable and help synthesis – putting work in a form that relates to other work.

By observing the conventions of the discipline, you're saying that you know what's important and therefore 'belong in the club'.

Show you have something worth saying

This is something to be done courteously and in a non-aggressive way. There's no sense in antagonizing your audience, but there is sense in sending out a signal that you are a professional and that you won't be wasting their time with second-rate garbage. A handy tip is to think in terms of asking your audience to 'look at this' rather than 'look at me'. If you start by identifying an interesting problem and an interesting possible solution, rather than by telling the audience about something which you find interesting and a solution which you think *might* work, then this is likely to be a good start. (It also has the advantage that if the proposed solution doesn't work, then that doesn't reflect on your judgement . . .)

A strategy which is often effective is to bring in a potential solution from another discipline. The other discipline needs to be credible in the domain where you want to apply it – this normally means that it has to be more formalized and more mathematical than the domain of application. It's advisable to have a good knowledge of the other discipline, since otherwise your proposed solution is likely to be shot down by an expert from that discipline as being just another example of a keen beginner who hasn't read the literature in depth and who makes classic novice mistakes, only one from a different discipline this time. (You might just get away with superficial knowledge of the other domain in a conference, where there's a slight chance that none of the audience know that domain. You won't get away with it in a refereed venue, because the editor will make sure the work is sent to referees from the relevant fields. It's also surprising just how knowledgeable academic audiences are about the most unlikely things.)

Know your enemies

Remember your enemies at this stage. The real enemies are the people you could be confused with. Differentiate yourself from them tacitly, not explicitly. If you mention them explicitly, then you have added an unwelcome item to the audience's agenda, namely deciding whether you really are different from your enemies, as you claim. If you do it tacitly, then that item shouldn't be an issue.

The keen beginner

One enemy is the keen beginner who hasn't read the literature in depth and who makes classic novice mistakes. You need to send out a strong signal that you don't fit into that category. The good old cup of coffee will help you to find out about classic novice mistakes. The good old reading through the classic literature back to the year dot will help you with the literature in depth. It's surprising what you find if you go back more than about 20 years – a lot of researchers are too hungry for fortune and glory to bother doing their homework properly, and to discover that they are reinventing the wheel. There's no long-term substitute for reading the literature. The short-cuts in this book are about identifying the best ways to do things efficiently and well, not about ways of avoiding the literature. The literature, like research methods, is your friend; the more you have in your repertoire, the more situations you can tackle confidently.

The intelligent layperson

Another enemy is the intelligent layperson. If general knowledge is enough to tackle the problem, then you shouldn't be bothering to tackle that problem. This is where counter-intuitive results from the literature are useful.

The snake-oil merchant and the self-proclaimed genius

Other potential enemies are the snake-oil merchant and the self-proclaimed genius, both of whom peddle their own patent panaceas. Claiming that you have solved a problem which has baffled the best minds in the field (including, by implication, the audience) is not something which will endear you to your audience, and is about as advisable as marching into a mediaeval Mongol war camp and shouting, 'Genghis is a sissy!' at the top of your voice.

Don't show weakness or doubt

You should never show weakness, apologize or ask for mercy. If you've done the work right, then there's no need to apologize or ask for mercy. If you haven't done the work right, then don't present it – go and get it right instead.

There are lots of words and phrases which indicate weakness. Some of these are of a type usually known as 'weasel words', whose purpose is to help you wriggle out of committing yourself to an assertion and substantiating it. Weasel words usually have no place in academic writing, and certainly not in a dissertation. It is not normally good enough to say that something 'seems' to be something else: is it or is it not? Similarly, 'probably' isn't good enough. Weasel words suggest that the author has not looked hard enough, or is making speculations which cannot be substantiated.

Whenever you justify something, you raise the question of why it needed justifying in the first place, and whether your justification of it was good enough. Anything which involves assumptions is also leaking blood (e.g. 'presumably the respondents believed that . . .') Words such as 'probably,' 'presumably' and 'must have' are another way of saying, 'I have no firm evidence for this, and am guessing'. If you have evidence, present it; if you don't have evidence, and the issue is important, then get evidence and find out whether you are actually right in your guess. Speculation is something which should either be explicitly labelled as speculation (and therefore of only tangential relevance) or saved for the closing stages of the discussion section where you are discussing future work, or preferably both.

Vagueness is not acceptable. From an actual examiner's report:

> In an academic argument the details should all be nailed down, as far as this is possible. Often it is best to omit things of which one is unsure. If this is possible they should not be present anyway. If it is not possible, they must be established definitively. Otherwise the conclusion will inherit the lack of precision. Then the whole work may simply become a piece of unproven speculation, which is unacceptable for a doctoral thesis.

One thing worth watching out for in this context is the temptation to use public-domain principles as explanations. The reason for this advice is that these principles are often untrue or seriously misleading. This is one case where the internet is positively useful – the sci.skeptic and alt.folklore.urban newsgroups are rich sources of widespread beliefs which have no basis in truth. Make sure you have a proper academic source for any explanatory principles you want to use. If you can't find one, then it might be because the principle just isn't true . . .

Don't bluff

If you don't understand something, make time and work on it until you understand it. If you try to use technical concepts without understanding them properly, the critical reader will spot it instantly.

One apparent exception to this is when you are using advice about specialist tests (generally in the context of choice of statistical test). The normal convention in many disciplines is that in such cases, where the expertise is outside what a researcher in the domain could be fairly expected to know in detail, it is acceptable to take advice from two or more independent authorities in the relevant area and follow that advice. If they get it wrong, then that isn't your problem, because you've taken reasonable steps. You'll still need to understand what the statistical results mean, though.

Academic style: an example

The example below is from a paper by one of the authors and a colleague. It has been chosen specifically because its topic will be unfamiliar to most readers, making it easier to demonstrate the way in which language is being used at both the explicit and the 'between the lines' levels.

Direct evidence for hemispheric asymmetry in human and proto-hominid brains is in principle obtainable via endocranial fossil remains. Unfortunately, the number of suitable skulls is limited, particularly for older species. Much the same problem applies to attempts to infer handedness from the weight and size of hand bones, on the principle that a more extensively used hand will be more robust (and therefore have larger bones) than the non-preferred one (Roy, Ruff and Plato 1994). There is evidence of such asymmetry in the long bones of the upper limb and shoulder girdle of Neanderthal specimens (Trinkhaus, Churchill and Ruff 1994; Vandermeersch and Trinkhaus 1995) but the paucity of suitable pre-Neanderthal material limits the scope for this approach.

There are several specific types of coded language in use here. These include the following.

Technical terms

Technical terms signal membership of the relevant research community: 'hemispheric asymmetry, protohominid, endocranial, robust, non-preferred, long bones, upper limb, shoulder girdle'. 'Robust' is a technical term, the converse of 'gracile'. 'Long bones' is also a technical term, contrasting with 'short bones'.

References

References signal familiarity with relevant literature: (Roy, Ruff and Plato 1994); (Trinkhaus, Churchill and Ruff 1994); (Vandermeersch and Trinkhaus 1995). All three are from within six years of the submission date of the article, and all are specialist journal articles.

General academic language

General academic language signals membership of the general academic community: 'in principle, via, much the same, infer, there is evidence of such, paucity'. Note how specific claims about inferring handedness via specific methods are supported by references, while a broad statement about lack of suitable fossil material is not supported by a reference. Within this research community, the lack of suitable fossil materials is a generally agreed truth which does not require a supporting reference; the authors have already demonstrated their membership of this research community via their familiarity with its literature and technical terms, so can make the broad statement without a supporting reference. Writing for a different research community, a supporting statement might well be needed (for instance, if the different research community had not reached a consensus about the lack of suitable fossil remains, or was completely unaware of the issue).

Note also how an entire approach is described and rejected in two sentences. The authors throughout assume that their readers will be familiar with a range of technical terms relating to physiology, such as 'endocranial' – this assumption is made because the paper is for publication in a journal catering for a well-defined research community (laterality researchers). This assumption reduces the need to unpack and explain terms; this in turn means that the writing can be terse and efficient. If the authors deal with terms unlikely to be known to the readers, then it is necessary to explain each term on the first occasion when it is used (as happens later in this paper when the authors describe flint artefact manufacture).

Writing as expressive behaviour

Style and voice – and indeed the selection of content – do have a role in expounding your central argument, but they have an even larger role in conveying what sort of author you are.

Bad things to communicate are:

- I am ignorant, clueless and in despair;
- I am lazy, dishonest and rude, and I deserve to be hanged and flogged.

Good things to communicate are:

- I know what I'm doing;
- I'm a professional with the right attitude.

How do you communicate these things? They vary in easiness.

I'm a professional with the right attitude (easy concepts, but hard work)

- I pay attention to detail in things like spelling and the layout of the references
- I've done all the work I should have done, and demonstrated this in the write-up
- I've done a meticulous job of work and demonstrated this in the write-up
- I've presented this work neatly and exhaustively, following the conventions of this area

I know what I'm doing (requires knowledge of your chosen field and hard work)

- I know all the key texts, have read them and have cited them correctly
- I have read other relevant things as well and have cited them correctly
- I know and understand the technical concepts in this area and have been careful to use all the relevant ones somewhere in my write-up

I am ignorant, clueless and in despair (all too easy to communicate, especially in the second year of a PhD)

- I have not read the key texts
- I have made classic mistakes without even realizing it, and have not had the wit to show my draft to a reliable mentor who would have spotted them ages ago
- My work contains apologies and pleas for mercy

I am lazy, dishonest and rude, and I deserve to be hanged and flogged (effortless, if you're a sinner)

- My work contains hardly any references
- My references are all from the internet, popular magazines or textbooks
- My spelling, grammar and presentation are dreadful
- I have attempted to conceal the dreadfulness of my spelling, grammar and presentation with jokes, clip art, a fancy binder, coloured pie charts and a grovelling acknowledgement to my supervisor
- I have misspelled my supervisor's name and got their title wrong in the grovelling acknowledgement to them
- There is no evidence in what I have written that I have done any work
- Some paragraphs of my text are much better written than others, and bear a strong resemblance to articles on the internet
- I have done things which my supervisor specifically told me not to do
- My text compares theory and academia unfavourably with the 'real world' but I have not put my money where my mouth is and gone away into the 'real world'

If these things apply to you, then you will probably not even be allowed to start a PhD – the initial selection process will almost certainly detect you and hurl you into the outer darkness (though you might manage to bluff your way onto an MSc, only to be failed when your dissertation erupts onto an unwilling world). It is unlikely that anyone fitting this description will be conscientious enough to bother reading this book anyway; we have included this section largely as a reassurance to virtuous but insecure students, so that they know they aren't as bad as they sometimes fear.

Getting it right

Avoiding mistakes is all very well, but what can you do that is positive?

One useful method is to go through your text with a highlighter, highlighting any words or phrases which would not be familiar to the average person on the street. This is particularly useful for your first page, and especially for the first paragraph, where first impressions count. An alternative is to delete any sentences which fail this test and see what is left.

Here are two examples. The first is fictitious, to protect the guilty, but closely based on horrible experience with MSc students. The second is real, to reward the virtuous, and comes from one of our MSc students. Both deal with the design of good web pages for commercial sites on the internet.

Example 1

The Internet is the fastest-growing technology that the world has seen. Its now possible to download movie clips and the latest music via the Internet from sites across the world, and to watch events like a Shuttle launch happening in real time. The Internet clearly offers many opportunities to a company to advertise its products around the world for a fraction of what that would previously have cost. However, with so many companies competing for attention on the Web, it is particularly important for companies to have Web pages which are eye-catching and memorable, and which convey the right impression to the customer. Otherwise, even if a customer does view the organization's Web site, there is the risk of conveying the wrong impression and losing sales and wasting money in the process. Although the design and advertising communities have considerable experience of doing this sort of task via traditional media, it is not safe to assume that the same principles apply to Web page design as to printed page design, and this area clearly needs to be researched.

Example 2

At the core of software engineering lies the issue of software quality and this has resulted in the growth of the software metrics field of research. Software metrics is based on measurement theory and there exists a comprehensive literature relating to both measurement theory and software metrics, [Fenton and Pfleeger, 1997], [Kitchenham *et al.*, 1995], [Hall and Fenton, 1997]. Traditionally software metrics research has been in relation to application software. However, the rapid expansion of the Internet and corresponding growth in the number of commercial web sites [Rupely, 1997], [Jones, 1997], has given rise to a new set of problems relating to the development of metrics for a new class of software products including web pages, epitomised in the question 'How good was my web site?'.

Numerous guidelines have been published with regard to the design of web sites but no recognised standards have yet been set with regard to the assessment of the quality of web pages [Nielsen and Molich, 1990], [Pfaffenberger, 1997], [Berk and Devlin, 1991].

Analysis

If we strip out the terms which would not be familiar to the person in the street, here is what we are left with:

Example 1

Example 2
software engineering
software metrics
application software
measurement theory
[Fenton and Pfleeger, 1997]
[Kitchenham *et al.*, 1995]
[Hall and Fenton, 1997]
[Rupely, 1997]
[Jones, 1997]
[Nielsen and Molich, 1990]
[Pfaffenberger, 1997]
[Berk and Devlin, 1991]

The first example contains absolutely no evidence that the writer has ever studied the area. Depending on the marker's world view, this answer might get a mark ranging from 'just fail', on the grounds that it was true and relevant but devoid of advanced knowledge, to zero, on the grounds that it contains no evidence of having studied the topic and could have been written by a member of the public who reads the occasional newspaper.

The second example shows that the writer has done his or her homework thoroughly, to the extent of quoting eight different sources, including a classic text and some advanced journal articles, in the first paragraph alone. This is the sort of thing which creates a good first impression. You don't need to write the whole piece at this level of density, but you do need to establish your credibility early on. If you put the heavy stuff on page 2, it's usually too late; the reader will already have formed a low opinion of you, and you will have the doubly hard job of undoing that low opinion and then persuading them to change it to a high opinion. (They'll probably think that if you're silly enough to have a lightweight first page, then there's no point in changing their opinion of you.) Note that this example does not contain any 'buzzwords' and that the English is pretty plain apart from the technical terms. It could only have been written by an expert, but can be read by a non-expert.

Spelling and punctuation

Get your spelling and punctuation right. If necessary, buy a dictionary and/or go on a training course. They will probably be the best investments you will ever make. If you're claiming to be a highly educated professional and you can't spell or use punctuation correctly, then you're off to a bad start.

Rhetoric and rigour

Most students know that a PhD requires good theory, good documentary evidence, good science or good engineering. Many forget that it also requires good storytelling. Both rigour and rhetoric are *essential* ingredients of a successful dissertation. At most institutions, rhetoric is an *explicit* criterion for a PhD, expressed as 'good presentation' or 'publishability'.

Books will tell you that the purpose of writing is to communicate. This is true. At the most crude and mercenary level, if you don't communicate anything about your knowledge and ability, you won't get any marks. (A blank sheet of paper, or a sheet of impenetrable waffle, get zero for being content-free, not full marks for having no mistakes . . .)

The dissertation

There are certain things that you're demonstrating through your dissertation:

- mastery of your subject;
- research insight;
- respect for the discipline;
- publishability.

Getting the form and voice of the dissertation right is just as important as getting the content right – indeed, they're essential to conveying the content. If you doubt this, remember the ground rules: a dissertation should stand on its own – if the examiner misunderstands it, then that's the candidate's problem, not the examiner's.

The dissertation is widely viewed as the highest form of academic writing, requiring content, precision, substantiation and mastery of context beyond what is normally required in individual published papers. It is a 'master piece', not in the sense of an 'ultimate work', but in the sense of a piece that qualifies an apprentice to be called a master through its *demonstration* of techniques, skills, form and function. (This is discussed in some detail in our section on cabinet-making – see p. 4.)

The red thread

At the heart of good presentation is a good 'plot' – not in the sense of fiction, but in the sense of a connected sequence of elements, each leading on to the next. The dissertation must have a clear narrative spine. Swedish academics use the image of a 'red thread' running through the text (like a red thread woven through plain muslin). The red thread – an appropriate structure, with a clear argument – is an essential ingredient of success. Although this is strongly linked with writing structure, we've included it in this chapter on style, since good style includes clarity and demonstrating that you know what's important and what's peripheral.

Thomas Green, a Wise Man, talks about this in terms of the 'Great Overall Scheme of Things' or 'GOST'. All of the elements of your dissertation must ultimately fit into the GOST – and work that doesn't contribute to the GOST should be left out. Thomas' advice is to 'Make friends with your GOST'. If you continually reassess your GOST, you'll be in a good position to make a coherent account of your work.

Style in academic writing again, from a different angle

As we said before, when writing you choose a style that fits the occasion. Style is conveyed through structure, voice, rhetoric, the way evidence is presented, the use of literature, the use of tables and illustrations and so on. The appropriate style for an academic research paper is very different from the appropriate style for a textbook, and both of these are different from the appropriate style for a business report. Learn (by analysing exemplars) how to use different styles, and learn which style is appropriate for what you are trying to achieve. If you're using the wrong style, then you're sending out a signal that you don't understand the ground rules of the area you're working in, and the reader will wonder what else you don't understand.

It's also important to realize that some parts of differences in style are there for very good reasons – for example, the insistence on use of references in formal academic writing, and conventions about reporting experiments. Beware of style guides intended for areas other than your own – what is a good style for a business report is not a good style for a thesis, and vice versa. Similarly, 'plain English' is nice in theory, but anyone who advocates it for specialist writing has probably never tried using it this way in practice. The best academic writing manages to achieve a pleasant, conversational voice while still providing the necessary clarity, sophistication and precision.

Voice

'Voice' is the quality of your writing that suggests what sort of person is writing, with what sort of attitude and for what sort of 'implicit reader'. Some texts come across as argumentative (with whom is the author arguing?), evangelical (who is the author trying to convert?), apologetic (who is the author trying to appease?), condescending (who is the author underestimating?), arrogant (who is the author dismissing?) and so on – those voices are reflections of the implicit reader the author has in mind.

Clarity, simplicity, authority and honesty are good attributes of voice. Imprecision, evangelism, defensiveness and arrogance are attributes to avoid. Find a paper you consider exemplary for presentation and consider what makes it so. See if you can characterize the 'voice' and 'register' the author's use.

Who is your audience? What are the conventions in the discipline you're addressing? What are the standards of reporting? One trick is to identify an intelligent, well-read, non-specialist reader and hold that reader in mind. It's easier to avoid some of the more damaging voices if you assume a reader who is capable, open-minded and interested in what you have to say. Can an intelligent, educated generalist understand the gist of your argument, even if the technical content may escape them?

Clarity is extremely important. You are demonstrating in your thesis or paper that you have a detailed understanding of your chosen topic. This is not the same as simplification, or inserting big words. A good paper will use technical terms where appropriate and, if written for a specialist audience, will quite possibly be incomprehensible to a layperson as a result; however, this does not prevent it from being clear to its intended audience. If you don't understand what you're trying to say, then you need to go away and try again until you do have a clear understanding; the writing will then be a lot easier. A technical term can be explained unambiguously so that the other person knows exactly what it means and what it does not mean – that is the whole point of a technical term. A buzzword fails this test. So do a lot of plain English terms.

Be wary of using a thesaurus. If you aren't familiar with the word which you proudly unearth from the thesaurus, then there's a good chance that you will use it wrongly and make an idiot of yourself.

Characterizing the appropriate critical voice

The appropriate critical voice is:

Clear

- Has a clear, coherent argument
- Avoids digressions
- Pares away unnecessary elements
- Language is 'lightly formal' – not too dense, not overly formal, not clouded with jargon but considered, readable
- Key terms are always used with the same meaning
- Examples are helpful and illustrative

Honest

- Provides 'audit trails' from data to conclusions
- Considers alternative accounts
- Addresses limitations

Neutral

- Chooses neutral formulations of questions
- Actively avoids bias in research and presentation
- Avoids emotive language

Authoritative

- Adept use of literature
- No weasel or waffle words
- Pre-emptive accountability
- Good coverage
- Terms are used precisely and appropriately

Substantiated

- Choices and assumptions are justified and accounted for
- No unsubstantiated claims or assertions
- Distinguishes data from results from discussion from conclusions

Critical

- Relates presented work to the literature
- Gives structure to the contributing ideas
- Identifies weaknesses or gaps in existing knowledge
- Doesn't just report, but adds intellectual content

So what?

- Articulates implications
- Articulates significance and importance
- Identifies further routes

Reading between the lines: some classic examples

As we explained in Chapter 8, examiners are highly skilled in reading between the lines of your thesis, and you need to avoid tell-tale and giveaway phrases that say one thing but will be interpreted as saying a quite different thing. Some examples of good, bad and ambivalent writing are given in Table 3.

Table 3 Reading between the lines: some classic examples

You say	Others read this as meaning
Smith says	I haven't read many journal articles
explains Dr Smith	I read too many magazines
enthuses Dr John Smith	I read too much Barbara Cartland
there is general consensus that (a)	there is some agreement that
there is general consensus that (b)	I don't have any specific references but this sounds like a plausible claim
it is clear that	I think
it is arguable that	I hope
a larger sample might prove	I don't understand anything about inferential statistics or survey methods
a recent study found that	I don't have a reference for this, but I'm fairly sure it's true
there is some anecdotal evidence that	some people told me in a bar that
exciting	I haven't grasped the point of academic writing yet
achieve it's potential	I want to look as if I've wasted years of education
excede it's potential. A serendipitous instance of such hegemony is	here's where I start plagiarizing stuff from real researchers who can use big words correctly
objective	I don't understand research methods properly
bias free	I don't understand research methods properly
I think	I am clueless, and also haven't heard about the third person passive

Table 3—*continued*

You say	Others read this as meaning
(though c.f. Green *et al.* (in press) for an interesting re-evaluation of this literature)	I've read the advanced literature, so sod off
e.g. Green and Brown 1998; Smith and Wesson 1999; Jekyll and Hyde 1999; Young, Gifted and Black 1999	I've read lots of stuff, but I can't distinguish among the papers
Smith (in press)	I'm on such good terms with Nobel Prize winners like Smith that they send me preprints of their papers
Smith (*pers. comm.*)	Smith mentioned this when we met in the toilets at Schiphol Airport on our way to the conference last year
a strong similarity to the debate in the 1950s over X	I'm thoroughly familiar with the literature back to before most people in this area were born, so sod off
per se	I had a proper classical education, so . . .

11   The process of writing

'Now just listen to this one, will you,' he said, *'and tell me whether it is good grammar and proper language.'*

Sooner or later, more or less every PhD student hits problems with writing. Sometimes the problem takes the form of writer's block – you sit in front of the keyboard, typewriter, paper or whatever, and you simply can't write anything. Sometimes it's an avoidance problem – you find all sorts of reasons for not starting to write. Sometimes it's a voice problem – you can write words about the topic, but no matter how many times you try, the words don't come out reading the way you want them to.

If this happens to you, the first thing to remember is that it happens to pretty much everyone else too. Successful researchers and writers are not ones who've never encountered these problems; they've encountered the problems, and come through. So can you. This chapter is about the process of writing, with particular reference to common problems, but also with reference to things that will help your writing process when things are going well.

If you're reading this chapter because you're going through one of these problems, and feeling bleak and low, then one thing worth remembering is the bottom line of writing the thesis: it doesn't have to be entertaining or elegant; it just needs to show you have the skills that merit awarding you a PhD. There may some day be researchers who win the Nobel Prize for literature, but it's highly unlikely to be for what they write as researchers.

Anyway, on to process. This chapter mainly consists of lists and tips, because of the nature of the topic (though we don't advise you to try that line in your thesis . . .)

Writing tricks

Removing distractions

The shoebox

Put your out-takes and extra ideas in a safe place, for later use. Then stop thinking about them while you write your dissertation.

Don't edit until you have a complete first draft

One exquisite paragraph is not much use out of context – better to flesh out a first draft before diverting yourself into a perfectionistic editing loop.

Sharpen your pencils

Writers, like tennis players, often develop 'rituals' to help them focus on the task at hand. The trick is to put a strict time limit and structure on the ritual, lest it become a distraction in itself. So, for example, sharpen three pencils and sweep the desk clear – then begin.

Getting started

Talk to a friend

Tell an intelligent friend the 'story' of what you're trying to write. Tape-record what you say, including how you answer your friend's questions. If you don't have a friend handy, imagine one, and talk to the tape recorder.

Write it 'wrong'

A number of 'tricks' have to do with moving as quickly as possible away from initial generation and recasting your task as rewriting or editing. Writing something that's definitely not what you want will give you something to react against and correct – which is often easier than starting from scratch.

Question–answer

Either with a friend, or by yourself, conduct a question–answer sequence, starting with, 'What's the message?' with each question following on from a previous answer and 'why' and 'how' featuring regularly.

Amanuensis

Get someone else to play 'amanuensis' and to write a narrative based on what you tell them. They may do a good job, or they may write something inaccurate; either way, you'll have something to respond to.

Throw away the first half hour

Promise yourself that you'll throw away whatever you write in the first half hour. That means that you can write garbage, a letter to your mother or a version of what you intend – anything, as long as it's prose. The idea is just to start composing sentences and paragraphs, without regard to quality. (If it's good, you can always keep it, but if it's bad, you promised yourself.)

Just start typing

Sometimes it helps to start up the 'subsystems' separately – for example, to start typing anything just to get seated in the right position with fingers moving, then typing canned text just to get a flow of words from mind to hand, and only then to start composing.

Don't start at the beginning

Skip the introduction and start with the material which is most familiar, or easiest to express. Alternatively, start with the most challenging part.

Extreme writing

Set a target, and then sit with a friend and write collaboratively, intensively, for a fixed period.

Surprising yourself

Change mode

Sometimes just changing the way the writing looks (e.g. type font, formatting) or the kind of writing (e.g. from academic paper to children's book), or the mode (e.g. visual instead of verbal), or the medium (e.g. paper instead of computer) can make the material look 'fresh' or expose something different.

Write the Ladybird version

Ladybird is a publisher of children's books, including early-reader non-fiction. Distil the most fundamental story and write it in very simple language.

Storyboard, with pictures

Follow film-making practice and sketch out a 'storyboard' of the narrative, with a frame for each of the key statements, using pictures instead of words. You can even talk through the narrative, acting out the frames. Hokey, as Buffy might say, but potentially inspiring.

Organizing ideas

Index cards

Write each of your key points on an index card, then spread them on the floor and sort them using spatial arrangement to indicate grouping, flow or relationship.

Mind maps

Use mind-mapping to elicit ideas and relationships. Start with a big enough sheet of paper or with a computer-based tool.

Finding a focus

Visit your GOST

Remind yourself what your 'Great Overall Scheme of Things' is before you dive down into detail.

Find a model

Find a paper or chapter that does the sort of thing you're trying to achieve (e.g. presents a study). Analyse what makes it exemplary for you: what it contains, how it's organized, what gives it its character. Distil a template from the model, then start filling it in with your own material.

Work backwards

Start by thinking where you want to end up: imagine the finished paper, or the finished chapter (you might use a model to help you, see above). Then work backwards from the product, identifying major components, sorting out critical paths to those components and so on, until you find a place to start.

Headings

Write the headings before trying to write the text. This allows you to fix the overall 'story' or structure in your mind and to work through the sequencing of presentation before you get bogged down in details.

Improving your thinking

Invert the question

Turn your key ideas inside out, upside down or sideways. If you're thinking 'does feminist discourse reduce smoking?', then consider: 'does smoking inhibit feminist discourse?'

Read aloud

What's it for?

For each section (or paragraph), write a comment on its *role* in the document (e.g. this is where I introduce my thesis; this is where I outline the major competing theories; this is where I give a precedent for the method I've used).

Look for the traps and pitfalls

When you review your draft, consider the sorts of things a reader might criticize (e.g. are your assertions justified? Is the terminology used consistently? Have you presented the limitations in a way that undermines your results? Does your illustration illustrate or obscure?)

Keeping going

Cookies

Give yourself mini-incentives (e.g. line up cookies somewhere nearby, and allow yourself one after each section that you draft; give yourself a play day after a solid week's writing).

Progress table

Set out your section headings in a table and fill in the word count and time as you complete each one. Total the word count at the end of the day.

Obstacles in writing

Writing is not a single activity. It is not just 'writing down', not just a simple transcription from mind to page. Rather, it is many activities: analysing, elaborating, remembering, synthesizing, mapping, ordering, articulating, clarifying, editing, criticizing, structuring, sense-making – as well as transcribing. With so many cognitive activities interacting, of course it's complex and demanding. Having the right expectations about it helps to make it less daunting. Having a few disciplines helps to make it manageable.

For many people, writing is associated with fear. Educators talk about 'fear of failure' (anxiety about the consequences of getting it wrong or 'not being good enough' becomes an obstacle to engagement and progress) and 'fear of success' (anxiety about the consequences – the increased expectations – associated with success becomes an obstacle). It's important to recognize and face your fears. OK, so it's scary. But it's not impossible. The key realization is that *any writing is better than no writing*.

Once you've written something down, you've reduced the number of activities you have to do. Separating the activities is one of the disciplines that can help in writing. Writing can be approached as a series of 'passes': dumping ideas, prioritizing ideas, putting ideas in order, elaborating an initial structure, generating sentences from notes, editing for structure, editing for language, checking for redundancy, editing for 'voice' and so on. One of the most important aspects to isolate is 'dumping ideas'. Once you've got something on paper, you can shift from generating to responding, and turn 'writing' into 'editing' for a while. A good tip to remember is: no editing until everything is written once.

Another discipline is Keep It Simple, Stupid (KISS) – a principle that applies to most design activities. The simplest language that does the job – the simplest vocabulary, sentence structure and rhetorical structure – is often the best. Keeping it simple is different from 'schematic writing'. Whereas schematic writing reduces expression to the barest essentials (leaving out much of the detail and often realism), good 'simple' writing provides all the necessary information and detail in the most direct way possible. Think of the difference between the London Underground map and an Ordnance Survey map. Both represent the key paths, but one does so realistically, maintaining the relationships of the paths to the surrounding context and indicating the nature of the terrain.

General advice

- Writing is a skill, and like most skills it improves and becomes easier with practice
- Make a commitment to write something every day and to produce a finished piece of writing – a couple of pages – every week
- Try to present material in writing at every supervision session
- When someone critiques your writing, take the time to analyse the critique: why did the critic make those comments or suggest those changes?
- If someone copy-edits or redrafts your writing, take the time to analyse the changes: why those changes, what do they change and how do they improve the prose?

Writing obstacles raised by students

Problem: starting to write anything; not starting to write because the subject is not 'good enough'.

Try just 'dumping ideas' as a first step. Remember: *any writing is better than no writing*. Don't worry about whether it's 'good enough'. It probably won't be until you finish writing it – writing it is part of the process of making it 'good enough'. (There's a research literature on this subject ...) Until you put marks on paper and let people scrutinize them, you won't be able to get feedback about how well you've managed to convey your ideas, or on how interesting your ideas are, or on what insights they inspire in others.

If you have trouble writing something, it probably means you haven't got it clear in your mind yet. Write whatever you can, and then consider why it's so uncomfortable or seems incomplete. Gnarled sentences often signal tangled thoughts – so look again at the dense bits.

Consider writing tricks such as:

- Tell it to a friend over coffee. You might also try having the friend tell it back to you.
- Play 'Eliza'. Eliza was a computer program that simulated a therapeutic dialogue. Actually, the program only had a limited number of conversational gambits, none of which added any new information, but those few could be, to coin a phrase, effectively elicitative. So to play the Eliza game, you simply start with an initial remark and then build on that through some simple-minded questioning. For example: 'I want to write about purple elephants.' 'Why?' 'Because purple elephants are more interesting than grey ones.' 'What makes them more interesting?' 'Because most elephants are grey, and purple ones are unusual.' 'Are all purple ones unusual?' Every so often you can throw in a *non sequitur* (although it doesn't have to be 'What do purple elephants have to do with your mother?' – the type of *non sequitur* which Eliza might use). What you're doing is asking yourself repeatedly: what do I think, why do I think it and why should anyone else care?

Problems:

- I know the main points but I don't know how to present them;
- I can't progress from the draft to writing the final version;
- lack of clarity;
- finding a clear structure;

Good writing is typically a process of drafting and redrafting. So don't expect to get from ideas to polished prose in one step. Going from ideas to *notes* is usually reasonably easy. So what's the difference between notes and prose? Usually: structure, order and complete sentences. The key is finding the right structure – first the structure of the ideas and then the linear structure of the argument or story you want to make about the ideas.

Try some of the tricks for structuring ideas:

- Mind maps. Once you've got all the ideas mapped out, then you can try to arrange them into a linear order.
- Put ideas on index cards – one to a card – and then 'sort' or arrange them in different collections or structures. Again, you can do this in a series of 'passes': grouping by relatedness of concepts, grouping in terms of dependency, grouping thematically, prioritizing, ordering . . . trying to sort the index cards in different ways can help reveal ideas that don't fit (so that you consider why they don't and why you want to include them) and also highlight the ideas that are focal.
- Outlining: experienced writers often advise writing a very detailed outline as a first step. Different sorts of outlines can help: content outline (just a detailed hierarchical structure for the content, e.g. headings and sub-headings); headings with small abstracts for each, indicating the storyline; headings with 'roles' (what the section is and why it's there, how it serves the overall argument).

Problem: using too many words to write something that my supervisor does laconically.

Solving this is a matter of practice, both of writing and of editing. Remember KISS. But also understand that 'simplicity' is not just a matter of word count – sometimes a few more words can make the writing simpler and more accessible. Work at the structure of the argument and review your draft for structure (the 'highlighter test' might help). Chaos and disharmony often result when you're not sure where something fits, and so you distribute bits of it all over the place.

Before you hand a draft to your supervisor, do an editing 'pass', looking specifically for redundancy or wordiness. When your supervisor does the cut, analyse the changes: what was expendable and why? What role had you thought that material played?

Problem: needing to develop an academic writing style.

Collect exemplars of papers that have a good writing style and an appropriate voice. Analyse the collection: what do the examples have in common? What makes them appeal to you? How do they handle tough aspects of writing? How do they highlight and present key ideas? How do they introduce vocabulary? When you're writing, consider how one of those authors might have structured or phrased your material. See if there's an analogous passage in one of them that you can use as a model.

Problem: it's easy to grasp my results from a table, but I find it difficult to explain the same thing in words.

Tables and graphs should always be introduced in the text. It's not enough to say 'The results are in Table 2'; Table 2 should be discussed in the narrative, and possibly also in the caption. This doesn't mean describing Table 2 exhaustively, item by item. It means leading the reader through the significance of Table 2 and its role in the argument. What does the table show? How do you intend it to be interpreted? The text should describe the key features of the table that lead you to a particular interpretation. It should relate the information presented in the table to the greater argument. What messages do you mean to convey by presenting the table? The narrative should summarize the table and articulate your messages about the table.

Problem: lack of consistency (e.g. reference style).

This is just editing. Style is various and often personal. The keys are:

- meet the requirements of whatever forum you're addressing (journals often have style guides);
- be consistent with whatever style you're using.

You can choose your own reference style for your dissertation, so choose one that makes sense for you and then use it consistently. If you use a tool like the bibliographic software, Endnote, you can easily alter the style for different uses.

Problem: deadlines (always missing them).

Writing is hard, and it takes a long time. Always allow at least twice as much time as you think you might need. Consider how long you think the job will take; double the number, increase the units (be they hours, days, weeks or even years (!)) and add one. So, if I first think a job will take five minutes, I can sensibly allow 11 hours.

Deadlines don't go away. As your career progresses, there will be more deadlines and more responsibilities competing for your time. Cynical readers may wonder whether skill in meeting deadlines will result in The System viewing you as a safe pair of hands and dumping more work on you, until you reach your level of incompetence. Readers versed in *realpolitik* might answer that this depends on whether you exhibit skill in meeting The System's deadlines as opposed to your own. We couldn't possibly comment on this.

12   Presentations

*My formerly silent tongue waxed voluble with the easy grace of
a Chesterfield or the godless cynicism of a Rochester. I displayed a
peculiar erudition utterly unlike the fantastic, monkish lore over
which I had pored in my youth . . .*

This chapter deals with 'live' presentations such as seminars and conferences.
Some of the issues relating to this topic are also relevant to written work –
for instance, how to deal constructively with criticism, whether from the
audience ('live' presentations) or the reviewers (written work). It would be a
good idea to read our chapters on writing as well as this chapter if you're about
to do a presentation.

There are two main things that you need to bear in mind when doing presentations. The first is the distinction between content and form. The second
is the three golden principles: don't lie, don't try to be funny and, last but most
important, don't panic and blurt out the truth.

Content and form

The distinction between content and form is summed up in a variation on a
song title: 'It ain't just what you say [content], it's the way that you say it
[form]'. Content is essential in a presentation. If there is no content worth
mentioning, then the best that you can hope for is to be viewed as entertaining. That does not help you in an academic research career, where you are

assessed by your peers in terms of how much interesting content you have to offer in your ideas and results. Speakers who give content-free talks can get pretty rough treatment from academic audiences. One such talk in an old university department was interrupted after ten minutes by one of the audience banging a fist on the table and saying, 'Are you going to say something worth listening to? Because if you're planning to continue with this bullshit then I'm leaving.' This is not the sort of reception that you should be aiming for. We will return to content soon.

Form is extremely important in a presentation. The form gives a lot of information about what sort of person you are, and what sort of researcher you are. There are plenty of popular books about public speaking which give detailed advice on what to wear, how to speak and so forth during a presentation. Unfortunately, the rules are somewhat different for public speaking, for teaching, for business presentations and for research presentations, so you need to be careful about which rules you follow for which setting.

Content in detail

The principles for content are fairly straightforward.

Most presentations are divided into three parts. The classic advice is: 'First, tell the audience what you are going to say. Then say it. Then tell them what you have just said.' This is usually very good advice. The opening section sets the context, explains why your topic is important to the audience and prepares them for what comes next. The main section contains the main content and is usually the longest section. The closing section summarizes what you have just said. Each of these sections may have subsections, depending on the length of the talk.

Classic mistakes involving content

There are various classic mistakes involving content. One is to misjudge the amount you can fit into the time available. The best way of avoiding this is to rehearse the presentation and time yourself, then add or (more often) subtract material and try again until your timing is right. For short presentations this is simple and effective. For longer presentations it is not much fun rehearsing an hour's worth of material for the third time, so a better strategy is to rehearse once, adjust the amount of material if necessary and have a plan about which bits to add or leave out depending on how the time goes.

A handy tip for timing is to have a master sheet in front of you which tells you which topic you should be covering at what time – for instance, '10.15 – slide about software failure rates'. This will give you an idea of how near you are to being on track. For very short presentations, careful rehearsal can make the timing much easier. One of us once had to give an eight-minute presentation as part of a job application, where ability to keep to time was one of the skills being judged. Our strategy was to rehearse the talk several times (including rehearsal to an empty room) and adjust the material until the talk took between seven and nine minutes. When we gave the real presentation, we deliberately did not check the time on our watch; instead, we watched the audience, whose expressions told us how near we were to the finishing time, and finished within seconds of the specified time without apparently needing to check the time. Showing off? Yes, but it made the right impression – most speakers have difficulty keeping to time on an eight-minute slot even with time checks, so keeping to time without looking at watch or clock was an indicator of professional skills.

There are various classic problems involving content. Probably the most frequent of these is the choice of appropriate level of material to present. Giving a highly technical presentation to an audience with only basic knowledge of the area usually results in a very bored audience. Giving a novice-level talk to a highly knowledgeable audience is extremely embarrassing for everyone concerned. The best strategy is to check with the organizer about this, and to find out the level of the audience well in advance. Most organizers are only too happy to help with this, and will treat such a question as a sign of professionalism on your part.

A related problem is how much the audience members already know. Again, it is worth asking the organizer about this. Then, if you have to cover a topic which is already familiar to the audience, you can include enough detail to show that you understand the topic, but move on fairly rapidly to material which is less familiar to them.

Texts about business presentations and public speaking usually emphasize the need to make the presentation interesting. There is often an implication that this should be done by keeping technical detail to a minimum and by using plain English. This is not a wise strategy for academic presentations.

If you are doing a PhD, you are likely to give two main types of presentation. The first is lectures to students on MSc or undergraduate courses, as part of your CV development. The second is talks to other researchers (for instance, seminars, conference papers, internal presentations on your progress and the dreaded viva). These two types have quite different requirements.

If you are lecturing to students, you will be expected to produce handouts with references to respectable journal articles, textbooks and other sources of information to backup your talk. This is all very laudable. You will also need to give a clear, coherent, simple overview of the area, based on established wisdom and with unnecessary detail removed for the sake of clarity. This is also very laudable. Unfortunately, the world is seldom clear, coherent or simple, so for lectures you will have to present a version of reality which is not a lie, but which is also not the complete story.

For presentations to other researchers, the requirements are very different. The purpose of these presentations is to demonstrate that you (a) know what things are like at the sharp end of research, (b) have been at the sharp end yourself, and (c) have achieved something at the sharp end which will be of use to at least some other researchers. An important point is that these other researchers will often not include your audience (e.g. in internal presentations on your research progress). For presentations of this sort, a simplified version is blood in the water, and an attempt to hide behind established wisdom is an even gorier metaphor, because you should be reporting work too recent for any established consensus to have been reached. Another important feature of talks of this sort is that you will have to present your own results to professionals who will usually know a lot more tricks of the trade than you do, and who may be hostile (for instance, if you have antagonized them by giving a simplified account). You therefore need to have your content right.

Form in detail

This section deals with the way in which you present the content of your talk. Form overlaps with content in places, but usually the distinction is fairly clear as well as useful.

The audience will usually have an impression of you before they even see you. This can come in various ways. In a job presentation, they will probably have seen your CV. (Do you have accomplishments in your CV and covering letter which create a good impression?) In an academic setting, they will have seen at least the title of your talk and probably a descriptive paragraph about it. (Are these interesting and sending out the right signals about you and your work?) A little homework and anticipation can make a lot of difference.

The next thing the audience know about you comes from the way in which you are introduced. An ideal start is an introduction such as, 'It's a pleasure to welcome Linda, whose work is already familiar to most of us here via her collaboration with Chris'. A less good start is when the person introducing you has to keep checking your details on a note card and gets your name wrong. If you take a proactive approach to your career, you can greatly improve your chances of getting the first sort of welcome.

The audience will also be forming impressions about you based on your appearance and behaviour. How formally are you dressed? How neatly? Are these both at an appropriate level for the setting of the talk? For a job interview in academia, appearance will usually be treated as significant; for a visiting seminar, the audience will usually be more or less indifferent to what you wear unless it is totally outrageous, and will be much more concerned with what you say in the seminar. If you aren't sure what the dress code is for your chosen venue, then find out. Observe job applicants in your department; go to departmental seminars and see how people dress. Ask someone about dress code over a cup of coffee.

Classic mistakes involving form

Most beginners start their talk by smiling nervously and then have problems working out how to use the audio-visual equipment, making them more embarrassed. It is a good idea to become familiar with audio-visual equipment well before your presentation – learn how to use as many varieties as possible. Also, assume that the equipment will cause problems and have a fallback ready – for instance, if you are using a PowerPoint presentation, have a set of overhead projector (OHP) slides ready as an insurance policy. One of us was once examining MSc vivas involving 15-minute presentations by each candidate. During one presentation the OHP machine broke down. The candidate didn't panic and the machine was replaced. The candidate carried on until the replacement machine also broke down. The candidate didn't panic and finished the talk with a third machine. Even by the standards of hardened professionals this was an impressive performance and sent out a lot of very good signals. It is extremely unlikely that you will have two machines fail on you, but it is quite possible that one will, and being ready for it will greatly help your peace of mind.

When you start talking, it is usual to begin by introducing yourself, normally with a slide giving your name and affiliation. This is your chance to check the focus of the audio-visual equipment and to find a good spot to stand. A classic mistake is to stand between the audience and your slide, so that you cast a shadow across the screen and have tables of results showing all over your face. You should get into the habit of standing to one side of the screen. You should also get used to pointing at parts of the slide on the screen using your shadow.

Beginners often try to put too much onto each slide. You need to use large print so that the slide will be readable at the back of the room, and white space so that the audience isn't overwhelmed by indigestible masses of information. It's usually a good idea to use bullet points on the slide for the key concepts and to explain the bullet points via what you say, rather than to read words off the slide.

Tables of results are a traditional problem in presentations: usually the figures in the tables are too small to be readable at the back of the room. It's a good idea to check the readability of your slides well in advance. It's also a good idea to prepare a handout which complements the slides – most audiences like a one-page handout of connected text covering your key points and a hard copy of the slides, with the slides reduced to a sensible point size so that they can scribble notes on the hard copy during the presentation.

You need to talk clearly enough and loudly enough to be understood at the back of the room. It's a good idea to check that you can be heard at the back of the room; it's a bad idea to do this by saying 'Can you hear me at the back?' because of the risk of some comedian replying 'Yes, unfortunately'. Beginners often start in a shout and then revert to a mumble after a few minutes. A simple way to reduce this problem is to write a reminder to yourself on your master sheet (e.g. 'Slide 2: are you mumbling?') A more difficult strategy, but one which is invaluable for many purposes, is reading your audience.

Reading your audience involves looking at the audience and assessing their response to your presentation.

Classic bad signs are:

- people looking out of the window;
- people telling jokes to their neighbours;
- people shaking their heads;
- people at the back craning forward to hear what you are saying;
- people at the back asking their neighbours what your slide says;
- people looking at their watches or the clock.

Classic good signs are:

- people taking notes;
- people nodding when you make a point;
- people whispering to their neighbours while looking at your slides or handouts in an interested way;
- people looking at your slides or the handouts in an interested way.

You need to send out to your audience the signal that you are a professional with a thorough grasp of the subject matter. You can send out some positive signals about this in the same way as when writing. For instance, when you quote one of the classic texts, you can mention in passing a more recent, more sophisticated critique of that classic text which is not widely known except among academic heavyweights.

You also need to master the low-level skills of organizing your materials. If you are using OHP slides, then you will need to keep them in order. This is a lot less simple than it sounds. You need to take each slide in turn off your 'incoming' stack. Once you have shown it, you then need to put it somewhere (usually your 'outgoing' stack). A useful habit is to work from left to right: incoming on the left, outgoing on the right, as with washing up and other craft skills. However, OHP slides have a bad habit of sticking to each other, making it difficult to stack them neatly without distracting the flow of your talk, and you will often want to refer back to a slide you showed previously, turning your outgoing stack briefly into an incoming stack. One way of reducing this problem, if you know you will be referring back to a slide, is simply to make two copies of the slide.

Conferences (including student conferences) can be an excellent place to observe different presentation styles. In some areas, such as safety-critical systems research, widely different areas of academia and industry are represented and the audience can be treated to a succession of speakers using extremely different approaches to the same topic. One of us once witnessed an eminent academic in a bright pink cocktail dress giving a state of the art PowerPoint presentation, followed by an equally eminent academic in well-worn tweeds using handwritten OHP slides which looked as if they had been written on the way to the talk in a taxi with dodgy suspension. (There is an allegedly true story of a very eminent academic with little concern about fashion who was arrested for vagrancy early one morning on the steps of the

British Museum, while waiting for that august institution to open. Not terribly relevant, perhaps, but it would have been a shame to leave the story out, especially since one of us was told it by someone who claimed to have heard it from the eminent academic in person.)

Other handy tips

A moment spent in reconnaissance is seldom wasted. If possible, check the room where you will be giving your presentation, once from your point of view and once from the audience's point of view. From your point of view, what equipment is there and do you know how to use it? How much space is there for you, for things like standing to one side of the screen? Are there trip hazards such as tangled cables on the floor? Can you see the audience clearly enough to read expressions at the back of the room? Is there space to put your bag, slides, etc.? Where will you keep the incoming and outgoing slides if using an OHP?

From the audience's point of view, how visible is the screen from different parts of the room? If visibility is bad, and you have the chance, then consider distributing hard copies of your slides so the audience won't miss anything, and remember to tell the audience that you are giving them hard copies of the slides (a lot of people won't bother to look at the handouts until the end, or a boring bit). Are there glare problems anywhere?

Some types of presentation, such as job presentations, are competitive. In such situations it is a good idea to think about what everyone else will be doing and work out a way of doing something different and better. Which topics will everybody else be emphasizing? What will they have failed to think about which you can take as an element in your talk?

It's also a good idea to get as much experience as possible of presentations by attending other people's – for instance, the departmental seminar series. Even if the topic of this week's seminar is utterly unrelated to your work, it is worth going if only to find out how other people do things. (There's also a good chance that sooner or later you'll encounter something from another area which has major implications for your own area.) If the content of a talk is of no interest to you, you can use the time to make notes on any tricks of the trade which the speaker uses, or any mistakes which they make, so that you can improve your own style. One of us learned a great deal about skilful presentation, with particular regard to scaring off questions before they were even asked, during a seminar on learning in rats, while studying media influence on western attitudes towards Arabs.

Attending other people's presentations, especially during the first few weeks of the new academic year, is also a good way of learning about professional etiquette at such events. Watching someone being savaged for asking a naïve question, or for giving a naïve talk, is painful, but it's a lot less painful than being savaged in person. You can learn what your peer group's attitudes are towards things such as falling asleep during a presentation (usually considered bad form, but occasionally used as a studied insult), asking hostile questions (frowned on by some groups, venerated as an art form by others) and knitting (usually viewed with considerable ambivalence).

Audiences who meet frequently (e.g. at departmental seminars or on a well-established conference circuit) often exhibit behaviour which looks odd to an outsider, as a result of group dynamics and history. For instance, a senior figure may savage an inoffensive presentation by a good and unsuspecting student as part of a long-term vendetta against the colleague who supervised that student. This will usually trigger off a retaliatory strike by the supervisor, and within seconds the scene can resemble the academic equivalent of a spaghetti western – a sleepy Mexican afternoon one moment and a high body count the next. An interesting aspect of this is that many members of the audience will be quite unaware that this carnage is going on, because it will be couched in academic language inscrutable to outsiders. (For instance: 'I presume that you allowed for the anchor and adjust heuristic in the design of your instrument?' 'There was no need for that, because a frequentist presentation was used, due to the inherent problems associated with single event probabilities.' This section is too short to unpack that one . . .)

Sidestep if necessary

You don't have to disagree with a critic. You can say: 'That's a really interesting point, and I don't think it's been properly addressed in the literature'. There's not really a lot that anyone can say to a reply like that without making a fool of themselves. You have shown yourself to be courteous and open-minded, and ready to take on board what they are saying; you are also implying that the omission is common to the literature in the area, rather than a failing on your part.

If your audience points out something which appears to be a genuine flaw, then thank them for it, go away and test out what they've said – they may be right, and if so the sooner you fix the problem the better. In such cases it's a good idea to ask them to work through the implications as a response to their question – it might well be that they are wrong, or bluffing, and if so this will become apparent in their response to your courteous reply.

Hypothetical example: you have just described a methodology for eliciting information about the beliefs and values of socially disadvantaged groups. Someone at the back of the audience says that you might find that the literature on requirements acquisition already covers this in more depth. You ask them politely to give an example. Response 1: 'Oh, I'm sure you'll find lots of examples in the literature'. Response 2: 'Well, for a start, there's the problem of missing various forms of semi-tacit and tacit knowledge, such as preverbal construing, taken for granted knowledge and implicit attitudes'.

Response 1 is quite possibly a bluff. Response 2 is either an extremely elaborate bluff or an indication that what you thought was a harmless squirrel in the bushes is actually a large bear.

Have comfort food and bandages ready

The world is not fair. Sometimes people will be gratuitously and unnecessarily rude to you even when you're in the right. Sometimes you won't think of the brilliant and correct riposte until years afterwards. (For instance: 'Prospect theory is descriptive, and assumes that people fail to make the normatively correct decision as a result of heuristics and biases; this version of possibility theory shows that there are justifiable normative solutions very different from those advocated by the heuristics and biases school, and which correspond closely with those which are actually used by people, and which are described in prospect theory'. Not exactly a line that trips readily off the tongue, and several years too late, but at least it's been said now, and one of the authors feels better for it.)

Sometimes the comments are justified – for instance, the occasion when one of us was writing a fairly esoteric paper about an obscure aspect of repertory grid technique and didn't bother to cite Kelly (the seminal text) on the grounds that nobody could have become familiar enough with the technique to write that paper without having read Kelly. One of the referees pointed this out as a mistake, and they were right. The change was made and that mistake not made again.

On other occasions the fairness of comments is more debatable. Here are some examples which happened to other people:

- Opening line in question from audience at conference (witnessed by one of us): 'That was the most ignorant and ill-informed talk I have ever heard'.
- Alleged opening line in PhD viva from external examiner who was allegedly taken away for psychiatric treatment soon afterwards (possibly urban myth): 'Can you give me one good reason why I shouldn't use this thesis to wipe my backside?'
- Suggestion from audience in conference to someone else in the audience who complained with gratuitous rudeness that the speaker's recommended approach hadn't worked for them (witnessed by one of us): 'Perhaps you should try doing it right.'

A good strategy (once you're out of the danger zone) is to feel utterly sorry for yourself for the rest of the day and seek solace in comfort foods and your personal equivalent of bandages – a small sherry, chocolate, watching a movie with a high body count, or whatever. That gives your psyche a chance to sort itself out. Then, the next day, you ask yourself what you are going to do about it and how you are going to move on. Were the comments a fair hit? If so, you need to work out how to fix the problem. If not, what are you going to do to reduce the risk of similar unfair hits in the future? Remember that the search for revenge can do you just as much damage as the initial wrong – quite often the best strategy is to get on with seeking fortune and glory, and leave your assailant behind you. (There's the added comfort that if you learn from the experience you might be able to wipe the floor with your assailant next time you meet . . .)

A closing point about strategy and fairness: although it isn't a fair world, there are quite a lot of fair people in it. If you're perceived as a nice person who does good work, rather than an embittered seeker after petty revenge, then more experienced researchers will be likely to talent-spot you and to put opportunities your way. This is something which doesn't usually happen to people who spend their lives in pointless wrangling.

A brief checklist for presentations

- Have you checked the level of detail at which to give the talk?
- Have you checked what the audience will already know?
- Have you rehearsed the talk?
- Are your slides readable?
- Do you know how to use the audio-visual equipment where you will be presenting?
- Have you looked at the room where you will be presenting?
- Do you have a master sheet showing when you should be at which stage of the talk?
- Do you have a backup plan in case of equipment failure?

Presenting a paper at a conference – some tips

Dealing with nerves

- **Preparedness:** being really well prepared won't stop you being nervous, but it will give you something to rely on as you overcome your nerves. If you've given a practice talk that was well received and that allowed you to sort out any glitches, then you are likely to be more confident in the conference presentation.
- **Crib sheets:** if there's key information you want to remember (e.g. key papers and who wrote them), then write yourself a 'crib sheet' (i.e. list of the key facts and points) that you can take along for reference in case you need it.

- **Anticipate your fears:** think through the things that worry you most. What's the worst thing that could happen? How might you deal with it? Ask someone else how they'd deal with it.
- **Find a friendly face:** it's easier to make the talk warm and conversational if you can view it as a conversation with someone – especially someone who is interested.
- **Pause for breath:** pauses during a presentation feel to you like they last for years, but the audience hardly notices them. Allow yourself pauses to think, to collect yourself, to catch your breath. Your talk will be better for it.
- **Introduce yourself as a student:** if you're really terrified, you can slip in the information that you're a student in a bid to get the audience to treat you gently. For example, you can credit your supervisor, and you should credit your funding body, if appropriate.
- **Study the question patterns in preceding talks:** many people ask the same sorts of question of all speakers (e.g. methodology, statistics, application, relationship to particular theories). So, if you have a chance, pay attention to what sort of audience is in attendance and consider how you'd answer similar questions focused on your talk.
- **Dress comfortably:** you'll have enough to think about without being distracted by shoes that pinch or clothes that feel inappropriate. So wear something that makes you feel good.

What sort of script?

Different people use different sorts of scripts or notes to guide their talks. Think about what sort of script will support you best.

- **Overheads:** your overheads should be a distillation of the key ideas in the talk. They can themselves provide the cues for your narrative.
- **Notes:** people keep notes of points they want to make, in the order in which they want to make them. Some annotate a photocopy of the overheads to include fuller information and an indication of the 'story' they want to tell about the overheads. Others keep a separate 'text', with indications of how the overheads relate to the notes.
- **Full script:** some people write a full script for the talk – not necessarily to read it (which is not a good plan), but to have a set of words to fallback on if they 'dry up'.
- **Time line:** it's a good idea to know how your talk fills the available time, so that you know how much material you should have covered by the halfway mark and so on. If you have a script, or a set of notes, or just a running order, you can annotate it with elapsed time. Then you can check your progress during the talk.

Handling questions

- **Practice:** if you've given the paper as a seminar, you'll already have met some questions and had the experience of being 'on the spot'. This will help.
- **Question patterns:** during seminars and other people's talks, pay attention to the sorts of question that people ask. See if you can discern patterns in what people ask about. That gives you a basis for anticipating questions that might arise after your talk, and you can prepare answers for those.
- **Fending off references to unfamiliar literature:** if you don't know the paper you're being asked about, you can throw the question back to the asker: 'I'm not familiar with that paper; what point does the author make?' Or you can ask the questioner to relate it to literature you *do* know: 'I'm not familiar with that paper; does it fall into the AI camp or the empirical studies camp?' or, 'Is that anything like the travelling salesman problem?' Don't fake it. Make a note of the questioner and ask for the citation after the session.
- Divert **overly technical questions** to private discussion. ('That's an interesting point, but it would take a while to answer. Could we discuss it at the break?')
- **Missed questions:** if you're not sure you've understood the question, then paraphrase it back to the questioner: 'If I've understood you correctly, you're asking me if . . .' and then answer *your* version. If you haven't followed the question at all, ask the questioner to repeat it – he or she may ask a simpler version.
- **Long questions:** have paper and pencil ready. If someone asks a multi-part question, or passes off an essay as a question, then making some quick notes will help you keep track of what you want to say in response.
- **Bizarre questions:** treat similarly to overly technical questions; something along the lines of, 'That's a very interesting point, and one to which I hadn't previously given much attention. I'll look into that once I return to the office'. *Don't* offer to discuss it in the break.

Get someone else to record the questions asked, preferably with the names of the askers. You're unlikely to just remember them and you may not have time to make notes. In general, it's a good idea to be prepared to take notes – of people to catch later, or of particularly good points (theirs or yours), or of things you want to follow up.

13   Research design

I have brought to light a monstrous abnormality, but I did it for the sake of knowledge.

This is a topic which requires a book in its own right, and excellent books exist on this topic, but it would be hard to write a book such as this one without some coverage of research design, so here goes.

The research question

This is not the same as a question you ask people (such as experimental subjects): in many disciplines, such as metallurgy, research is performed on things, not people. Asking the right research question is a key academic skill. Bad research questions are a common cause of (at best) wasted time and (at worst) failed research, or (occasionally) of tragedy when a mistaken result is used for public policy making. A good research question reduces the problem space in an area. This means that the answer, whatever it is, eliminates one set of plausible possibilities. The next research question will then further reduce the possibility space, and so on, until there is only one sensible explanation for the problem which corresponds with the facts. Good examples of this approach can be found in the history of medicine – for instance, Pasteur successively eliminating possible answers for the cause of decay in foodstuffs.

Bad research questions come in various forms. The most common are listed below.

Seeking supporting evidence for a preconceived idea

It is surprisingly easy to find large amounts of evidence for even the most silly ideas. One exercise we use to demonstrate this to students involves dividing them into groups, then giving each group the name of a living thing which may or may not be a human (for instance, it may be a kangaroo or an ant). Each group then has to list as many arguments as possible for their living thing being a human being (for instance, that it has two legs, or that it constructs homes), with the other groups trying to guess whether or not they are describing a human.

A frequent version of this problem involves setting out to measure an effect, without thinking about (a) whether that effect exists or (b) what the wider context is. For instance, a lot of research by computer science students involves setting out to measure how much better their software is than the previous industry standard; if their software doesn't perform better, they end up with several years' worth of embarrassment and wasted effort staring them in the face.

Asking an unanswerable question

A question may be an important one, but unanswerable. For instance, do different Palaeolithic tool assemblages reflect (a) different activities within the same group or (b) different groups of people, such as different tribes or cultures? Both explanations fitted the facts equally neatly for a long time, until techniques were invented for identifying how tools were used.

Asking a useless question

Just because a question can be answered, that does not mean that it is of any use. For instance, discovering that a particular group of people (e.g. those with low scores on the Smith & Wesson dance test) have particular difficulty in learning foreign languages is unlikely to help anyone who is trying to teach them a foreign language – the teacher will be much more interested in finding out about better ways of teaching them. A well-formed research question will usually have very clear practical implications for someone. An improbable-sounding instance involves research into flamingo breeding. Captive flamingos are often reluctant to breed. Research indicated that this was because flamingos would only breed when they believed that the flock size was large enough. The practical implication of this was that putting mirrors beside the flamingo enclosure would make the flock appear twice the size, which did in fact encourage the flamingos to breed.

It is a good habit to work out the possible answers to your research question before you start your data collection, and to make sure you know (a) why each possible answer would usefully reduce the problem space and (b) what the practical implications would be. The latter is also very useful if you are looking for funding.

Useful questions about your question

There are some simple useful questions you can ask yourself about your research question. If the questions (or the answers) make you angry or nervous, then you should rethink your research design. (Hint: the answer to each question should be 'yes'.)

- Are you trying to find something out, rather than prove something?
- Do you ever find yourself being surprised by what you find in your data?
- Do you ever decide, on the basis of your data, that your previous ideas about an area were wrong?

Choice of method

Most research uses the traditional methods for that field. The number of researchers who take the time and trouble to learn the tools of their trade thoroughly is woefully small. A useful test is to list in detail the steps in your plan of research and then ask yourself, 'Why?' for each. For instance, why use a questionnaire rather than any other method (and what other methods are there)? Why use a sample size of 300 rather than 298 or 154? Why is a p value of 0.05 treated as statistically significant, whereas one of 0.051 is not? What does 'statistically significant' mean anyway? All these questions and more have been extensively researched for decades, and the more you know about research methods the more likely it is that you will be able to carry out good research with minimum wasted effort. This section looks briefly at these issues, as an illustrative example rather than an exhaustive list.

Data collection method

This is usually treated as synonymous with 'questionnaire' or 'interview'. Both of these are very easy to do badly and very hard to do well. They also both encounter serious problems with external validity (i.e. how well the answers obtained correspond with reality in any sense of that term) and usually also encounter problems with the representativeness of the sample (particularly in the case of questionnaires, where it is completely usual for over 80 per cent of recipients to throw away the questionnaire). Trying to argue that (a) analysing the results from the 20 per cent which were returned is in any way a meaningful exercise or (b) that everyone else in the field does the same, so it must be acceptable, are both pretty shoddy arguments.

There are many techniques for eliciting information from people, most of them much more useful for any given research question than questionnaires and interviews, and you should have enough basic knowledge of the main techniques to make an informed choice between them. These techniques include: participant observation, shadowing, direct observation, indirect observation, critical incident technique, scenarios, structured interviews, unstructured interviews, depth interviews, group interviews, card sorts, laddering, repertory grids and various forms of content analysis.

You should also be aware of the concepts affecting choice of technique, such as external validity, reliability (test-retest, inter-observer) and observer effects. You should remember to make sure you have ethical clearance if needed.

Sampling and sample size

Your sample needs to be either a total sample of an entire population or (much more often) a representative sample of a larger population. This is not always the same as a random sample, and you should know the difference between the two concepts. You should know how to select your sample in such a way as to make it representative.

There are statistical tests which allow you to say how likely it is that your sample is representative. Once your sample is big enough for you to be reasonably sure that it is representative, you do not need a bigger sample. You should know what level of likelihood is acceptable in your field, why it is considered acceptable, how this level of likelihood is calculated and what it actually means.

Types of research

Overview

- Size: small versus large
- Style: informal versus formal
- Focus: hardware, software, interface, people, the literature
- Data collection methods
- Data analysis methods

Size

Most students assume that a big study is better than a small one, and that a huge study is even better than a big one. Most students also don't know much about statistics.

You can use statistics to tell you how likely your results are to be the result of chance. You can also use statistics to assess how likely you are to find anything more by extending your sample size. After a certain point, extending your sample size is simply a waste of resources.

It's also important to realize that increasing your sample size won't magically transform bad data into good data. If you are collecting bad data (for instance, with a particularly awful questionnaire) then collecting more data simply means that you have even more bad data, and have wasted the time of even more long-suffering respondents.

It's possible to work out statistically in advance how much data you will need to collect for a particular experiment. The method for doing this is too lengthy to fit in the margin of this page, but if you sweet-talk a statistician there's a good chance you can persuade them to do it for you. The result will probably make you happy, the statistician happy (especially if they're going to be involved in the data analysis at the end) and the general population happy because you won't be bothering so many of them.

If you ask the right sort of question, you can get away with surprisingly small sample sizes. One of the authors once got a paper into a good international conference based on data collected from one respondent, which is about as small a sample as you can get. (Some of the referees even said nice things about it.)

Some sample sizes, and things to say about them, are listed below. The letter 'n' refers to the size of the sample: an n of 3 means that the sample size is three, for instance. Disciplines, as usual, vary. If you tried using an n of 2 in epidemiology, for instance, people would probably still be talking about you when your grandchildren had become old.

Use some discretion, and look at what the norms are in journals in your field.

n = 1 to 5: case study
Typical examples: in-depth study of an organization, demonstration of concept, 'white crow' study (demonstrating that an improbable-sounding effect exists).

n = 5 to about 20: pilot study or small study
Typical examples: gathering rich data from a small sample; extended fishing expedition; extended demonstration of concept.

n = about 20 to about 50: study
Typical examples: field experiment, formal experiment.

n > about 50: survey
Typical examples: gathering information about the incidence of a particular condition, belief etc. Surveys usually consist simply of gathering information, without any experimental manipulation of the respondents. It is possible to do experiments of this size, but the logistics quickly become horrible.

Style

There is a traditional divide in most areas between 'neats' and 'scruffies'. The 'neats' concentrate on formalisms to provide clean, abstract descriptions of the area; the 'scruffies' concentrate on understanding what is actually going on, even if they can't express it very neatly. Relations between the two groups usually vary between cool disdain and bitter feuding. 'Neats' typically have more academic street credibility, because they typically use intimidating mathematical representations. 'Scruffies' typically have more credibility with industry, because they typically have a wonderful collection of 'war stories', and know just what sort of things go on when the Health and Safety Executive isn't watching. Some people straddle the divide and have both a wonderful fund of stories and the ability to use intimidating representations. These people frequently end up as the 'gurus' in a field, and apparently get quite a few free meals and invitations to nice conferences as a result.

Anyway, returning to planning research, there is a spectrum of research types ranging from formal to informal. At the formal end of the scale are abstractions: for instance, mathematical modelling of an area, or trying different representations of the same topic. For this sort of work, you usually won't need to worry about sample size because you won't be collecting data as such; instead, you'll be assessing how well the formalism performs.

Next along the scale is the formal controlled experiment, straight out of the textbook: for instance, comparing the responses from two groups which you have treated in different ways. For this, you will know which variables you are manipulating and which you are measuring; you will have thought carefully about sample size.

Around the middle of the scale is the field experiment, where you are not able to control all the variables that you would like to and are trading that off against the realism of experimentation in the outside world. For instance, when redecoration time comes round, you might manage to persuade your establishment to paint the walls of one computer room a tasteful shade of green to see whether this calms down the users and reduces the number of complaints they make about the computers, compared to the users in the standard-issue hideous orange rooms. For this, you will know which variables you are manipulating and which you are measuring, but you will be horribly aware that other variables may be scurrying around looking for somewhere to cause you trouble.

At the scruffy end of the scale is the collection of squishy subjective data with a very small n. A good example of this is the eminent sociology professor who allegedly studied tramps via participant observation (i.e. passing himself off as a tramp and socializing with them). The result can be extremely interesting insights into an area, plus data that nobody else has, plus clothing that smells of methylated spirits.

Focus

Research can focus on a variety of things. In computer science, for instance, the research may focus on hardware, software, interfaces, people (either as groups or individually) or the literature. There is a useful conceptual divide which can be applied to most fields, consisting of research into (a) inanimate things (b) people/animals/plants and (c) concepts/the literature. Each of these has different implications for research design.

Research into inanimate things is a Good Thing. Much of physics, chemistry, geology and similar disciplines involves work of this sort. These disciplines usually have their own well-established ways of doing things and we have no intention of trying to teach them how to suck eggs.

Research involving people (and other living things, which we will ignore from now on, for brevity) is also a Good Thing. However, although there are many relevant disciplines, such as psychology, sociology, ergonomics, history and the like, most of which have venerable histories, it has to be said that there is still room for improvement in their methods. This is particularly the case with students, who usually appear not to have encountered any methods other than interviews, questionnaires and reading books or internet articles. (This issue is discussed in more depth below.)

Research involving concepts/the literature can be a Good Thing, but is a lot harder than it looks. If you are doing research involving collecting new data, then it is pretty easy to find something which is in some way new – even a change of wording on a questionnaire can be enough. If you are doing research involving concepts and/or the literature, however, then you need to know what is already known before you can start looking for something new. This means that you are giving yourself the task of reading the literature, including the most recent and the most advanced work in your chosen area, and then trying to find something that the best minds in the area haven't thought of yet. This is not advisable for a beginner. It is also not advisable to believe that simply reporting what other people have found will count as original research – it won't. At PhD level you will need to take on the literature and show that you can do original work, but it's wiser to do this via new data or new methods rather than head-on.

Data collection methods

Data can be collected using a wide range of methods. It is a good idea to become familiar with a range of these, since this can make your life a lot simpler.

If you're dealing with people in your data collection, you might want to find out more about the following. Some of these (particularly physical measures) may involve ethical or licensing issues:

- **physiological measures:** response time; ECG; EEG; skin galvanometer measures; physical force used on instrument;

- **behavioural:** responses to various situations, such as smoke coming from under a door, or whether respondents post a dropped letter (may involve ethical issues);
- **observation:** direct, indirect; participant; shadowing; time lines;
- **interview-like:** interviews; scenarios; critical incident technique;
- **personal construct theory:** repertory grids, laddering, card sorts, implication grids.

Data analysis methods

There are numerous ways of analysing data and it is usually possible to analyse the same data in quite different ways for different purposes. You might want to find out more about the following, which come upstream of any statistical analysis you might want to do: content analysis; coding into categories; time lines; discourse analysis; causal assertions; semiotics; deconstruction; grounded theory.

Classic pitfalls in research design

The biggest obstacle to research is researchers' own assumptions. Ignorance and isolation are the enemies of research. Here are some other common pitfalls to watch out for:

- Leaping before looking: failure to reflect (think; reflect on assumptions, evidence, techniques, what can go wrong).
- Ignorance: often manifest as reinventing the wheel (a day in the library can save six months of redundant research).
- Putting the cart before the horse: trying to choose techniques before refining the questions and evidence requirements (do first things first).
- Great expectations: also known as eyes bigger than stomach, or biting off more than you can chew (if the question is too big, ask a smaller question; a life's work takes a lifetime, but it's achieved one step at a time).
- Sand through the fingers: for a precise study, you need a precise question, but by the time you've got your experiment sufficiently controlled, you've lost sight of your purpose and possibly of your big question (back off and remind yourself why you started, then review your inference chain meticulously; maybe what you really need is some coarser-grained approach to help you refine the question).
- Bias: be vigilant, be honest, go and read a good book on the subject.
- Confusing anecdote with fact: what 'everyone knows' is often wrong (let anecdote help shape your questions, but then seek independent evidence in order to find answers).

- Confusing statistics with rigour: find out what statistics can and cannot do, then go and find a good experimental statistician to consult. The point is to know what can and cannot be shown with different sorts of evidence.
- The false seduction of the definitive experiment: sometimes you need a different research method.
- Lack of respect for failure: Nils Bohr said, 'Science is not "that's interesting" but "that's odd" '. Great research often comes from surprise. The only bad study is one that doesn't inform you; what information does your 'failure' provide?
- Shortage of theory: back to the library.
- Overgeneralization: take care in your storytelling and be meticulous about your inference chain.
- Fatal independence: trying to be an expert in everything (cultivate a social life; have coffee with a genuine expert).

Planning a body of research

So there you are, newly appointed, with a desk in your shared office, with the world in front of you, not sure quite what to do next apart from react to what your line manager is telling you, and wishing that you hadn't read out the checklist item about the key to the departmental wheelbarrow when you worked through the list of things you needed with the departmental secretary. What do you do?

The first step

The first priority is the cockroach principle. Cockroaches have been around for a lot longer than human beings, and are likely to be around for a long time to come. They didn't last this long by having maladaptive strategies. One of their key principles is to make sure they have a nice, safe hole to scuttle into when things get scary. From your point of view, this means that you should make sure you have a protector and/or bolt-hole. Ideally, these should be your boss and your job, respectively. A good boss will protect staff and treat them as valued assets. If you have such a boss and you're being given needless grief by some idiot with more power than you, then your boss should be able to sort things out. It's a very comforting feeling to be able to say: 'You'll need to discuss that with my line manager' and to know that you will never hear that request/threat/inappropriate command again.

Humans, however, face a problem which cockroaches are spared: human bolt-holes are organizational rather than physical, so humans need to maintain them. This is done, not by grovelling or bribery, but by honouring your end of the bolt-hole deal – you do the work which you are supposed to and support your boss in their daily struggle against the forces of chaos and darkness. This need not be a scary process; some very successful bosses get their way by a reputation as friendly, helpful, useful people to have around. This can occasionally lead to odd situations, such as your helping someone in a different faculty with some work which appears to have no visible connection to your official role, but it all helps the world go round.

Sometimes, unfortunately, your boss is either unwilling or unable to protect you. A classic example is when your boss is the head of department and you are the newest lecturer, viewed as fair game for organizing the departmental tea money, teaching the class of 300 unruly second years that nobody else will take, and so forth. That's neither particularly fair nor particularly fun, but nobody seems to have any good solutions. The best bet is to assess whether this is an initiation by fire, after which things will become reasonable, or whether you have just landed in the educational equivalent of one of the later chapters of Dante's greatest work. If the latter, then it's a good idea to find a new job as soon as possible.

Assuming that you are staying, and have reasonable prospects, what do you do next?

The second step

Having made sure that you do the main things required by your boss and The System, you need to make your own plans. It's your life, and your career; nobody else owns it except you. If you decide that you want to win a Nobel, or that you'd rather have a quiet life studying Walloon neologisms, that's up to you.

If you decide to build a career in research, then you need to put together some integrated plans. It's tempting to grab at any opportunities which are passing, and to do the most obvious and/or easiest things which flit into your mind. These temptations should be resisted. They lead to frittering away time and effort which could be better spent in other ways – for instance, doing an excellent piece of research in half the time which most people would take, and then spending the time you've saved having a pleasant excursion in the park, or whatever works as an antidote to workaholic tendencies for you.

Some parameters of your plans are largely determined for you by the norms of your discipline. If you want a career in research, then you need to bring in income, and to get out successful PhD students and good publications. Experienced colleagues will be able to tell you the figures for acceptable, good or outstanding performance in each.

Although these parameters are largely predetermined, you still have enormous flexibility in what you research in order to achieve your goals. Your two journal papers a year (for instance) could be on pretty much any topic imaginable. So, how do you decide what to tackle?

Schemata and other forms of mental organization

Experts aren't significantly better than novices at logic and abstract reasoning, other things being equal. They do, however, have much better organization of their knowledge about their area of expertise than novices do, and they also know a lot more facts than novices do. In addition, they have better strategies for tackling their domain than novices do. There is a well-established literature on this topic, which is useful reading.

One useful way of organizing knowledge is to use schemata, which are mental templates for a 'standard issue' case. For instance, the usual schema for getting started in research is a first degree, followed by a PhD, followed by several years of postdoctoral research, followed by a lectureship. Schemata are useful because they provide ready-made solutions to many problems, without much need for original thought.

A standard schema for a piece of research is to find something in the course of one piece of research, and then use it as the basis for a student research project. If the results are sufficiently interesting, the student project can then form the basis of a journal paper, and the student becomes a potential PhD student after they graduate. The paper establishes priority of publication in that area, so the PhD won't be marred by worry about whether someone else will get there first. If the PhD goes well, then you and the PhD student write a research proposal in the final year of the PhD, to employ the student on postdoctoral research.

What happens if you're not sure which area you really want to have as your main focus? One way of reducing the problem space to manageable proportions is to have a series of strands of research. It's a good idea to start with just one strand if you're new and/or nervous.

Another handy part of expertise involves knowing how to fit things together. For instance, if your research has several strands, you soon won't be able to keep on top of it all. A good way of handling this problem is to delegate. For example, your PhD student could supervise some undergraduate projects on topics which complement their PhD, which in turn would be one of your strands.

Ethics

Ethics are pretty damned important. The trouble is, everybody has a different idea about what is ethical. We can't give you a set of bullet points and top-ten tips on hot ethics. What we can do is give you a focal concept, say something about background context and discuss the implications of things that people do in research, so you can think about it for yourself.

Duty of care

The focal concept in research ethics is 'duty of care'. As a principled researcher, you owe a duty of care to a variety of parties, including your predecessors, your research community, your colleagues, your subjects and, interestingly enough, yourself. For example, if you are gathering confidential information from respondents about their most embarrassing experiences, then you have a duty of care to these respondents, which includes making sure that their names remain out of the public domain. If you remember nothing else, remember to ask yourself: to whom do I owe a duty of care, and what is it?

Subjects

There's a line attributed to a German researcher from about a century ago, who allegedly said: 'We must not be anthropomorphic about human beings'. It's a line with more depth than first appears, and bears thinking about.

However, when you are dealing with human subjects, you have to take into account the effect that your research will have on them. Milgram's experiments into obedience to authority would almost certainly not get past an ethical panel today, because of the psychological effect they would have on subjects who discovered that they were capable of giving someone what they believed to be a fatal electric shock, just because an authority figure told them to do it. That's an extreme example, but useful for making the point clearly.

It's tempting to think that your own research couldn't have that effect on anyone. The trouble is, Milgram didn't think that his research would have that effect. He asked his colleagues, professional psychologists, what his subjects were likely to do. The consensus opinion was that the subjects would refuse to give shocks at quite an early stage of the experiment.

Research into humans involves finding out about how they work. People don't often have a very accurate image of themselves, for various reasons. It can be profoundly disturbing to become aware of aspects of oneself which had previously been unsuspected. That's what happened to Milgram's subjects.

The obvious answer is not to do research which might lead to disturbing the subjects. However, that's too simple an answer. There's a strong case for the argument that making people aware of their weaknesses and shortcomings can help them to come to a better understanding of themselves, and in the long term be of benefit to them – that's what psychotherapy is all about. Understanding human strengths and weaknesses also helps us as a society to do things better.

There isn't a clear, God-given answer to all of this. You need to think it through for yourself. It will make you a better person, especially if you can resist the temptation to kid yourself. Some thoughts which might help you with this include the following:

- Are you claiming that the end justifies the means (a trusty favourite)?
- Has your professor/tutor/boss said that it's OK (as with Milgram's subjects)?
- How would you feel if your most despised enemy outlined this experiment and you were on the ethics panel deciding whether to approve it?

- How comfortable would you feel if you received notification that one of your subjects was hiring Wolfram and Hart to bring a lawsuit against you for unethical research?
- How would you feel on your deathbed looking back on this bit of research? Proud of it, or ashamed?

Attribution

It's probably no accident that proper research only got going after duelling was outlawed. Arguments over publications can assume an intensity and bitterness which has to be experienced to be believed.

There are good reasons for this. You need to remember the conventions about how references are cited in the text. If it's a one-author citation (e.g. 'Smith 1999') then it's 'Smith 1999' every time it's mentioned. If it's a two-author citation (e.g. 'Smith and Jones 1999') then it's 'Smith and Jones 1999' every time it's mentioned. However, the situation changes the moment there are three or more authors. Then, the first time it's cited, all the authors are named (e.g. 'Smith, Jones and Cobbley 1999') but all subsequent citations are abbreviated to 'Smith *et al.* 1999'. This is compounded by a widespread convention that the first author in the list is the one who did most of the work. There's a very big difference between being a first author and an *et al.* in terms of the prospects for getting attention from other researchers who read that paper. People therefore argue bitterly over the order of names.

There are some simple ways round this:

- agree on authorship, and who writes which bits, before you even start the research – if you can't agree at this stage, don't bother starting the research;
- only work with people you like, trust and respect;
- work out a system which you all agree to be fair, and stick to it;
- only write one-author and two-author papers.

Anonymity

Normal practice is to keep your respondents truly anonymous. This is different from not mentioning their name(s). If it is possible for someone to identify a respondent (whether an individual or an organization) then that respondent is not being kept truly anonymous. This is a Bad Thing. Unfortunately, there are situations where it is very difficult to describe a respondent while maintaining their anonymity (for instance, 'a major UK non-commercial television broadcasting company'). If such a problem is likely, then sort it out before starting data collection – that's a lot preferable to sorting it out in court . . .

Credit and acknowledgements

You should give due credit for the contribution of other people. This includes previous researchers in the area and people who have helped and collaborated with your research. It includes (for instance) technicians who helped prepare equipment needed for the research and statisticians who advised you on the analysis of your data. Where the contribution was a significant component of the work described in your article, the person has a claim to co-authorship of the article. Where the contribution was one which was a routine part of the person's job, involving no input to the overall design and nature of the research, and was done to order for the researcher (as in the case of a technician following a specification for equipment needed) then this is usually credited in the acknowledgements rather than in the authorship.

The situation with research assistants in this respect is not clear-cut, and is the source of numerous battles on research projects. If you've spent years developing a body of theory, you would feel understandably reluctant to hand over first authorship of the first publication to a research assistant who might never have heard of the area before you hired them. If, on the other hand, you are a research assistant who has contributed a significant proportion of the research design, carried out the actual research and analysis, and written the first draft of the paper, then it is a bit galling to be excluded from the authorship.

IPR

This stands for 'intellectual property right' and is a growth area, especially for lawyers. It relates to who has the intellectual ownership of an idea and is entitled to money from its exploitation. Again, the issue is far from clear-cut. If you have been working for 20 years on a cure for Alzheimer's, and finally find one three weeks after starting work at St Winnifred's College, you might not be too pleased if the College claimed that they owned IPR on the idea because you were working for them at the time, and would be even less pleased if they set out to become the richest college in the world while not paying you a penny of the profits. Conversely, if you are the vice-chancellor of Rutland University, and have been pouring large amounts of money into a long-term institutional drive to find a cure for AIDS, you might be a bit annoyed if someone who has only recently joined the institution runs off and sets up their own private company based on your university's work. What is the situation if you have been using a series of different research assistants over a period of 15 years before the latest version of your work finally strikes gold? Would a research assistant from 15 years ago have a good claim? No idea. Nobody else knows yet either.

It's worth thinking ahead about this one, and deciding what you really want out of life. A wise institution will make sure that the pay-offs suit both parties. It will be interesting to see how many wise institutions there are out there as IPR issues become more prevalent.

Truth

Truth, according to Vance, is a precious jewel, the more precious for being rare. It is not a researcher's job to keep the price up by keeping the supply down.

However, as any social scientist know (the phrasing is a dry allusion to several classic texts, which will probably be missed by everyone except the diligent copy-editor, but never mind), truth is a tricky and relativistic thing to pin down. There are good grounds for arguing that truth in the strictest sense is a meaningless concept. There is also the small matter of the first and third golden rules ('don't lie' and 'don't panic and blurt out the truth' respectively).

A neat way out of this is to argue that there is an asymmetry, derived from the mathematics of infinity. There is an infinite set of propositions which correspond with a given slice of reality and can therefore be described as 'true'. However, this is not the same as saying that all propositions are equally true and valid. There is a different and also infinite set of propositions which do not correspond with a given slice of reality and can therefore be described as 'not true'. You should not publish work which you know to be not true.

That particular idea is so neat that it leaves the uneasy feeling that there must be a catch somewhere.

14   The viva

Once I sought out a celebrated ethnologist and amused him with peculiar questions regarding the ancient Philistine legend of Dagon, the Fish-God; but soon perceiving that he was hopelessly conventional, I did not press my inquiries.

The viva (short for *viva voce* or 'living voice' examination) occupies a place in PhD student myth and legend which offers immense scope to writers with a taste for scary metaphor, but tact and common humanity prevent us from exploring that area as fully as we might. In one sense the folklore is right. The viva is one of the two essential outputs from your PhD. If your written thesis and your viva are both good enough, then you get a doctorate. If they're not, you don't. Nothing else comes into play – not how hard you've worked, or how bright you are, or how much you care about your topic, or how important it is to the world, or how much you've suffered, or how much you want that PhD. It's perfectly possible to write a decent dissertation and then make a disastrous mess of the viva. So, what do you do about it?

The first thing is to understand the purpose of the viva from the examiners' point of view. The PhD is a rite of passage, showing that you are worthy to be admitted to the clan. In terms of the cabinet-making metaphor, it's the point where you leave apprenticeship behind and become a fully-fledged cabinet-maker, if you're good enough. The key point in both metaphors is that neither of them contains any mention of perfection. PhDs don't have to be perfect. They only have to be good enough, where 'good enough' means that you have demonstrated a satisfactory command of the skills required for a professional researcher in your discipline. The level of 'good enough' will be high, but that's different from perfection. Nobody will be expecting your thesis to be perfect

– in this context, the whole idea of perfection is only meaningful as a convenient shorthand term. By definition, when your work involves new discovery, there is uncertainty and no absolute right answer. Your work will build on previous work and on established techniques; all of these are ultimately derived from approximations, assumptions and consensus in the field, rather than from God-given absolute truths. Part of becoming a mature professional researcher is being able to accept uncertainty, and to deal with it in a way which is appropriate for the situation in hand. Sometimes an uncertainty is the whole point of the research (for instance, 'Why is this mould growing on my Petri dishes?'), but on other occasions you have to accept that you have to work with an uncertainty which is not likely to be clarified in the foreseeable future (for instance, 'Why do things so often form Poisson distributions?')

The obverse of this cheering thought is the implication that your thesis will contain *questionable things*. These provide a starting place for the examiners to do some poking around, to check the extent of your skills. They don't want nasty surprises. They want to be reassured that your mastery of your field holds up adequately under scrutiny. They do not want to discover that your thesis is brilliant because your supervisor wrote all of it for you under the influence of desperate, unrequited love. They do not want to discover that you didn't mention an obvious point because you'd never thought of it, rather than because you didn't think it was worth mentioning because it was so obvious. Two stories illustrate this. We have chosen stories which are probably apocryphal, so as to spare the feelings of those involved in definitely true stories.

Stories of nasty surprises

The mushroom story

The mushroom story concerns an agriculture student whose undergraduate dissertation involved looking at growth in farmed mushrooms, a topic of little interest to most of the world, but of considerable importance to mushroom farmers. Much to his surprise, he found that the mushrooms did not grow either continually or in diurnal cycles; instead they grew in cycles of a few hours. This finding was so unexpected that he went on to do a PhD on the topic, producing large amounts of data and analysis. The day of the viva arrived, and went beautifully up to the point where the external examiner asked a gentle, ground-clearing question, namely: 'I take it that you allowed for the central heating going on and off in the mushroom sheds?' After some seconds of horrible silence, it was agreed that the viva would be postponed until after the student had done a post-pilot study to check that the effect was not due to the central heating going on and off. The results of the post-pilot were sickeningly predictable: the student had just spent several years of his life measuring, in effect, how often the central heating went on and off in mushroom sheds.

The woodpecker story

The woodpecker story is similar. We include it partly on the grounds that it's wise to be wary of principles which are always illustrated by the same example – this raises the nasty suspicion that there is only one example – and partly on the grounds that one of us used to wear a safety helmet in the course of a previous day job and can personally testify that they come in very handy when someone drops a bucket on your head. The woodpecker story is also useful because it demonstrates a more subtle and far-reaching effect than the mushroom story.

According to the story, the developers of safety helmets decided to look to nature to find inspiration for a new approach to design. One of them wondered whether there were any animals which experienced powerful blows to the head without suffering brain damage. Inspiration struck, in the form of the woodpecker, which spends much of its waking life banging its head against trees with considerable force. The team accordingly read up on the anatomy of the woodpecker and discovered that it had a spongy base to its beak which absorbed the force of the impact. The team used this inspiration to come up with a design for a helmet which was not designed to stop objects from penetrating the helmet (as with First World War military helmets, for instance), but instead was designed to absorb the blow by deforming harmlessly, preventing most of the energy of impact from reaching the wearer's head (unlike helmets designed to prevent penetration). The designers were proudly demonstrating their concept when, according to the story, a member of the audience asked: 'How do you know woodpeckers don't suffer brain damage?' Painful silence ensued . . .

In the mushroom story, the student failed to identify a relevant variable (the central heating). In the woodpecker story, the design team had not checked a key assumption (that woodpeckers don't get brain damage). The woodpecker story in fact had a happy ending; the current design is demonstrably good and the designers were proved right (even though, as far as we know, nobody ever did check on brain damage rates in woodpeckers). In other cases, however, unchecked assumptions have led to years wasted in pointless research, which could have been spent instead in a useful area. This is quite a different proposition from reducing the problem space by eliminating one set of plausible possibilities.

For this reason, external examiners are likely to poke around in the foundations of your research, checking that you have neither missed anything which you should have thought of, nor made an unwarranted assumption.

An example from popular culture might provide a more cheering return to the plot, namely the comic-book character the Incredible Hulk. According to the story, the Hulk was created when a mild-mannered scientist was trying to find the source of people's astonishing strength in emergencies, such as the woman who lifted a car off her child after a crash. That story is fiction and obviously silly, because – dramatic pause – people *don't* have astonishing strength in emergencies; the story of the woman lifting a car off her child is an urban myth. (Try checking the website www.urbanlegends.com if you're thinking of applying for a research grant of your own in this area, before you start budgeting for high-stretch shirts and non-rip trousers . . .)

Most students collect horror stories about vivas, using them to nurture their nightmares. In our experience, failure at viva is rare and is almost always attributable to one of two things:

1 The student didn't listen to their supervisors, or any other advisers for that matter.
2 The supervisory relationship had broken down and the student hadn't compensated for it.

Therefore, failure at viva is in principle avoidable, given two protective behaviours:

1 Listen to your supervisor.
2 Build up an effective personal network and expose your work through seminars and publications in advance of your viva, so that you'll be alerted to oversights early.

What happens at the viva: the things that go before

Anyway, back to the main story. External examiners are there to check that you know how to make cabinets; how do they set about doing it?

The story normally starts before you see them. At some point in your PhD, you and your supervisor need to choose an external. For some PhDs, this is done before you even register for the PhD; for others, it happens after you've written up. For most, it's somewhere in the last year or so. There are various factors in choosing the external. They should not have a conflict of interest – if they're co-applying with you for a Nobel prize, for instance, then they will have a substantial incentive to pass your thesis, whether you deserve it or not. Similarly, if your last conversation with them started with you saying: 'Wake up, darling, or we'll be late for my viva,' then questions might be asked . . .

Once the external has been chosen, they will get on with their life until your thesis arrives in the post, accompanied by the appropriate forms and other paperwork. What do they do with it? That depends. Most externals will read the thesis in detail, at least once. Many will read it line by line, making notes page by page. They will look in detail at the references and appendices (the equivalent of hauling the drawers out of a cabinet and checking the joints that were never intended to be seen in normal use). They will check references or assertions which don't look right. They will probably spot the reference to Young, Gifted and Black (1976) which felt so amusing at the time. And so forth. At the other end of the spectrum, there are persistent stories about externals who read theses on the train, on the way to the viva. Either way, you want their initial reaction to be the same: you want them to feel the nice warm glow that accompanies the thought: 'Well, this doesn't look like a fail'. So, make sure that the pages which they will look at first are all reassuring – all the pages up to and including the second page of the introduction; the references; and the concluding couple of pages.

The examiners will usually read the thesis independently and then contact each other to discuss it. They have a limited set of options about marks, since you either get a PhD or you don't: you don't get a percentage mark like you do with a final-year project. However, this apparent simplicity derives from a more complex assessment process. The examiners can pass your thesis without changes (unusual, but far from unknown); they can fail it completely (far from unknown); they can recommend that it be considered for an MPhil instead; or, more commonly, they can accept it subject to specified changes of varying degrees of severity. If they all agree that it looks like a straight pass, a straight fail or an MPhil, then their life is simple; more often, however, there are changes required, which means that the examiners have to discuss what needs to be changed. This can be time-consuming and irritating, especially if the changes are needed because your thesis is vague or otherwise badly written. After this, they will need to agree on the game plan for the viva itself – who will handle which bits, and how? Note that they don't simply put together a list of changes ready to give to you. The provisional list will be modified in the light of the viva. If it turns out, for instance, that an apparent problem is simply a matter of your using an unusual name for something instead of a more familiar one, then the change might only involve putting in a parenthesis to explain that your term is the same as the more familiar one. Conversely, if the viva reveals major and inexcusable ignorance on your part, then what initially looked like a minor change can turn into a major one, or even a fail. This shouldn't normally happen, but it may happen in cases where a student vanishes into the wilderness, does some research, then writes up and insists on submitting against the advice of the supervisor (rare, but unfortunately not unknown).

The day itself: the opening stages

The examiners normally rendezvous in or around the department some time before the viva, and have a pre-viva meeting to confirm their plan of action. They will usually not show much interest in meeting you at this stage. This is nothing personal: they have a job to do, and they need to concentrate on that. Many vivas are held in the afternoon, to give the examiners time to get to the venue; in these cases, the examiners are normally taken off to lunch by your supervisor before the viva. You probably won't be invited: this is etiquette, not a snub. (You may be invited to lunch if you had a successful viva with them in the morning, but that's different.) There are persistent rumours about relationships where the supervisor treats the examiners to a few drinks at lunchtime to get them in a good mood; if true, this is the exception, not the norm.

When they are ready, you will be summoned, and will go into the room, looking and feeling distinctly nervous if you are anything like most other PhD candidates.

Opening gambits

Since you are likely to be nervous, most examiners will make an effort to put you at your ease. Since the viva usually takes place in your department, with the external as the visitor, there isn't much scope for the traditional opening gambit in meetings, namely asking whether you had a good journey. Similarly, the bit where they introduce themselves will usually go past you in a nameless blur, like the following bit where they say how they are going to conduct the session. There are various other gambits which are more likely to get through to you, most of which are open to being misconstrued by nervous candidates.

An example of this is the external who offers you a couple of sheets of A4 listing the typos they have found. This is easily misconstrued as trivial, petty nit-picking which misses the great philosophical points behind your thesis. Not so. It's actually a graceful courtesy. For one thing, it shows that the examiner has paid you the compliment of bothering to read every page in such detail that they have found the typo on page 174 which your spell-checker missed. For another thing, it is much preferable to have that list by you when you fix the typos, rather than being told that there are numerous typos which need to be fixed, but not being told where they are. A third thing is that in some cases the examiners only ask a few token questions and use the list of typos as an indirect way of saying that you've done such a good job on the thesis that it only needs very minor alterations (in such cases, the list of typos is an indirect way of saying that they're not simply going for the minor alterations option because they're too lazy to do anything else).

Another opening gambit which is widely used is to say something about your thesis along the lines of how interesting or readable it was. This gambit can actually mean several very different things. For some academics, 'readable' is a low-grade insult, referring to the sort of thing written by scientists who popularize science (an activity viewed with condescension by many academic researchers). For others, 'readable' is a compliment, meaning that it's possible for a human being to work out what you're on about, unlike most of the turgid grot perpetrated by people writing in your area. How can you tell which meaning you are encountering? One indicator is the reputation of the examiner. If they're notoriously sadistic, then you're probably about to encounter trouble, so don't let that opening sentence lull you off your guard. If the examiner is known as a considerate soul, then you're probably being given a gentle start to the session. However, it's worth remembering that even the most considerate examiner is also a professional academic and likely to take the viva pretty seriously, so don't presume too much. If you encounter this gambit, a fairly safe response is a dry smile and a 'thank you' in a polite tone which implies that you're no idiot.

A third opening gambit which can be misconstrued is asking you to give a brief overview of your thesis. One perfectly understandable response to this is anger: surely if the examiners have read your thesis properly they shouldn't need a brief overview of it? Again, not so. The brief overview is a pretty good way of getting a nervous candidate to open up: they usually become so absorbed in the topic that they forget their nerves. It's also a good way of finding out which aspects of the thesis they find most important, which tells you a lot about their professionalism. In some cases, it's also useful for finding out just what the thesis is supposed to be about, if it's been written up in a particularly vague or unreadable style. Quite often, a thesis will contain stuff which looks promising but which is poorly structured and badly described. If the content is good, then a few skilful changes can make a surprising difference to the thesis; if the content is as bad as the style, then the whole thing needs to be consigned to a nameless pit and erased from human memory. Either way, this opening gambit helps the examiners towards a decision.

It's tempting at this stage to break the third golden rule, by panicking and blurting out the truth about things you did wrong. Don't give in to temptation. Instead, give a clear, previously prepared overview, listing the main findings and the main ways in which this work is a contribution to knowledge. You might want to use a few gambits of your own to show that you know the rules of the game – for instance, a discreet reference to your latest paper in a major journal, or a mention of ongoing work with a major figure in the field. Don't overdo it, though – remember that you're a candidate, not an examiner.

The mid-game

After the opening exchanges the real business begins, and vivas begin to differ. Examiners have four main options available to them in terms of outcomes: straight pass, pass subject to minor changes, pass subject to major changes and fail. They have many more options available to them in terms of how they conduct the viva itself, and it's important to remember that a viva can feel like a grim interrogation to you, but end up with a straight pass.

The straight pass

At one end of the cosiness scale is the situation where the examiners make it clear from the outset that there's little doubt this will be a straight pass, and then ask a few questions for courtesy's sake before heading off with you and your supervisor to lunch/coffee/the pub. You may be asked to fix three or four typos, for form's sake. This outcome typically occurs when you have a good supervisor, when you and your supervisor both know how the game is played, and when you've done a thoroughly good job on your dissertation.

Minor changes

Next down the scale is the viva where you are asked a few technical questions to check on specific points. You probably won't be able to answer all the questions either to your satisfaction or to theirs. Don't let that shake you: nobody can answer all the possible sensible questions, or have done all the relevant reading. An example of this is as follows. You have done a PhD which involves a new taxonomy of human error types. You have done the essential reading (Reason, Hollnagel, Rasmussen and so on). You have also done some good further reading by looking at the literature on formal taxonomic classification in biology. The external examiner asks you whether you have read the literature on use of multidimensional statistics for classification. You haven't. What do you do? Well, for a start, you don't panic. Although the question is a valid one, you have already gone beyond standard best practice in your area by bothering to read up on formal taxonomy. The leading literature on human error isn't based on multidimensional stats and cluster algorithms. Although you could in principle have investigated that route, it's only one of many routes which you could have taken, and it's physically impossible to take all of them. Saying that you could have taken it is very different from saying that you should have taken it. So, you can bounce the question back at the external by making some of the points above, and politely asking what they think that the multidimensional approach would offer to this area. You can then get into a debate with them which allows you to demonstrate your ability, which is the main point. To conclude this example, if you make a good case in the debate, you may be asked to add a sentence saying that you chose not to use multidimensional stats, and giving the reason for not using them: a pretty minor change.

Major changes

A more serious situation would be where the examiner's question identifies a serious area of ignorance on your part. A good example of this comes from statistics. Suppose you have looked at different groups' perceptions of how car crashes are shown in the popular media, and have gathered some numeric data on the respondents' perceptions. You write this up in neat tables and mention in your discussion that the difference between two groups is significant, and that another finding is highly significant. The examiners reach this point in your thesis and the external examiner says that you have described results as significant and as highly significant, but haven't mentioned the tests you used or the p values involved.

None of the options at this point are good. The least bad is that you tell them which tests you used and what the p values were; the examiners will wonder silently what sort of idiot you were to omit this information and will be on the lookout for further signs of idiocy, but you may well get away with simply adding the missing information. The two other main options are about as bad as each other. One is that you tell them that you use only qualitative methods and don't agree with quantitative methods on principle; you then look like an idiot for choosing a non-qualitative external examiner, and for having gathered quantitative data but not analysed it quantitatively. This issue relates to some serious debates about which skills in a discipline are essential rather than optional, which go beyond the scope of this book: to use an extreme (and genuine) example, should someone be allowed to graduate in French if they refuse on ideological grounds to use standard French spelling and punctuation? If you don't approve of cabinets, that's fair enough, but to undertake an apprenticeship in cabinet-making when you feel that way is a decision that falls somewhat short of being sensible.

The last main option involves your admitting that you have never heard of statistical tests or p values, and asking what p values have to do with significance anyway. This approach might be perfectly acceptable in some disciplines, but in others where statistics form a core skill (e.g. experimental psychology) it would be disastrous. If you've ended up in a situation where your external is asking this sort of question and where your answer is an admission of total ignorance, then you've made a serious mistake in your choice of external, in your choice of discipline or in your approach to your subject. The best that you can hope for with either of the two latter options is some serious revisions. Even if you wriggle out of this particular question, the session will have shifted from a fairly routine check to a serious investigation of whether or not you deserve to pass, and there's a strong likelihood that one of the next questions will sink you fair and square.

The fail

At the bottom of the cosiness scale is the viva where the examiners think that you've made a serious mess of things, and where you exacerbate matters by being gratuitously offensive, ignorant and/or stupid. Usually, but not invariably, these cases occur when the student submits their thesis against the advice of the supervisor. A typical example might be a part-time PhD student who has a fairly influential day job as a manager, and who cobbles together a dissertation topic on job satisfaction based on reading textbooks and professional magazines, then goes on to conduct a badly designed questionnaire and/or some badly designed interviews, and who talks about 'getting all this airy-fairy academic stuff out of the way'. (Yes, this sort of thing has really happened, and more than once.) There isn't much that can be salvaged from such cases. The literature review is too simplistic to lead to an interesting research question; the methods are too boring to form the basis of a decent rewrite; the data will probably be untrustworthy or uninformative because of the flaws in the methods. Work of this sort will fail, and deservedly so. Again, if you think that cabinet-making is overrated and that MFI flatpack furniture is just as good, then you're entitled to that opinion but you would be pretty silly to apply for an examination as a would-be master cabinet-maker and bring along a poorly assembled flatpack as your alleged master piece.

The end game

By the end of the session, the examiners will probably have reached a conclusion about what to do with you. 'Probably' because they will need to check with each other and reach an agreed verdict. They will politely ask you to leave, and will do whatever examiners do while you are pacing around in the corridor, feeling nervous.

What examiners do is to check with each other, reach an agreed verdict and have some breathing space. If your thesis is a clear pass or a clear fail, then they will check explicitly that they all agree. If it's a clear pass, they won't necessarily summon you back 30 seconds after you've gone out; quite a lot of examiners believe in keeping the candidate waiting for a few minutes, on the grounds that it is good for the candidate's soul.

If there's consensus that you'll have to make changes, then nice examiners will draw up a clear list. This might be a longhand list written there and then, or it might be emailed to you a day or two later.

If there's not consensus, then the examiners have to slug it out among themselves. At this point, you can reap what you have sown much earlier. For example, if you have produced a couple of decent journal papers out of your work, then that demonstrates that your work is of adequate professional quality, which strengthens the case for anyone wishing to argue that your thesis contains good stuff, even if it's been badly written up. Similarly, if you have done a solid literature review, then that shows that you have a proper professional knowledge of your area, even if your data collection was a bit tatty. Both these examples involve starting early; they're not something you can cobble together in the last week. It's a good idea, a year or so into your PhD, to read your institution's regulations and then get someone knowledgeable to translate them into English for you, so that you can find out about things like indications of acceptable quality in the thesis. If there's something about 'publishable in a peer-reviewed journal', for instance, then getting a couple of publications in a peer-reviewed journal will help your case in the event of a debatable verdict after the viva.

When all of this has been done, the examiners will reach an agreement with your supervisor about the next stages, and summon you back. Some will say the magic words: 'Congratulations, Dr Smith'; others won't. Strictly speaking, you aren't Dr Smith until you've formally graduated, so don't read anything too much into it if they don't use those words; externals are the sort of people who will probably know about the distinction between 'doctor' and 'doctorandus' and who may phrase their greeting accordingly. The rest of the session will quite probably be a bit hazy. If you and/or your friends have been efficient, there may be champagne ready. The examiners may or may not participate in the festivities; the day will end and in the fullness of time the first day of the rest of your life will dawn.

So, that's what happens from the examiners' point of view. What happens from your point of view? This section is briefer, partly because much of it is covered above and partly because it's also covered in depth in all the other books on this topic.

Before the viva

Early in your PhD, discuss with your supervisor whether or not to go for a journal publication or two. Supervisors, and disciplines, vary in this regard. When you write-up, allow plenty of time to do a decent job, and pay particular attention to displaying your cabinet-making skills in the thesis. Choose an appropriate external in a sensible way: by this stage in your career, you should have a reasonable idea of the relevant rules of the game and of the main relevant players.

The week before

In the days before the viva, reread your thesis and your data, plus some of the key literature. You'll probably be utterly sick of all of them long before this stage, so reward yourself with chocolate, or whatever currency works for you. Organize a mock viva, including a presentation at the start, with at least one mock examiner who knows the craft skills of doing a good viva and presentation. If they're good, they won't be gentle with you in the mock viva, and they will give you constructive feedback about what to change for the real event. A lot of this is likely to involve blood in the water – you'll probably panic gently in the mock session and blurt out needless admissions of weakness such as: 'I know now that I should have used a larger sample size' rather than something like 'My next study will extend this and will use a larger sample'.

The day before

The day before the viva, check that you are sure where and when the session will take place (there may have been a last-minute change which you missed). Line up a trusted friend to be available for you during the viva day. They will probably organize a tactful bottle of champagne and glasses in a way which doesn't look too much as if it is tempting fate, and whisk you away if it all gets too much – even a pass with minor changes can leave some candidates feeling like a thoroughly wrung dishcloth. Do not go out for some serious drinking the night before: you'll need to be fresh on the day. Check that you know the examiners' names, titles and main publications. This is not to help you grovel; it is to show professional courtesy and to improve your chances of anticipating the direction of their questions. Make sure that you have appropriate clean clothing for the next day and a hard copy of your thesis. Ask your supervisor politely if they will make sure they have a copy of any required changes, in case you forget in the excitement of the moment. (They will probably be planning to do this anyway, but it doesn't hurt to make doubly sure.)

On the day

On the day, turn up in plenty of time, and have something to do while you wait. Don't be offended if you aren't introduced to the examiners, invited to join them for lunch or if you are kept waiting before the session begins. All of these are perfectly routine features of the viva process and reflect neither discourtesy nor inefficiency. You might, for instance, be kept waiting because some idiot has been illicitly using the viva room for an unofficial seminar, and has had to be evicted, leaving the examiners with the thrilling job of rearranging all the furniture.

At the start of the viva, be polite and do your exercises for staying calm if you need to. If you aren't asked to do a presentation or an overview, don't fret: the mock session won't have been wasted, because it will have helped you to pull together your thoughts about the thesis in a way which will come in very useful during the viva.

The first question or two will probably be fairly light, and used for breaking the ice. With these and the subsequent questions, you need to remember the three golden rules (don't lie, don't try to be funny and don't panic and blurt out the truth) plus a couple of other things.

One thing is that the viva is quite a lot like fencing practice. The session is used to assess your fencing skills, so you are expected to defend yourself in a way which shows your skill in fencing. You are neither expected to let your opponent hit you every time, nor to attempt to kick your opponent in the groin and then pummel them to death. What matters is how you answer the questions, rather than whether you happen to know a correct answer. At this level, there often aren't any unambiguously correct answers.

Another thing to remember is that you don't need to reply instantly. You can buy yourself some thinking time by using tactics such as raising an eyebrow, saying 'Hmmm' in a thoughtful way, or saying 'That's an interesting question; I'll need to think about that for a moment'. There's also nothing wrong with asking the examiner to clarify something in the question (as long as you don't ask something silly, like the meaning of a term which is a central part of your discipline). When you've given your answer, there's nothing wrong with checking whether it's answering the question which they intended.

After the viva

After the viva, make sure that you don't vanish off the face of the earth; it's a good idea to borrow a friend's office to retire to, but a bad idea not to let anyone know that you're in there, so that the examiners have to scour the corridors looking for you. If you've failed, take the news calmly, be polite and read our section on what to do if things go wrong after giving a presentation (see p. 142) (in brief, go away and feel sorry for yourself for the rest of the day, then do some sensible advice-gathering and planning the next day – a fail is not the end of the world). Statistically speaking, though, you will probably be passed subject to some changes to the thesis. There is no point in arguing about the changes at this stage – argument would only show that you don't understand the way things work on a PhD. Instead, be grateful that you've passed subject to changes, thank the examiners and your supervisor politely and go off to celebrate. Don't worry about remembering all the changes; you should have arranged with your supervisor beforehand that they will make sure there is a clear written list which you can collect from them the next day. If you've passed without changes, then be sure to thank your supervisor – they will have earned it. You can now go out and have that large drink, or whatever form of celebration takes your fancy.

Handling revisions

The day after the viva, possibly nursing a hangover, you need to present yourself at your supervisor's door and work out precisely what needs to be done and by when. A surprising proportion of candidates give up at this stage. Doing corrections is not much fun, but it's a lot better than failing. Work out a clear timetable, with some contingency time, and get cracking on the corrections. If you want to have a break first, that's up to you, but don't put the corrections off; do them at the earliest possible opportunity and make sure your supervisor okays them. Write a covering letter detailing where you have made which changes and how – that makes it a lot easier for the examiners to check that you have done everything required. In most institutions, minor changes will only need to go back to the main examiner, but major changes will need to be approved by the whole examination team, and a covering letter makes life easier for everyone involved in such situations.

During or after the viva, you need to get the examiners to be very specific about the changes they want. Which chapter, which section of the chapter, which paragraph in the section need to be changed? Can they give you an example of the change they mean? How is this different from what was addressed in section X of the dissertation? You need to show judgement and discretion – if they say something like 'This whole chapter is unclear' then there's a limit to how much precision anyone can give.

You also need to check that you know the date by which the corrections are due. Do not aim to have everything ready five minutes before the deadline; you will need to liaise with your supervisor about the revisions and give your supervisor a reasonable amount of time to check the revisions before you hand them in. This is particularly important if you're near the end of your time as a registered PhD student. The last thing you want to do is to miss the deadline for the revisions because (a) your printer broke down at the last minute or (b) because your supervisor spotted a fatal flaw requiring days of work on your revisions when you finally handed them over for inspection the day before the deadline.

Doing the revisions can produce surprising feelings of revulsion for some students – it's a bit like washing up greasy plates in cold water the morning after a wild party when you have a massive hangover, or so we are reliably informed by friends who attend wild parties. It's worth knowing about this so that if you find yourself engaged in displacement activities rather than doing the corrections, then you can spot this and do something about it. The standard motivation techniques, plus strong support from friends, are helpful here.

Once the changes have been approved, you can plan for graduation. Most institutions allow you to have two guests at the ceremony, which normally means that the candidate's partner and one parent attend while the other parent remains in outer darkness – a source of potential annoyance, and one which it's wise to address as early as possible. Many candidates end up wishing they had better photos of themselves in the formal gowns; it's worth thinking about hiring the gown for a week instead of just a day, and then arranging some decent photos somewhere scenic (especially if you graduate in winter and it's chucking down rain outside on the day of the ceremony).

After all of this, you will probably never want to see your thesis again, and will be seriously tempted to burn it to ashes. Don't do that: the thesis is like a mask: where you see only the inside with all its imperfections, the rest of the world sees the glittering, burnished exterior. Yes, that's a somewhat over the top metaphor, but you've earned a bit of praise by the time you reach this stage.

The viva: hints, lists and things to remember

Despite the reputation of the viva, the truth is that, by the time you get there, you've already done the hard part. Remember: a viva is pass–fail. Most examiners are looking for a reason to pass the candidate. Your job is to make it easy for them. Perfection is not required. Competence is.

What you're doing in a viva

- Showing respect for the academic system and discipline
- Showing general mastery of the domain and its intellectual tools
- Demonstrating intellectual independence
- Joining the academic discourse
- Undergoing a rite of passage

How to fail a viva

- Assume that the viva doesn't matter
- Answer any question about what you did with, 'My supervisor made me do it'
- Stick to one-word answers
- Display intransigence
- Display rampant cynicism
- Display flippancy
- Display a lack of interest
- Persist in an inability to describe your own work
- Persist in an inability to define fundamental terms
- Persist in an inability to talk about the papers you cite
- Call the examiner rude names

These are tried and true methods; we've seen students fail using them.

Also, don't waste time second-guessing the examiners. A professor in our acquaintance tells the story of a brilliant student who, having seen him write 'fail' in his notes, decided that he had made a decision and 'died' through the latter half of her viva. He couldn't understand the dramatic change in her previously flawless performance and asked about it afterwards. When she explained, he was horrified; he'd actually just been making a note to follow up on an interesting idea in one of her answers.

How to impress your examiners

- Come prepared
- Listen; comprehend the questions and address them directly
- Make eye-contact
- Show enthusiasm for your work
- See your work in the bigger picture
- Be able to refer directly to your text (highlight key passages) in answering questions
- Be able to refer directly to seminal texts by author and with accuracy
- Be able to articulate the nature and scale of your contribution
- Think forward – think beyond the research to further work and implications
- Be reflective – be able to articulate both what was good about your work and what could be improved and how

These are tried and true methods as well. Students who show command of their material – both their own research and the prior work that frames and contributes to it – and who engage in the examination dialogue with knowledge, interest and courtesy are able to impress their examiners, even though they may also make some errors or sometimes answer falteringly. Examiners like lively and interesting examinations.

Preparing

Obviously, the best preparation for a viva is an excellent dissertation.

- Mark up your dissertation. Put tabs (Post-it notes or similar) on the pages you're most likely to want to refer to.
- Decide if there's any supporting documentation (e.g. key papers, design notes, data examples) not included in your dissertation that you want to have along. You'll almost certainly never refer to any of it, but it might make you feel safer.
- Go through the 'generic viva questions' and think up answers.
- Make a list of the questions that frighten you most and compose answers to them.

- Get experienced people to do a mock viva and to debrief you afterwards about what they liked and what they thought could be improved. (Understand that mock vivas are often much tougher than real vivas; mock examiners often play extreme roles so that you'll know you can withstand the worst.)
- Skim through your five key references. If you don't already have adequate notes in your annotated bibliography, then make notes on the key papers: what they did, why they are important, how your work relates to them, implications they have for your work. Be able to refer to the papers by the names of their authors.
- Skim through a couple of papers by your examiners, noting their topic area, approach and style.
- Prepare a publication plan for the material in your dissertation (which material, parcelled how, for which venue).
- Having done your preparation in good time, do something utterly relaxing and diverting the day before: sports, a walk along the coast, your favourite classic film, a full-body massage, whatever. This does not include drinking binges, extreme sports or anything else which might leave you feeling bad the next day.
- Get a good night's sleep.

Fending off panic

- **Pause:** you're allowed time to think.
- **Breathe deeply:** three deep, 'centering' breaths, making sure that you exhale slowly, usually help.
- **Take a drink:** there's usually water on the table.
- **Make quick notes** to yourself, especially if you have more than one point to make.

If you don't understand the question or don't know the answer:

- Ask the examiner to repeat the question (chances are, they'll simplify it as they do so). This is best when you simply didn't take the question in.
- Rephrase the question back to the examiner: 'I think you're asking me about X' – and then answer it.
- Offer alternative interpretations: 'I'm not sure if you mean X or Y. Could you clarify?'
- It's much better to offer an interpretation of the question than to say 'I don't understand', but once or twice you can do that too.

Keep it simple, stupid. When you hear yourself saying the same thing for the third time, just *stop and smile*, or say, 'Sorry, I'm repeating myself'. We all get nervous. Once (certainly never more than once) in a viva, if you really can't help yourself, you're allowed to relax the stiff upper lip entirely and say

something like, 'I'm sorry, I'm feeling very nervous, I just need a moment . . .'
The examiners are likely to back off a bit and ask you a warm-up question
before carrying on in earnest.

Questions examiners ask

- **Warm-up questions** to calm you down. Often of the form, 'So how did you
  come to research this subject?' Or, 'Can you summarize your core thesis for
  us?'
- **Confirmatory questions** to let you demonstrate your knowledge. Often
  of the form of asking you to reiterate or define something in your
  dissertation.
- **Deep confirmatory questions** to let you demonstrate that your knowledge
  is more than skin deep. These are usually follow-ups to confirmatory
  questions that take up some point in your answer. Just keep your head and
  continue to address the questions.
- **Calibration questions** to help the examiner check their own understanding of your work.
- **Scholarship questions** to let you demonstrate that you know the field as
  well as your own research.
- **Salvaging questions**, when you've written something badly, to let you
  show you do know what you're talking about after all.
- **Pushing the envelope questions** to see how far your knowledge goes.
- **'This is neat' questions** to give the examiner a chance to discuss your
  interesting ideas.
- **Redemptive, 'lesson learned' questions** to give you a chance to admit
  some awful blunder in your work so that the examiner can 'let you off'
  without worrying that you'll make it again. A typical example is, 'Would you
  take this approach again if you were pursuing this issue?' when a student
  has applied an inappropriate method that yielded little.
- **'This is a good student; how good?' questions** – a little 'sparring' to let you
  really show your stuff.
- **'Give me a reason to pass you' questions** – often, if the examiners
  continue asking about the same topic, it's because they're interested; if so,
  then cooperate actively with them, rather than trying to change the topic.

These are all moderately benign questions. If you arouse the examiners'
anger or a suspicion that there is something wrong with your work, however,
you may be asked some hard, sharp questions. The next section lists some
classic 'killer' questions and suggests some ways of responding effectively
to them.

Killer questions and how to survive them

In this section, Q = question, A = suggested answer, C = our comments on the question and/or answer.

Q: How does your work relate to Jim Bloggs' recent paper? (when you've never heard of Bloggs)
A: 'I'm not familiar with that paper. Does he take an X approach or a Y approach?'
C: Show something you do know that's relevant; then, when the examiner offers a précis: 'Ah, so it's like so-and-so's work?'

Q: Isn't this obvious?
A: Well, it may appear that way with hindsight, but there was surprisingly little work on this topic in the literature, and the question needed to be properly answered.
C: Many dissertations codify what people think they already know but which has never been properly established. 'Obvious' can be good; it can make a contribution. Marian's *external* examiner asked her this and, fortunately, her internal examiner answered him that it was only obvious because he'd read her dissertation. You might try a modestly phrased version of this answer yourself if nobody offers it for you.

Q: Isn't this just like Brown's work?
A: It differs from Brown's work because . . .
C: Everyone worries that someone else is going to 'gazump' them and publish exactly their work just before they do. Forget it. There will be something – a difference of approach, of technique, of sample – that distinguishes your work and protects your contribution. If you know Brown's work already, then you should have already identified how it differs from yours; if you don't, ask about Brown's work until the answers reveal a difference.

Q: You use the term X in two different ways in Chapters 4 and 6. What do you mean?
A: In Chapter 4, I was using Smith's definition, which was most appropriate for that part of the thesis. In Chapter 6, I was using Brown's . . .
C: Answer the question, giving a concise clarification. Make a note of what you say because you'll probably be asked to amend the text with the clarification when you do your corrections.

Q: Why didn't you . . .?
A: Because . . .
C: This is why you reread your thesis and have a mock viva. Rereading your thesis will remind you of why you did things the way you did (and, conversely, tell you why you didn't use the other options). This will also give a sanity check that you haven't missed anything obvious. If the suggestion is

something little known in your field, then you can reply along the lines of, 'That's interesting, and it sounds as if it should be more widely known in this field'. You can then turn this into a discussion of methods in the field and an opportunity to talk about the things you *do* know about.

Some ways of addressing weakness

Sometimes, you just have to admit that you were wrong. Occasionally, just making the admission with humour is effective. (As with the student who, when asked if she would use the same (fruitless) survey technique again, said with feeling: 'Hell, no'.)

More often, it's safer to follow the three-point plan:

1 Reiterate why whatever you did was a justified choice at the outset.
2 Explain, as simply as possible and without apology, that you understand why it failed.
3 Make some alternative suggestions about what you'd do instead next time that would improve your chances of getting it right.

No one expects doctoral research to flow smoothly without errors or hitches. Indeed, it is rare for any research to do so – research is opportunistic and (happily) full of surprises. What examiners expect is that students will respond to the errors and hitches with intelligence and by learning from them.

Generic viva questions

We haven't suggested answers to these, for obvious reasons. You may find it reassuring and useful to have a friend ask you these, and then see if you can answer them. The friend doesn't need to understand your answer; if you can answer swiftly, confidently and concisely, then you'll probably be okay. If you can't, then some time thinking about possible answers should prove very useful.

- How did you come to research this topic in this manner?
- What are the main achievements of your research?
- What has your thesis contributed to our knowledge in this field?
- What are the major theoretical strands in this area: what are the crucial ideas and who are the main contributors?
- What are the main issues (matters of debate or dispute) in this area?
- Where is your thesis 'placed' in terms of the existing theory and debate? How would the major researchers react to your ideas?
- Whom do you think will be most interested in this work?
- What published research is closest to your work? How is your work different?

- Why did you choose the particular research methodology that you used?
- What were the crucial research decisions that you made?
- If you were doing this research again, would you consider using any other research methodology?
- What do you see as the next steps in this research?
- What was the most interesting finding in your results?
- Isn't this all obvious?
- Were you surprised by any of your results (if so, why, and what was surprising)?
- What advice would you give a new student entering this area?
- What is your plan for publication?
- What haven't I asked you that I should have done, and what would your answer have been?

15   Conferences

When I drew nigh the nameless city, I knew it was accursed.

Researchers have three main ways of keeping in touch with what is going on in their area of research. A swift and efficient way is the grapevine – if Smith and Jones have solved the most important question in their field, then most of the major players in that field will know about it via phone calls and emails within a few hours of the news going public (and probably much sooner, given the way that gossip works). This is fine if you are a major player with good connections to the grapevine, but not so fine if you are a struggling PhD student who still has an uneasy suspicion that the major texts in your field are produced by superhuman figures who live somewhere on the middle slopes of Mount Olympus.

A more feasible way of keeping up to date for most PhD students is reading the journals, which are, depending on your favoured metaphor, the gold standard, the touchstone, or some such indicator of quality. Unfortunately, the lead time for journal papers is about two years, so the journal freshly appearing on your library shelves will contain accounts of work done about three years ago. This is not an ideal situation. However, help is at hand in the form of conferences. Every year, most research fields witness a batch of annual conferences at which researchers from around the world meet to present their work and to listen to other people's presentations of their work. They also, more importantly, socialize and build their social networks, usually over a drink in the bar. A conference therefore gives you the chance to find out about research which is no more than a year old, and is probably considerably more recent, as well as a chance to meet colleagues from around the world.

So much for the basic context – how does this translate into specific things that you need to know? We will start with the process, from the viewpoint of the absolute novice, then move on to the process from the viewpoint of the long-suffering organizers, and conclude with some advice about how this knowledge of the processes can be used to help you make the most of conferences.

The conference process: a novice's perspective

There are two capacities in which you can attend a conference. One is as someone presenting work; the other is as someone who is not presenting work. For simplicity, we will proceed with the assumption that you are presenting work, since this includes what you need to know about being in the audience.

There are several main routes into presenting at a conference. One is that you want to publish something and have a vague idea that a conference might be a good place to aim for; this usually leads to some unsystematic searches on the internet and the high-tech equivalent of sticking a pin into the list. Another, more sophisticated, route starts with a desire to see Hawaii or some other exotic place at someone else's expense; this produces some more focused research into possible venues. The most sophisticated route starts with a desire to get a paper into a particular conference because that is the main conference for this field; by a fascinating coincidence, the main conferences are surprisingly often held in places like Hawaii, and are in consequence able to be very selective about which papers they accept.

Whatever the route, it will end up at the same place, namely the call for papers for that conference. The call for papers will specify which types of paper will be accepted, will state the guidelines for each type of paper and will also give the deadlines for each. The main types usually include some or all of the following:

- full papers (what they sound like: full-sized papers);
- short papers (also what they sound like: short papers);
- abstracts for papers, which may be full or short;
- posters (where you stand in the lobby at coffee and lunch breaks next to posters which you have previously prepared, describing your work).

The main thing to remember about abstracts is that if your abstract is accepted you will need to write the paper at some point. It is horribly easy to forget this and to realize with a chill dread that you will have to write the paper during the fortnight when you have to mark several hundred exam scripts. The other main risk about being accepted is that you will have to live up to the wild claims that you made in the abstract, in the hope of being accepted. The main thing to bear in mind about posters is that most of the people at the conference will walk right past you and your poster; this is nothing personal, but it can feel pretty grim. The other main thing to bear in mind about posters is that most of the people who do ask questions will leave you with a faintly uneasy feeling, either because they've asked questions to demonstrate their own greater knowledge of the field, or because they are strange individuals. Again, this is nothing personal.

So, having written your paper or whatever, you stick it in the post, think about it for a few days and then get submerged in routine tasks. At some point you will receive a verdict on your submission and decisions need to be made. If the verdict is unfavourable, then the decisions involve what to do with the paper (perhaps submit it somewhere else, or throw it away) and whether to go to the conference anyway purely as a spectator, if you have the money. If the verdict is favourable, then you need to do assorted logistical things. If you are a complete novice, or have a taste for the grey side of ethics, then you will face some interesting decisions about how to persuade The System to pay for your travel, conference fees and accommodation for a week in the Hawaii Hilton. If you have not previously checked with The System whether this is OK, then you will be asked to explain just why The System should fork out a couple of thousand pounds for you to have a nice holiday, when the state of the departmental budget means that better researchers than you are only being funded to go to a two-day workshop in Skegness. A wise supervisor will have made sure that the funding for your PhD includes allowance for a conference per year; a realistic supervisor will be aware that this allowance will usually not stretch to a major conference in somewhere exotic.

Assuming that the funding has been approved, you still need to arrange travel, accommodation and the like, which can be pretty stressful if the conference is in (say) Spain, and your Spanish is minimal. If you have acquired a reputation as a pleasant and reasonable person, you may discover at this point that one of the secretaries or research assistants speaks fluent Spanish and is willing to help. If you have acquired a less inspiring reputation, then the likelihood of making such discoveries is significantly less.

We will draw a genteel veil over that stage, plus the stage of finding your hotel and booking in, probably at two a.m. local time, and will proceed to the point where you step off the bus at the conference venue, stressed out from the journey, trying to carry a briefcase and a coat simultaneously while opening doors with your third hand. What happens next? You follow the signs for your conference; if your conference has more than one set of signs, then you follow the ones marked 'registration'. At the place of registration, you will usually be issued with a badge, a programme of events and a pack of information; from this point on, you can follow the crowd, and not have to make any decisions for the immediate future. There is a non-trivial possibility that the registration people will claim never to have heard of you, especially if you have left booking till the last moment, which is a good reason for (a) not leaving everything till the last moment and (b) going with someone who is familiar with conferences.

Problems of this sort usually get resolved somehow, but they're something you can do without.

When you find a suitable quiet corner, you can decide which sessions to go to, and so forth. Many conferences use two or more lecture halls so that two or more talks can be in progress simultaneously ('parallel streams'), in which case you'll need to decide which stream to attend. You don't have to go to every talk every day unless you really want to.

We now move for a little while to the organizers' viewpoint, which should help you to understand the niceties of conference procedure more clearly.

The organizers' viewpoint

Why do people organize conferences? There are three main reasons, namely fortune, glory and (in quite a few praiseworthy instances) the good of the discipline. A good conference can bring in a substantial profit to the institution involved, and can bring fame and power (within research circles at least) to the academics organizing it. A well-planned conference can also be an excellent way of revitalizing an area of research which has gone stale, or of starting a new area of research.

So, if you want to start a new area of research, or revitalize an existing one, you might organize a conference. One of the first problems to tackle involves how to attract enough people to make the conference viable. A standard solution is to invite some key speakers, whose talks will be a significant attraction. This is particularly effective if one or more of the keynote speakers gives a talk which either summarizes the current state of the field, or (preferably) suggests some really interesting new ideas. A nice venue is another attraction worth trying. The third classic attraction is to publish the conference proceedings; an added enticement is to strike a deal with a journal editor to publish the best papers in a special issue of the journal. The reason that this is a significant inducement involves the way that departments fund conference-going. If several researchers ask for the same amount of money to go to a conference and there is not enough money for all of them, then the pecking order is as follows: published proceedings plus special issue, as first choice; published proceedings only, as second choice; no proceedings as third choice.

We will draw a tactful veil over most of the logistical processes and concentrate on the ones involving papers and posters. If you are organizing a conference with published proceedings, then you will need to liaise with printers, and this can rapidly lead to all sorts of interesting and potentially stressful constraints about word lengths, deadlines and the like. Printers usually work on a basis of having slots set aside for each client, rather than of doing each client sequentially, so if you miss your agreed slot because your copy isn't ready you need to book another one. It might not surprise you to know that this will cost you more money. You are therefore likely to be twitchy about whether your speakers will provide copy on time and in the correct format, including correct word lengths. For many conferences, the proceedings are printed before the conference, so that delegates have the proceedings with them when they listen to talks. This is a very visible deadline, so as an organizer you might be less than sympathetic to authors whose copy is not submitted on time, or is submitted electronically in a format which nobody outside Nebraska can read.

Even if all the copy arrives on time and in the right format, the presentations themselves leave considerable scope for interesting things going wrong in strange ways. Talks are normally grouped into batches – the early morning batch between the start of day and the morning coffee; the coffee till lunch batch; the lunch till afternoon tea batch; and the afternoon tea till end of day batch. Each batch will usually be coordinated by one of the organizers, and may be introduced with an overview talk as well as, or instead of, a keynote talk from an invited speaker. Each batch will usually overrun, partly because of starting late because delegates trickled in at the last possible moment, partly because of equipment malfunctioning and mainly because of speakers overrunning by two or three minutes – not a big deal individually, but multiply that by the number of speakers and you soon start running seriously late. Each batch will also usually include at least one speaker who is inaudible, incomprehensible, boring or has unreadable slides.

The implications of this for you as a presenter are pretty obvious, but it's surprising how few presenters treat them as seriously as they should. The main implications are:

- submit your copy in plenty of time;
- follow instructions for authors;
- practise your talk so that you can keep well within your time slot;
- be considerate and try to see things from the organizers' viewpoint;
- if you encounter problems, let the organizers know as soon as possible, so that something can be arranged.

Miscellaneous good advice

Your very first conference is a glittering opportunity to make a complete idiot of yourself in front of the main players from your research community before you have even finished your PhD. There is, unfortunately, an asymmetry: there is not much scope for making yourself look amazingly wonderful to the same audience, for the simple reason that at this stage in your career you will probably not have anything remarkably novel and interesting to say. (Interesting, yes; novel, yes; both interesting and novel is a possible combination; *remarkably* interesting and novel is much rarer.) Some classic ways of making an idiot of yourself include the following:

- getting drunk in public;
- being sick in public as a result of a hangover from getting drunk in private;
- having wild sex with someone in the fond belief that (a) nobody else will know or (b) that it won't matter – in reality, everyone will know by coffee break the next morning, and your bedmate will probably turn out to be a dreadful mistake;
- asking the same inane question that gets asked every year by a new PhD student who thinks they're being original.

Your first conference is a good opportunity to practise your listening skills, even if you're sure that you have a brilliant solution to the problem that's bugging everyone. If you're right, then you'll still be right tomorrow, and learning to be patient is an invaluable research skill. (So is getting your idea into print, rather than blurting it out in a conference and then seeing it appear under someone else's name a few months later . . .)

Your first conference is a good chance to meet people and strike up friendships which might well last for the rest of your professional life. The best way to do this is over moderately sober conversations in the bar, with people who are willing to talk to you (the keynote speakers and other major players may be willing to talk to you, but are understandably wary of being buttonholed by every loon at the conference, especially if the major player in question has come to the conference for a long-awaited chat with a close friend from several thousand miles away whom they haven't seen since 1992).

If your first conference is also the first conference at which you are presenting a paper, then you might be excused for feeling a bit stressed. One good way of reducing the stress is to get some experience at public speaking before you go – for instance, departmental seminars, which should be treated as a useful opportunity rather than as an unwelcome obligation to be avoided till the last moment. You can also try running unofficial postgraduate seminars at which you present your work to each other in a constructive, supportive atmosphere (persuading a wise and supportive member of staff to come along and give constructive criticism can be very helpful). Another strategy is to co-author with your supervisor and persuade your supervisor to give the talk, with a promise that you will do the talking next time. You can then learn from your supervisor's experience. If you are talking, then it's a good idea to read the chapters elsewhere in this book on writing and presentations. Remember the three golden rules: don't lie, don't try to be funny and, above all, don't panic and blurt out the truth. At this point in your career it's wisest to go for an unpretentious, solid talk which reports what you did in a level tone, neither claiming too much nor too little. Your mission is not to entertain or dazzle the audience – that's the job of the guest speakers. Your mission in your first conference is reconnaissance, so that you'll know what you're doing at your second conference.

Getting the most out of a conference – a checklist

Strategies for covering conferences of different sizes

- Small: aim for comprehensive coverage (i.e. talk to everyone there)
- Medium: aim to talk to as many people as possible, but target those doing related work
- Large: make advance arrangements to ensure contact with key people, and focused targeting during the event

Take your business cards and write some specific information on the back that will help your contact recall your conversation.

Making contacts at the conference

- Use activities (workshops, working groups, tutorials, 'birds of a feather' sessions, first-timers' events)
- Present a paper (which introduces you to everyone in your audience)
- Ask a good question (others who find your question interesting may introduce themselves to you, and the author will be more likely to remember you)
- Attend demonstrations
- If you hear a conversation that's really interesting, then stand visibly on the periphery until you get a chance to make a contribution (a short question or a joke is good) or ask if you may join the group
- Get your supervisor or an existing contact to suggest people and make introductions
- Make early contact with a key person (e.g. someone on the committee, someone well established in the area) and be around when they make contact with others; ask them to make introductions
- Talk to the person sitting next to you in a session – ask a question about the last presentation
- Make it a habit to have lunch with different people every day
- Make connections for other people – refer to other conversations and work and be ready to make appropriate introductions
- When you're in a conversation, avoid 'sounding off' or entertaining people with your opinions – it's much more effective to phrase ideas as questions rather than statements

Have your 'cocktail party introductions' (i.e. brief description of who you are and what you're researching) worked out and ready to mind.

Following up

- Conference contacts tend to have a high attrition rate – but making contacts is still worth it if you make one good, lasting connection
- Always keep the promises you make: do send that paper, or email that information
- Follow up great conversations with a thank-you email
- Suggest visits or specific further interaction to good contacts
- Invite good contacts to your institution – perhaps to give a talk
- If you didn't get a chance to speak to an author during the conference, do it via email afterwards

Doing your homework

When you get your conference pack:

- Have look at the attendees list. Who's on the list that you'd especially like to meet? Are they giving a paper?
- Have a look at the sessions and at the paper titles and plan your attendance. Which sessions are not to be missed? When are there openings for conversations? Who is the first contact you want to target?
- It's usually a good idea to attend the plenary sessions.

  Each night-before:

- skim or read the papers for the sessions you plan to attend;
- have a look at the papers for the other sessions (you may meet their authors at coffee);
- check your plan for the next day.

  Take your proceedings to the sessions and:

- refer to papers for clarification;
- annotate the papers: for instance, if the authors add information during the presentation (there are often extra website addresses that are handy to file with the papers), or if there is something specifically resonant with your own work;
- figure out questions to ask;
- have something to do (i.e. read other papers) if the session turns out to be a dud.

The message

What you get out is related to what you put in – if you 'work' the conference, working at staying engaged, at seeking conversations and at keeping track of information, then you're more likely to make good connections. Remember, much of the 'real' value of a conference isn't derived from the sessions – it comes from conversations in the bar. If you don't drink alcohol, then remember that bars also serve non-alcoholic drinks . . .

16   What next?

This terror is not due altogether to the sinister nature of his recent disappearance, but was engendered by the whole nature of his life-work . . .

So there you are, through your viva, corrections finished to everyone's satisfaction and waiting for graduation day, without the thesis filling your life. At this point many students realize with growing unease that they haven't given much thought to the topic of what to do next with their lives. This chapter discusses some issues relating to that topic.

One issue is career structure within the academic world. We discuss this so that you can observe the lifestyle of people who have followed various career routes and then think about which of these routes, if any, might suit you. This should help you decide which jobs to apply for (though in practice your options will probably be a research assistantship or a lectureship – we include the big picture because it comes in useful for all sorts of other purposes).

Once you know which job to apply for, you need to know how to handle job interviews – what to do before interviews and during them. Most people take the perfectly understandable view that this involves thinking about what they have to offer; we describe a better strategy, and give various other hints and tips. We've phrased this in terms of applying for a lectureship, to help your morale, and because if you can handle that then you should be able to handle interviews for other jobs, with appropriate changes to our advice.

After that, we discuss ways of approaching niggling existential worries such as what you really want to do with your life, or how to break out of your feelings of misery and uselessness. At low points in your PhD, these things will be significant issues to you. We don't claim to have all the answers, but we make a few suggestions. We also give some suggestions about CVs.

Career goals

In order to make sense of academic careers, you need to understand what motivates successful researchers. According to Indiana Jones, the answer is, 'Fortune and glory'. That, however, is fiction. The reality is more subtle. Successful researchers are driven by a need for two or more of three things: status, power and satisfaction of their curiosity.

Satisfaction of curiosity

Satisfaction of curiosity is an important theme in research – you can be paid (not well, but paid) to be nosy. If you are shrewd, you can use this to get funding for things such as travel to exotic places to study the behaviour of holidaymakers on sunny beaches. Wise geologists are aware that some types of lava are only found in a few places, such as Hawaii. Researchers crop up in all sorts of unlikely-sounding places – for instance, digging holes through bits of frozen wasteland in the Arctic, sitting in the control tower of an airfield watching the air traffic controllers and on patrol with the local police, to mention just a few examples of things our colleagues have done. However, nobody will pay you for long if you just satisfy your curiosity and do nothing more; you also have to let the world know what you have found, which leads on to the other two goals.

Status

Status in the academic world is not quite like status outside it. The status that really matters to a researcher is status in the research community. Research investigates areas – for instance, glacial geomorphology, prion structure, criminal behaviour among teenagers. Within each research area there are well-established conferences, journals, newsletters etc. and there is also a body of researchers who are working in that area. These researchers form the research community for that area. They will usually read the same journals as each other, attend the same conferences etc. Within each research community there is a fairly clear pecking order, from beginners that no one has heard of, through moderately well-known researchers to the major authorities whose names and work are known and revered by everyone in the area. (The other researchers may not always agree with them, but they know them and acknowledge their status.)

Status in the research community does not derive from the prestige of your institution, or the impressiveness of your title (though these can help a bit). What matters is the quality of your work. If you are doing boring, routine work which produces no surprises, then the research community will be utterly unimpressed by your being Professor of Computer Science, Mathematics and Hard Concepts and will simply think that you don't deserve that post. If you are doing work which produces interesting findings and opens up new research directions for your colleagues, then you will be taken seriously, even if you are a research assistant at Fenlands College. Some academics actually make a deliberate choice to work in little-known places, on the grounds that a high-profile successful academic in such a place is more likely to be allowed to get on with their work in peace without being messed around by The System. Status of this sort is spread in various ways, but mainly through word of mouth and social networks. It is recognized at a formal level in various ways within the research community: for instance, being invited to give keynote talks at conferences, journal editorships and positions on funding bodies.

Unfortunately, there can be quite massive mismatches between someone's status in their research community and their status in their home organiza- tion. As a broad generalization, this is more of a problem in new universities, where the administrative system is not used to dealing with research, and equates status directly with position in the organization's official hierarchy. In such a situation, a professor with no standing in the research community will be treated as quite important, whereas a lecturer with a huge international reputation in the research community will be treated as a nonentity. This can feel quite surreal to the individual involved – being treated with deference at an international event one day, and being harangued by minor administrators at work the next day – and can also become extremely annoying. For this reason, most researchers sooner or later start a dalliance with the concept of power.

Power

Power is extremely useful. For most researchers, the initially attractive aspect of power is the power to refuse to do things which are an annoying distraction (e.g. paperwork or teaching a topic about which the researcher has little knowledge and even less enthusiasm). Contrary to what Theory X managers believe, most researchers, if left to their own devices, would happily research for as many hours a day as they could manage. Having power allows researchers more time to get on with what they really enjoy, which is a seductive prospect.

Where does power come from? In the researcher's home institution, power does not come from status in the research community: it comes from the ability to influence things in a way which matters to the host institution. This may come from official roles – for instance, if you are on the funding panel for a major grant-giving body, then some parts of your institution will be unlikely to want to antagonize you too much. Other parts of your institution, however, couldn't care less – for instance, the parts which are concerned only with teaching, and to whom research funding bodies are of no interest whatever. For these and other reasons, therefore, a more potent source of power is money. If you bring large amounts of money into the institution, then you will be viewed as a valuable asset. The more money you bring in, the more valuable you will be, and the better your chances of being treated well. Money in the accounts today is visibly useful to an organization in a way which the prospect of money tomorrow from a funding body is not. If that cash flow is being threatened because you are annoyed with the way that someone in administration is treating you, and you are thinking of moving somewhere where you will be better treated, then that person in administration is likely to receive a word from someone in the hierarchy, and the problem is likely to go away.

So far, all well and good. However, what happens when you are bringing in lots of money and become locked in conflict with someone else in the institution who is bringing in even more money? The answer is that you will probably lose. On a more virtuous level, what happens if you realize that your work can make the world a better place, but there aren't enough hours in the day for you to do all the things that are needed? The answer to both these questions is 'more power'. The prospect of having a few research assistants and perhaps a small research centre, possibly with just one or two colleagues, starts to become appealing, and you begin to flirt with the concept that having an empire is not an inherently Bad Thing. You realize that having an imposing title, a large office and numerous underlings allows you to deal with petty bureaucrats in the institution more effectively, and to get on with the important things in life, such as research. You become aware that you have reached a new phase of your career, for which you will need new skills and values. You begin to understand how much von Clausewitz was misunderstood, and start to read his classic text *On War* (in the original, in case you missed anything in the translated version). You wonder what was so wrong anyway about displaying the severed heads of your enemies on stakes in a prominent place . . .

Career types

In heroic times, the hero was traditionally offered a choice by Fate when at an impressionable age. The choice was between a short, brilliant life and a long, unremarkable one. The legends which survived were invariably the ones where the hero chose the short, brilliant life. This may be because heroes were all predictable when it came to that choice, or perhaps it's simply that legends about people leading long, unremarkable lives did not have a great deal of staying power.

Anyway, the relevance of this to the would-be researcher is that there is a similar choice in academia. At a certain point in your career, you have to make a decision. It's not quite the same as for heroes, but it's similar. After being a lecturer long enough to notch up the appropriate points on your CV, you can either take the route of becoming primarily a researcher or primarily an administrator and teacher. The former is usually the glamorous route; the latter is normally the route followed by invaluable people who hold institutions together, and who are usually overworked, badly treated and unappreciated until their stress rating reaches the point where they take early retirement. This is not particularly fair, and we do not greatly approve of it. One crumb of consolation for those who take the worthy, unglamorous road is that they might some day become a head of department, perhaps a dean, maybe even a vice-chancellor, and have the prospect of wielding a fair quantity of legitimate power over those who took the other road. A nasty chewy bit in that crumb of consolation, however, will be the discovery that eminent research professors with high-profile research groups can wield a large quantity of less officially recognized power, and can play dirty organizational politics just as well as anyone else. So it goes.

There are various classic career patterns for academic researchers. None is right or wrong *per se*, though each has its advantages and disadvantages.

The empire builder

One classic route is through the various formal levels of academic seniority towards a research empire of your own. You start off by doing a PhD then work as a postdoctoral research assistant for a few years, get a lectureship and work at that level for a few years, become a Reader for a couple of years and then get a chair (i.e. become a professor). In the process of becoming a professor, you will have built up the start of an empire (research assistants and PhD students of your own); after becoming a professor, you will build up a research group, perhaps a research centre with lecturers, research assistants and PhD students attached to it, possibly a research institute. This will make you a considerable power broker in your department, since you will be bringing large amounts of prestige and money in, so a wise head of department will not antagonize you. Most people who follow this route will not want to be a head of department; it's too much hassle, with no reward. They might possibly take on the role for a couple of years just so they have it on their CV (it can come in handy, and can also make the point to any subsequent head of department that there is some-one else who is perfectly capable of running the place if the newcomer gets any silly ideas about throwing their weight about). There is much to be said for this route if you want to get things done, and to wield some power; the drawbacks are the politics and the administrative effort involved. If these are not for you, you might consider something less fraught, such as the wandering scholar route.

The wandering scholar

Wandering scholars may wander geographically, or in academic discipline, or both. This has a long and honourable history. In the Middle Ages, scholars would move from university to university around Europe (having Latin as a common language made this considerably easier). During the Napoleonic Wars, it was considered completely unremarkable for eminent British scientists to give visiting lectures in France, even while the two countries were at war. This tradition is still very much alive, and good research groups are often populated by bright researchers from around the world. For practical reasons, people following this route usually don't build up substantial formal empires, though they may build up formidable reputations. A word of warning, though: it's easy to build up a formidable reputation if you wander about geographically, as long as you publish your work in respected venues within your chosen research area – the journals and conferences that everyone reads and attends. It's very difficult to build up a formidable reputation if you wander about between research topics. It takes time to establish a reputation (a rule of thumb is three years from starting a piece of research to seeing it in print in a reasonable journal and even longer in a high-status journal), and if you change fields frequently, then you won't be able to do this. One apparent exception to this generalization occurs if you use your wandering between areas as a way of building up a substantial body of expertise in related areas, then settle down in one area and apply concepts from other areas. That can be extremely productive, but does have an initial cost attached.

The geographically wandering scholar approach is a good way of working with the brightest minds in your area (and building your own reputation, if you have something good to offer), as well as seeing the world. However, if you have commitments which make this route difficult, or you dislike travel, then you may wish to consider a non-wandering career, described here as the hermit scholar approach.

Hermit scholars

Hermit scholars are, in fact, usually not celibate and usually do not live a life of austere contemplation in caves, but the mediaeval metaphor was too tempting to abandon. The term is used here to describe someone who conducts their own research, without a formal research group around them in their base institution, and whose research remains within a single theme. This is a perfectly respectable route and has quite a few advantages to offer, if played correctly. It can also be quite as social as the other routes, because of the nature of fame in academia, described above. People working in this tradition are quite likely to collaborate with researchers from other institutions around the world, and can build up a formidable reputation because of their in-depth knowledge of their chosen area.

Various other things

The classic fast track for research involves something along the lines of a First at Cambridge in something prestigious like mathematics, followed by a PhD with someone who has an outstanding reputation, followed by some post-doctoral work somewhere prestigious, and then a progression along the lines described above. Someone following this track will usually become more and more specialized in one or at most two areas as they progress.

However, it's important to remember that this is just one route. Another important fast track route can be described as a delayed-action fast track. It involves becoming expert in one area, then transferring concepts from that area to solve problems in a new area (the classic example here is John Maynard Smith's importation of game theory into evolutionary ecology). It is also important to remember that the race is not always to the fast: research reputations are built on quality of research, not speed of promotion. Becoming a professor by the age of 40 is a sign of achievement, but is not much use to the world if you don't come up with any particularly interesting research after becoming a professor. It also won't cut much ice with the rest of the research community – it's the content of your research which matters to the research community, not how quickly you climbed up the slippery pole.

It's also worth mentioning at this point that the research community is a strange place as regards status symbols. Students tend to worry a lot about what class of degree they will get. This is sensible at one level, since you are unlikely to be accepted for a PhD unless you have an Upper Second or First. After that point, though, other researchers won't be particularly interested in the class of your degree.

Another oddity as you proceed up the research pecking order is that the field of your first and subsequent degrees will become less and less important. This is particularly apparent in broad fields such as psychology, where it is quite normal for researchers to have started off in other fields such as mathematics, statistics or musicology before the direction of their research interests led them into a psychology department. Many borderlines between disciplines are debatable at best, and debated at worst – for instance, fields such as cognitive modelling, artificial intelligence and human-computer interaction are on the borderline between psychology and computer science, and it is often a matter of chance whether a researcher in these areas happens to be located in a psychology department or a computer science department.

Reputations

Finally, a note on reputations. The positive side of a reputation within the research community is that it makes your career; the negative side is that a bad reputation can destroy your career. The extreme case is academic fraud.

The entire edifice of research is based on a foundation of basic starting points (data, methods etc.) When you do some research, you start from what is already known in the field. If it turns out that one of those starting points is wrong because someone deliberately faked it, then the time you spent in your research was wasted. In some areas, such as medicine, delays in finding the answer can lead to people dying.

Such instances are extreme. More common instances involve grey areas – for instance, trying to claim more credit than is strictly justifiable, or making exaggerated claims. There are also personality issues, such as people who are needlessly aggressive or rude to colleagues. Although such bad habits can to some extent be outweighed by good-quality research, nobody actively wants to work with someone unpleasant and untrustworthy if there is an alternative. Such people tend to suffer what might be called passive damage to their careers. This takes the form of things which do *not* happen, particularly where a career marker involves invitations – for instance, invitations to join editorial boards, to give keynote talks at conferences or to collaborate on major research proposals. An interesting feature of this is that the people involved may be quite unaware that it is happening.

Anyway, that concludes our section on careers. A closing thought is that you can do worse than to imagine your own epitaph and then work towards that. Most people would favour the epitaph which describes the deceased as widely revered, fair, honest, brilliant, kind, supportive and things of that sort, and there are people in the research community who fit that description. We just wish there were a few more of them . . .

Job interviews

Some day, unless you do something very wrong or very silly, you will find yourself sweating outside an interview room, waiting to be interviewed for that all-important job. (They all appear all-important at the time – the first lectureship, the first permanent contract, the senior lectureship that shows you've made your mark, the Readership that shows you've made your mark, the chair that shows you've made your mark and so forth.) So, what do you do to help your chances of getting that job?

As usual, it's worth stepping back and having a careful think. This is one context where the virtual cup of coffee is a better idea than an actual cup of caffeine-laden mocha. People get very stressed about interviews, and unfortunately caffeine isn't good for lowering stress levels. You need to think about things such as whether you really want that job. When you're near the end of a PhD/contract/course of medication for stress-related illness, it's easy to grab for any straw that passes near your bit of the torrent, and to persuade yourself that the job you're applying for is exactly what you need to make your life perfect. There are some very nice jobs out there, but they're a minority, and are usually guarded with limpet-like tenacity by the incumbents (and who can blame them?) So, have a long hard think. If you realize that you're desperately clutching at a straw, then bear this in mind when you go for interview, and treat the interview as a chance to practise your technique.

This has various advantages:

* you will be less stressed, which is helpful in itself;
* you will get some useful interview practice;
* you will probably perform considerably better than usual, which is useful in itself and also as practice for the future (there is, in fact, a real risk that you will be offered the job).

On to the interview itself.

The stages you go through

In theory, the process starts with a fat first-class letter arriving in the post at your home address. In practice, some institutions may try more creative approaches such as emailing you at your work address. Most places now tell you that because of cost they won't notify unsuccessful candidates. Such places will also tell you that if you are shortlisted, they will definitely contact you, so you don't need to worry about letters going astray in the post. If you believe that, you might be interested in some real estate in Florida which we are thinking of selling, far away from the strains of urban life . . . It's a good idea, if you're reasonably sure you're appointable and you haven't heard anything after a decent interval, to check politely with the relevant part of the institution (usually the personnel department) to see whether you've been shortlisted.

The fat first-class letter will contain information about how to get to the place, and about the time and the format of the interview. You can now start panicking about how to get there, about what to put into your presentation, what they will ask you at interview, what you should wear, and so forth.

The following sections proceed through the things that happen, and then return to the question of the preparations you need to make before going for the interview.

What to wear

There is a cynical belief that if you're female, then it's simply a case of wearing something which shows excessive amounts of thigh and cleavage. This is not true. Some interviewers do respond positively to that approach, but more react pretty negatively (and that includes males, many of whom dislike cynical attempts at manipulation). With that issue out of the way, what do you wear?

As with academic language, you need to think functionally. What is the function of interview clothing? There are, in fact, several functions. One function is simply to show that you have reasonable social skills, and can be dragged out to help liaise with outside bodies if need be. This is sometimes referred to by expressions such as, 'They wear a good suit', meaning that they can look reasonably professional and presentable in a fairly formal context. For instance, if some people are needed to show moderately important visitors around, are you presentable enough to be turned loose? If you dress like the village idiot, then the answer is likely to be 'no', and that's one less possible use for you in the organization's scheme of things (and therefore, one less tick in the boxes that record your good points).

Academic dress conventions are usually fairly relaxed compared to the rest of the world during the working week, but interviews are different. The panel will assume that what you wear to interview is your idea of what you would wear to a formal occasion. It's a good idea to attend presentations by job applicants in your own department – these are usually open to everyone – to see how they dress. It's also useful to see what they do in their presentations.

Some minor details, in no particular order:

- Some interview panel members look to see whether your shoes are immaculate, or scruffy and tatty. If the latter, then they'll suspect you of being the sort of person who does bad work and then tries to dress it up.
- Most interviewees wear dark clothes. The reason for this will become apparent the first time you spill a drink in your lap two minutes before the interview, or have to sprint across a muddy car park to get to the interview room in time.
- One game played by some panel members in boring interviews is spotting which interviewees are wearing a tie/suit/dress for the first time in a couple of years. It's usually a fairly easy game. If about to be interviewed, and planning to dress formally, then practise beforehand so the clothes don't distract you.

How to get there

Usually, the convention is to do presentations in the morning and interviews in the afternoon. The candidates who come from furthest away are usually given the latest slots, to take some of the pressure off them in terms of travel. You will usually be sent a map, or a website containing travel information.

There's no single right answer about whether to use public or private transport. Whichever you use, allow plenty of time for things going wrong, and take plenty of cash. That way, if you have a disaster, you might well be able to rescue the situation.

Some examples:

- train breaks down a stop too soon: get a taxi (which is why we recommend cash);
- disastrous spillage on your best shirt: buy a new one.

It's worth thinking about what to wear during travel. If you're driving along an unpleasant, unfamiliar route during rush-hour, then you might want to wear one shirt for the journey and change into the interview shirt on arrival. You might also want to think carefully about just *where* you propose to change your shirt – car parks and public toilets may send out unintended signals and could also lead to interesting situations if you drop your best shirt onto an oily rag on the floor of the car, or the floor of a particularly squalid toilet. If the journey looks like being really horrible, then consider travelling the day before and staying at a hotel overnight.

When you finally reach the site, it's a good idea to make your way to the contact point as soon as possible, to check that it really is where it appears on the map. Some universities have two sites at opposite ends of the town, for instance, and these regularly have trouble with candidates going to the wrong site. You can identify yourself to the secretary handling the interviews, to let them know that you've arrived, and then say that you'd like to stretch your legs for a while. That's usually OK, but some places have heavy security and might not let you wander unescorted. In that case, you need to park yourself in a corner and read the good book that you brought with you for just this sort of situation, or read your notes about the institution/department/post.

You will be offered coffee (and sometimes tea); you will usually not be told where the toilets are. If you are asked how you like your coffee, don't say, 'Whatever is least trouble' since that is an unhelpful reply. You might want to learn to drink coffee without grimacing, if you're a tea-lover.

If they haven't told you where the toilets are, then find out; either use your initiative, or ask in a polite, unapologetic tone. You can then do important things such as checking whether you have oil stains on your shirt, hair sticking up at the back of your head, and so forth. It's also useful for when the coffee works its way through your system shortly before the interview starts – you don't need to rush frenziedly round looking for a toilet. Beware Supataps – they can jet out water in a sudden spurt that leaves your lap soaking wet in an embarrassing way. (This is another reason why interview clothes are usually dark colours.)

Your presentation

You will often be asked to give a presentation summarizing in 10 or 20 minutes your academic achievements and/or past, present and future research. You may also be asked to give a presentation as if it were part of a lecture to a specified group. The value of this for detecting good candidates is questionable, but it's surprisingly good at detecting some of the loons whom you would not want in your department at any price. (Not all of them, unfortunately, but some, and that's better than nothing.)

Things to bear in mind:

- Remember the cabinet-making metaphor – what skills do you need to demonstrate in your talk?
- Are you demonstrating all of the essential and most of the desirable skills from the job/person specification that came with the job details?
- What would encourage you about a candidate if you were on the interview panel?
- Have backups – if using PowerPoint or equivalent, then have OHP slides as backups, and be prepared to use a whiteboard if all else fails.
- Do as many practice sessions as it takes to get the talk down to the right length, days before the interview. Give the talk to an empty room if you have to (though feedback from more experienced colleagues is very useful).
- Think about what the sensible, obvious approach to the topic is. That's what everyone else will be using. Then think about a sensible, non-obvious approach which they won't be using, preferably one that shows you are more mature and far-seeing than the competition.

Your interview

The interview panel will have a make-up determined by a variety of factors. The roles usually include some or more of the following:

- someone from personnel to see that procedures are duly followed;
- someone external to see that the level of appointment is appropriate and that the panel isn't appointing someone underqualified out of desperation;
- someone from the department, who might have some idea what you're talking about;
- someone else from the department, to pad the department's vote and reduce the risk of the panel appointing someone disastrous as a result of its ignorance of the department's field of interest;
- yet another person from the department who disagrees with the first two, wants to appoint someone with diametrically different skills and who is too senior to keep away;
- one or two senior people like the dean who want to keep an eye on what's going on and make sure the department is fitting in with the master plan;
- someone reliable and sane who wears a good suit and has stood in at short notice for one of the above, to make up the numbers.

The panel will usually operate more or less in turn, and will usually ask you the same questions that they ask the other candidates. If one of the other candidates has some odd characteristics, then you may in the interests of comparability be asked the same question that the panel will ask them. The results can sometimes seem rather odd to the candidates who have not got a complex and obscure status regarding their nationality and work permits, for instance. If you're thrown by the question, you can always try asking the panel to expand on it a bit, on the grounds that you're not quite sure what they're trying to ascertain.

The panel will (in theory) have agreed on their sequence and their questions beforehand. They will also (in theory) have a copy of the 'essential and desirable characteristics' list in front of them, and will tick off one by one the characteristics which you appear to have, with varying degrees of discretion. Some panels then simply count the number of ticks and use that as a basis for appointment, which can lead to some scary decisions (hence the way that departments like to make sure they have the right people on the panel). There are all sorts of legal implications if a panel appoints someone who appears to be less qualified than an unsuccessful candidate, which is the reason for some of the more odd-looking decisions. The great bonus about this, from your point of view, is that if you're clearly much better than the internal candidate, then you have a good chance of getting the job.

You need to make very sure that you get as many things ticked as possible: read the list of 'essential and desirable characteristics' with care, and refer explicitly to particular characteristics if you think that the panel might not realize that you have those characteristics. Don't assume that they will have read your CV in detail; err on the side of spelling things out explicitly. Anyone senior enough to be on the interview panel will usually have a ludicrous work-load, and can be excused for forgetting that you're the candidate who worked for six months with the Bristol research group.

At interview, you will be concerned with showing the panel how wonderful you are, with a view to furthering your career. The panel will probably not give a damn about that. They will be concerned with their own agendas. These include things like the following:

Departmental members

- finding someone who can help out with teaching the SOD2001 module which nobody on the current departmental team can teach;
- finding someone to teach pretty much anything to the first years;
- finding someone to teach the complicated stuff to the final years and the MSc students;
- finding a good safe pair of hands who can help with departmental firefighting;
- finding someone who can strengthen the next RAE submission;
- finding an ally for their long-running power struggle with another member of the department;
- finding someone pleasant to lessen the baleful presence of Professor Jones and Dr West;
- making sure they don't appoint anyone like Professor Jones and Dr West.

Other panel members

- making sure the proprieties are observed and the forms are filled in correctly;
- making sure the institution can't be sued by dissatisfied candidates;
- making sure the department doesn't appoint someone dreadful out of rampant cronyism like they did with Professor Jones;
- making sure the department doesn't appoint the first person who looks vaguely suitable out of sheer desperation from lack of staff, like they did with Dr West;
- getting the whole business over with as soon as possible because there's too much else to do;
- having a leisurely break from the ludicrous volume of routine admin tasks.

The departmental agenda is usually the more important one from your point of view, and can be summed up in one question: what can this person do to make our lives better? If you come across as someone who can clearly fit one or more of the department's needs, then that's a very important step. If you ascertain what the department wants (reading the information for candidates is a good start) then that makes life a lot easier for you.

Knowing your enemy

As ever, knowing your enemy is extremely important. If you're keen on research, then the standard researcher is one of your enemies, as the lists below should make clear.

Standard researcher criteria for a good job:

- little or no teaching;
- little or no admin;
- few or no committee meetings;
- as much autonomy as possible.

These differ subtly from the criteria which most departments use to describe a good candidate:

- willing to do a reasonable amount of teaching;
- willing to shoulder their share of the admin;
- willing to help out with those boring committee meetings;
- a team player.

The positive way to view this is to look at the phrasing in the departmental criteria. In a fair department, you will be expected to do your share of everything. That's not unreasonable. In an unfair department, you will be expected to do too much of everything. In a pathological department, you will be expected to do things which are a total waste of your time and expertise, and which damage your career and health. How can you as a novice tell which category your prospective department falls into? You probably can't. That's . . . why you have a supervisor, and wonderful people to whom you can turn for advice.

Other enemies are enemies for pretty much any sort of job. They include the following:

- the plausible idler (who will appear keen and conscientious until the day after their probationary period ends, and will then never do another stroke of work);
- the plausible crook (who appears honest at interview and then does questionable or downright illegal things after being appointed);
- the clueless amateur (who is clueless, and therefore unlikely to be appointed in the first place);
- the dead wood (who did something good years ago, and will rest on the decaying laurels of that achievement until retirement).

Nobody wants to hire someone who turns out horribly different when they're on a permanent contract and difficult to fire. A department which has experienced one of these types will usually be extremely sensitive to the slightest suggestion that you might be another such case. Most panels have had experiences such as discovering that the two missing years on a CV represent time when the candidate was in prison. It's therefore a good idea to (a) check your CV for gaps and (b) avoid lying. If you lie, there's also the horrible risk that you might get the job, and then have to try teaching several courses on topics about which you know nothing.

Questions they might ask

Classics include the following:

'Did you have a good journey?' which means, 'You're probably feeling nervous; let's start gently'. It does not mean, 'We would dearly love to hear about the roadworks at junction 14'.

'Would you like to tell us about yourself?' can be asked for various reasons, such as reminding the over-worked panel whether you are the one from Southampton, or giving you a chance to describe yourself more coherently than you did on your CV. Whatever the reason, this is a good chance to summarize why you fit well with the essential and desirable skills.

'Why did you apply for this job?' can mean either, 'Why are you so clearly desperate to flee your present job?' or, 'Do you actually want this specific job, or would you settle for the first job that came along?' You need to be careful about the first of these, since you don't want to look like a vindictive failure. It's better in such cases to use a neutral phrasing which acknowledges that the present post is not for you, and that you've decided to move on.

For the second meaning, you need to phrase your reply to show a well-informed appreciation of the good things about the department, and to show how you can help it.

'Where do you see yourself five years from now?' is a cliché, but a good one. It shows two main things, namely whether you're the sort of person who plans ahead, and what your schemes are for using the department to further your career. If you're either short of planning skills or moving in a direction which will leave a trail of havoc through the department, then your chances of being appointed will probably dwindle.

'What would you teach if appointed?' Possible answers include the following, ranging from dreadful to good:

- 'Me? Teach?'
- 'I hadn't really thought about that.'
- 'Something to do with human factors.'
- 'Human-computer interaction; quantitative methods.'
- 'I've taught system analysis and design at all levels from HND to MSc, so I could teach your SOD1001, SOD2001, SOD3001 and SOD4001 modules. I could also . . .'

Questions you can ask

There are various questions you can ask. These are useful for two purposes. One is to find out things that you need to know, the other is to demonstrate to the panel that you are bright enough to ask the right questions, and shrewd enough not to ask the wrong ones. There are plenty of things that you need to know (for instance, how likely is it that you will have an enormous teaching load dumped on you?) but which nobody in their senses is going to tell you; if you ask questions along these lines, then you show yourself as someone who does not understand the rules of the game. A better way of finding answers to these questions is via the grapevine. Questions which demonstrate that you have the right stuff will vary depending on the precise job, but if your question demonstrates a clear understanding of the department's teaching and research, then you probably won't go far wrong.

Once you've been offered the job, you can ask post-offer questions. This is where you negotiate, wrestle, wheel and deal with your potential employer. There's a trade-off here between getting what you want in the short term and antagonizing your employer in the long term.

Preparation

A moment spent in reconnaissance is seldom wasted, to quote the sponsor of one of the earliest major scientific expeditions. It doesn't do any harm to know the department personally; you can do this via things like giving a seminar there, or striking up friendships with members at conferences.

If you're applying for a postdoctoral research post, then you need to use the grapevine and read between the lines of CVs on websites etc. to find out what your potential bosses are like to work with. Will they work you like a dog, leave your name off publications and ditch you as soon as the funding runs out? Are they pleasant people who will look after you, give you first authorship of a paper or two, and do what they can to look after you once the funding ends – for instance, by finding more money for a follow-on project?

You also need to find out the impersonal stuff – what courses they teach, how many staff they have, how many students they have (so you can work out staff–student ratios and therefore workloads), how much they have published, and so forth.

Once you've done this, then you will have a better idea of what line to take for your application. More importantly, you'll have a better idea of whether you want the job in the first place. A closing note well worth remembering is that the job application process is two-way. You don't have to take the first job you're offered; you don't have to fit in with the requirements of the prospective employers if they're clearly inflexible and unreasonable people. It's your life, not theirs.

On that cheering note, we move on to the next topic.

Life planning

So there you are, thinking that you really ought to sort your life out, and all too aware that you haven't a clue where to start. How do you plan the next ten years, or even the next ten months? How can you know what you will want out of life ten years from now? Why do things seem to keep going wrong for you, unlike those glittering other people that you see all round you? Why do all your socks look tatty? Answers to these and many other questions can be found in this section.

Time and sensible planning

The first thing you need to accept is that things take time. There are different sorts of time. One sort is elapsed time; another sort is task time. A lot of things take quite a short time for the action itself (task time) but involve a lot of waiting around until the action itself can begin (elapsed time). For instance, you're organizing something with someone else by email. The actual exchanges of information only take a total of five minutes at the keyboard, but the elapsed time to make the arrangements totals up to several days because you're having to wait for each other's replies. So, slow down a bit, stop rushing, and slow down a bit more. You will then be in a better position to do some sensible planning.

Sensible planning is a very different activity from two familiar enemies, namely displacement activities and expressive behaviour. Sensible planning is often quite difficult to do when you're stressed out by life events and hassles. The best thing to do initially is to buy yourself some time, plan how to buy yourself some more time, and bootstrap up a bit at a time. How do you do that? Ironically, a good start is via displacement activities. One of us was once given some very wise advice by their supervisor, namely that if you are going to engage in a displacement activity, you should make sure that it's a useful one. Here are some useful displacement activities.

Useful displacement activities

A long soaky bath

Once a week, instead of slumping despondently in front of the television, run yourself a long, hot, soaky bath. Lie in the bath with a wet cloth over your face. This will calm you down. It will also lead surprisingly often to your seeing your situation in clearer perspective, and realizing some better ways of handling things.

Weed your clothing

If your clothes look tatty and cheap, you'll feel tatty and cheap. Replace one item of clothing each week or month, whichever you can afford. Start with socks and underwear, which don't last forever, and which don't cost a fortune to replace. With more expensive items, if in doubt, buy one good-quality item rather than two mediocre ones. If you think this advice sounds extravagant, try dumping a batch of your clothes on the bed and asking yourself which items you genuinely like. The results can be surprising. It's a good idea to have at least one smart outfit suitable for interviews etc. and to get used to wearing it. It can make a surprising difference to your self-esteem if you wear smarter clothes than usual for a few days.

Get rid of some junk

Most of us have large amounts of clutter. Look through your belongings, get rid of the things that are neither useful, loved nor beautiful, and create some storage space and some swap space. Swap space is another useful concept: it's space needed temporarily while you rearrange things. For instance, if you're tidying shelves, you'll need at least enough swap space for the contents of one shelf so that you can empty that shelf, clean it, and decide which contents to put where. Hardly anyone has enough swap space or storage space. Don't try to do all of this at once; have an evening per week or per month when you do a bit.

Tidy and file

Most people don't tidy and file enough. Tidying and filing, if you do them in manageable doses, can be very soothing activities and can give you a feeling of control. They also make a practical difference to your life – it's a lot easier to be efficient and to have some spare time if your tidying and filing are under control.

Read a book about something different from your PhD topic

This will help you to break out of the cycle of worry about your PhD, will help you to see things in perspective and will quite probably one day provide you with the key insight that changes your life.

There are some excellent books available on planning, time management and self-development. They will give you a lot of ideas about ways of organizing yourself in the medium term, and a fair few ideas about developing yourself as a person. What you will probably find is that you start off fired with good intentions, take on too much and gradually slip back into bad habits. One thing you can do about this is to start on a manageable scale, without trying to do too much. Another is to try a variety of approaches until you find some that work well for you. For some jobs, for instance, traditional time management doesn't work very well because the job involves too much unpredictable firefighting (i.e. dealing with serious immediate problems caused by people other than yourself). In such situations, what you have to do instead is priority management, which involves a different set of skills. Another thing that often happens is that you find that one way of structuring your time (e.g. planning the day as a series of time slots) just doesn't work for your personality, but that another (e.g. planning for the week, with the days as the units – an admin day, a research day etc.) works well for you.

This is all useful stuff for organizing yourself in the medium term, so that you can get the day job and your immediate situation under control. It doesn't give you so much help about planning for the longer term, which is a useful and surprisingly soothing activity.

The main thing to remember about long-term planning is that as long as you haven't signed any forms, your plans aren't legally binding. You can change them; it's a good idea to update them periodically. When you start off, you can't know what you don't know. You can't realistically plan your career until you've worked in the area long enough to know whether this really is what you want to do with your life. It would be silly to commit yourself so totally to one career plan that your life would feel utterly pointless without it. You can, however, sketch in some main points along the way.

So, what do you want your death to be like? How do you want to be remembered? And, most importantly, what do you want to look back on in your life? You don't want to look back on a pile of 'if only' thoughts and unfulfilled dreams. Think about what achievements and memories you would really like to look back on. Once you've done that, you can start thinking about how to achieve them. Surprisingly few things are impossible if you are sensible, determined and keep trying. This approach also helps you to identify which things you will need to do as preparation for longer-term goals. For instance, if you want to have a wilderness holiday in Canada, then learning to canoe and getting fit would be highly advisable preparation; we are assured by colleagues who have relevant experience that learning about the habits of bears is also highly advisable. That, though, is another story, and a sign that perhaps this section should draw to a close.

Writing a CV

What's a CV for?

The main purpose of a CV is to get you 'across the threshold', typically to get you an interview. What story do you want to tell about yourself; what do you want to emphasize? The story will change with the purpose, and so the CV will change for each use as well. Think about CVs as 'effective or ineffective' rather than as 'good or bad'. Read other people's CVs and consider what they say to you about the person, and why.

Key features of an effective CV are:

- continuity;
- evidence of development and progression;
- consistency;
- accuracy;
- accessibility.

The private 'repository' CV versus the selective purpose-written CV

A good strategy is to keep one, private, up-to-date 'repository' CV containing anything that might possibly be useful, from publications through to course attendance. Things like key projects, seminars in other institutions, doctoral events, consultancy work, refereeing, conference organization, awards including studentships and so on can be relevant, so keep track of them.

Then make strategic selections from the collection to tailor a CV for a specific use. Use a structure that reflects the purpose (e.g. one that maps onto the job requirements).

How will the CV be read?

Imagine that your CV is one of 50 – or 500 – submitted for a position. Most selection panels first skim-read CVs in order to identify those worthy of further scrutiny.

Write your CV to be skimmed.

Interview panels are trying to divine what sort of candidate you are. They will read CVs strategically to glean particular sorts of information (e.g. specific skills, particular experiences, evidence of team work, evidence of individual initiative), to look for 'danger signs' (e.g. lots of chopping and changing, inconsistencies, significant omissions), to examine continuity and to look for indications of development or excellence.

Write your CV to be scrutinized in detail.

The significance of CV design choices

When you design your CV, you make choices about selection of information, emphasis and style of presentation.

Selection

What you choose to include can give your interviewers something to ask about. But *anything* you include is open to discussion. Don't include things you'd rather avoid discussing or that might be misunderstood. Think carefully about whether you really want to include personal information (e.g. marital status) or religious or political affiliations, and even consider what your hobbies say about you before you decide to include them. Sometimes, this 'peripheral' information can make all the difference – either for or against you – so make sure that what's there is how you want to be seen. Also consider what your omissions may say about you, especially omissions that relate to the purpose for which you're preparing the CV.

Emphasis

Choices you make about things like how you record dates, how you describe previous jobs and how you report your education can convey what you think is important. For example, when you're listing your degrees, do you prioritize the subject or the institution?

Style

The way you present your information can show that you understand what the employer values. For example, if you're going for an academic post, it's a good idea to present your publications in a way that reflects the RAE categories. If you're going for an industry post, it's a good idea to make accessible the technical qualifications that relate to the post and to emphasize any indicators of customer or market awareness.

Academic CVs tend to be different from industrial CVs. There are times when you need to emphasize your technical qualifications and times when you need to show what a versatile and well-rounded person you are. The trick is to understand enough about the context you're sending your CV into in order to emphasize the appropriate things.

CVs change over time, as people develop. CV design choices will change over time, too. Choices that are appropriate for an early career CV will be less appropriate for a mature career CV, and vice versa.

Writing for the skim-reader

- Make every word count. Don't use 'Curriculum Vitae' as your major heading – it's a waste of words. Your name should be the principal heading.
- The first page is key. Imagine that someone is trying to review half a dozen candidates and has spread the six CVs on the desk as an *aide mémoire*. A good first page can make you more memorable, more impressive, more accessible. What you put on the first page should reflect what you think is most important for the purpose.
- Be thoughtful in your use of typographic design; good design can help make important information accessible. White space and highlighting 'guide the eye' – make sure the eye is guided to important information. If you just scan down the emboldened words, what do you read? Indenting and spacing can help group information. For example, ex-dented dates can make it easy to scan for continuity.

Writing for the scrutinizer

- Proof-read! Then get someone else to proof-read!
- The use of narrative trades off with scan ability. Hence, use narrative sparingly and strategically, offering one or two lines to amplify or describe (e.g. indicating the significance of your doctoral work or highlighting the skills and responsibilities embodied in a previous job).
- Review your CV in the context of particular questions. Does it show continuity of activity? Are there any periods unaccounted for? Can the reader relate jobs to skills or outcomes in some way? Take questions from the job specification: what evidence does the CV provide that you meet the selection criteria?

What to avoid

- **Never lie in a CV:** but make the most of your history, selecting and high-lighting relevant and important information. Don't call attention to things you'd prefer not to discuss.

- **Focus on content, not dressing:** don't get fancy or cute, it almost always backfires. Conveying information is the goal, not impressing with your decorative flair.
- **Don't leave gaps:** if you do, employers will assume that you're concealing something, such as a spell in prison. If you were unemployed, then it's better to say so than to leave a gap; say something about how you used that time to prepare for the next job.

Useful principles and the like

I know just where the sea-elephants are stored

More top tips

These probably fail to include some incredibly useful tips which we've taken for granted; with luck, we'll catch some of those in a later edition. Anyway, here are some of our favourites.

Aim to have about 75 per cent of your bids/papers/job applications rejected.
If you're successful 100 per cent of the time, you're setting your sights too low. A rejection rate of about 75 per cent means that your calibration is about right. (Don't treat the 75 per cent figure as set in stone – it will vary across disciplines, but the underlying concept remains valid.)

Work backwards from where you want to end up.
If you know where you want to end up and work backwards from that, then you're likely to get to your goal efficiently. If you blunder off in a random direction, hoping to find a goal, then you're likely to end up lost.

When planning research, aim to reduce the problem space, not to find The True Answer.
If you gamble on finding a result, then you're probably doing things wrong.

You should phrase your research question in such a way that, whatever you find, it tells you something useful. You should work on the metaphor of the ship's captain making maps of an unknown sea, rather than the metaphor of the ship's captain gambling on finding El Dorado. Knowing that a stretch of sea is empty is just as useful as knowing that there is an island in it. Don't set out to collect data in support of your belief. Ask yourself: 'How could I tell if my belief was wrong?' If you can't answer that question, then you're doing politics, not research.

If bright people have been looking at a problem for more than three years and still don't have a solution, then the solution is probably somewhere unlikely.
Two to three years is about the time span for several bright professionals to try the obvious approaches, write-up their findings and present them in a conference. If no solutions are being reported after three years, this is probably a significant absence. In this situation, don't rush in trying the obvious approach, especially if the area is a hot topic: do some lateral thinking about different approaches.

Know the tools of your trade in detail.
Most researchers learn enough about the tools of their trade to get started. This isn't good enough. The more you know about them, the better the work you can do.

Aim to be genuinely nice to people.
It makes the world a better place and it pays off in the long term – people will remember you and put things your way. This is not the same as being silly or a victim, or as being mercenary.

A cup of coffee with a knowledgeable, supportive person can be the best investment you ever make.
Asking advice from the right person at the right time (usually before you get started) can save you a lot of tears and a lot of wasted effort. Remember to ask someone knowledgeable about the relevant area – a fellow lost soul, or someone knowledgeable about a different area, may be comforting but is unlikely to be much help in getting you out of the problem.

If you have any choice at all, only work with nice people whom you respect. You achieve much more this way and you have a nicer time along the way.

If you don't know what you're doing, then stop and find out.
Another cup of coffee can help at this point.

Go through important documents that you write (first pages of papers, covering letters for job applications etc.) with two highlighters.
Highlight in one colour anything that an intelligent layperson could have said and anything where nobody would think of saying the opposite. Highlight in another colour anything that only someone with detailed knowledge of the field could have said; anything an intelligent layperson could not have said; any tangible facts (such as references or data) or achievements; any other signs of excellence (e.g. advanced reading, or having done homework on the organization where you're applying to work). Delete the former, and make sure there is at least one of the latter per paragraph.

Remember, blood comes first.
Keep a sense of perspective. Life is more important than money or fame.

The three ignoble truths (with apologies to the three noble truths)

First ignoble truth: hardware will break and software will crash.
Second ignoble truth: resources won't be there when you need them.
Third ignoble truth: people will get sick, die and fail to deliver.

The three golden rules of public speaking

First golden rule: don't lie.
Second golden rule: don't try to be funny.
Third golden rule: don't panic and blurt out the truth.

Some useful terms

Only yesterday I learnt, to my surprise, that you trice puddings athwart the starboard gumbrils, when sailing by and large.

Standard terms are well described in the standard textbooks. This section concentrates on non-standard terms which you may find useful, and terms which are not as widely known as they should be. We have also included some terms which you may be guiltily aware that you're not sure about, even though you know you should be (for instance, what is the difference between a journal and a magazine, and how do these relate to periodicals?)

big name: someone with a considerable reputation in the research community. Also known as 'an authority'.

blood in the water: unnecessary indication of serious weakness in your work.

bounced (of paper submitted to a conference or journal): euphemism for 'rejected'.

buzzword: fashionable but usually content-free word. If you are working in an area which is currently popular in the media (e.g. biotechnology or nanotechnology) then you need to make it clear in your writing that you understand the area thoroughly and are not just waving buzzwords around without understanding.

cabinet-making: the thesis is like the master piece produced by apprentices in The Past. It is the piece of work which demonstrates that you have attained mastery of your chosen field. Like the apprentice, you need to make sure that your chosen piece of work, your thesis, gives you the opportunity to demonstrate the whole range of skills that you should have.

chair: professorship.

cup of coffee: this is shorthand for an informal chat with someone. This usually does take place over a cup of coffee – the best departments are well aware of the importance of coffee rooms as places for informal exchange of information, and for introducing PhD students to tacit information about the academic world.

eyeballing the data: this is an informal term for having a look at the raw data. This is a good idea if you're doing statistical analysis – if the results from the analysis don't look consistent with your impression from eyeballing the data, then there's a chance that you've made a mistake with the analysis. It's surprisingly easy to make mistakes, so eyeballing the data is a good habit.

field, the: has two meanings, which may be confusing for beginners.

Sense 1: a discipline, or area of research.

Sense 2: place, somewhere outside the lab/department, where data collection is conducted.

funded research project: if you want money to do some research, you can apply to various bodies for money (for instance, various research councils). Such funding bids range from a few hundred pounds for travel or equipment up to millions of pounds to set up a research institute. One common form of funded research project involves hiring a research assistant for one or two years to carry out the research specified in the funding bid. Bids of this sort bring money into universities and are an important part of research.

Good Thing: from the book *1066 and All That*. This is an ironic reference to things which are currently fashionable, with the implication that before long they will be out of fashion and replaced by some other fad.

Great Departmental Annual Report: most departments publish reports on their teaching and/or research at various intervals. This is usually because they are required to do so by some higher authority, such as the faculty or university, rather than because they want to. These reports are usually a thorough irritation to everyone involved, not least because they usually want information from you in a format which is as inconvenient as possible. They will also probably want to know the exact dates of any conferences at which you presented a paper, and the ISBN or ISSN for any publications. If you haven't kept records of these, then The System will probably hound you mercilessly until you track them down. The moral is to keep neat and complete records of publications (or, failing that, complete records – just putting all the paperwork from the conference in a folder to sort through later will probably be adequate).

harmless: a low-key insult. Describes something which is devoid of any particular good or bad features, but which will attract so little attention because of its mediocrity that it will do no harm to the world (e.g. 'a harmless paper').

inaugural: formal lecture given to colleagues and invited guests by a newly appointed professor, to mark their appointment.

inflating your *p* value: using an unnecessarily large sample size, so that a weak effect is statistically magnified to an unjustified extent. In some fields, weak effects are extremely important; however, in most fields the majority of weak effects are trivial and not worth bothering with.

journal: a learned periodical, aimed at a particular discipline. Differs from a magazine in several ways. Journals are intended for specialists, not general readers, and normally journal articles are written by academics, not journalists. More prestigious academically than magazines, having one of your articles published in a good journal is a sign of professional achievement.

named candidate: when you're writing a funding bid (to ask for money for a research project), some funding bodies like to know that you have already lined someone up to do the work if you get the money – it can be difficult to find someone with suitable skills for a specialist area of research, and a surprising number of projects fail because nobody suitable could be found to do the work. The named candidate is the person lined up to do the work; wise researchers are usually on the lookout for potential named candidates, such as PhD students who appear to know the unwritten rules.

Past, The: we've capitalized this in places to mark ironic humour. People tend to think of The Past as a fairly homogeneous time of slow changes, whereas the reality is rather different. In the case of the PhD, for instance, the nature of the PhD has been changing at a noticeable rate throughout living memory, and probably throughout history. This misconception of The Past can be a serious issue if a central part of your thesis involves claims of unprecedented changes in some area within the last few years; fortunately, a full discussion of this is outside the scope of this glossary.

periodical: a publication which comes out periodically, usually several times a year, such as a journal or a magazine, and in contrast to one-off publications such as books.

PhD: formal abbreviation for Latin *philosophiae doctor* (doctor of philosophy). Highest regular university degree, usually given to a candidate who has successfully presented a written thesis on a research topic and passed a *viva voce* examination. There are also other doctoral qualifications with different abbreviations in disciplines such as theology. As usual, conventions vary across institutions and disciplines. People with a PhD can call themselves 'doctor', a rich source of argument with medical doctors, with each side viewing the other as interlopers.

practicalia: low-level practical things, like making sure you have enough paperclips, or getting a form filled in by the deadline.

professor: academic title; the top academic (as opposed to administrative) title. You do not need to have a doctorate to be a professor, though it is usual. Becoming a professor is equivalent to becoming one of the senior elders in a traditional clan society. Becoming a professor before 40 is usually viewed as a sign of a bright young thing.

questionnaire: usually refers to a collection of poorly validated questions assembled without much thought about how they will be analysed, and with even less attention to the literature on good practice in data collection and in surveys. Much favoured by those who believe that it is better to collect large amounts of meaningless data than the right amount of meaningful data.

RAE: research assessment exercise. In the name of quality control, The System periodically asks universities to present data about their publications and other research activities. The better a university's research, the more money it is given by The System. What does 'better' mean? Good question. Shrewd departments have a fair idea of what will count as 'better' and will encourage it (usually papers in top journals and substantial income generation from research are in this category).

Reader: academic rank intermediate between lecturer and professor, specializing in research rather than administration. Usually Readers go on to be a professor fairly soon. We have spelled the term with a capital 'R' to reduce confusion and the scope for witticisms.

reducing the problem space: eliminating plausible but wrong possibilities so you can narrow down the set of possibilities which might be correct.

research assistant: a person who is employed to carry out research on a funded research project. Most PhD students go on to work as a postdoctoral research assistant for a few years after graduating, as a useful way of gaining experience. Once tellingly described as a 'research grunt' by a cynical colleague in that role (an allusion to the US Marine Corps which will probably be lost on most readers, but which might bring amusement to some).

research community: research in any given area involves a number of researchers; usually this number is surprisingly small, since fields tend to subdivide into manageably small subfields. All of the big names, and most of the leading researchers, will usually know each other, at least by name and reputation; they will normally meet at conferences each year. The usual career path is to find a research area which interests you and then to build a reputation within that research community.

research fellow: means different things in different institutions, ranging from a research assistant with a PhD to a very senior and very prestigious research post at a prestigious university.

sample size: usually a very large number, selected for no obvious reason, and without reference to the various statistical tests which can be used to show when diminishing returns have been reached and when there is no point in collecting more data.

sanity check: a test, usually informal, to check that a claim or a finding is not obviously silly. Useful when you are using statistical software for the first time and there's a risk of an error producing output which is in the correct format but which is completely wrong.

significant: has a specialized statistical meaning, which can lead to serious misunderstandings for students who are unaware of this and who use the word in the loose, popular sense. In statistics, 'significant' means 'the likelihood of this happening by random chance is at most 1 in 20'; this is normally accompanied by naming the statistical test which was used. 'Highly significant' and 'very highly significant' involve the same principle, but with odds of 1 in 100 and 1 in 1000 respectively.

significant absence: something whose absence tells you something significant. In a Sherlock Holmes story, the main clue is that the watchdog did not bark when the criminal entered the premises. This absence of barking was significant, and showed that the dog knew the criminal. If the dog had been a friendly creature that never barked at anyone, then the absence of barking would not have been a significant absence. Academic significant absences usually take the form of no reputable published accounts of a particular phenomenon or effect. Learning to spot significant absences takes time, but is an invaluable skill.

System, The: ironic reference to the image, widespread among students and supervisors alike, of the higher reaches of the university as being an unholy hybrid spawned by the imaginations of Kafka, Lovecraft, Orwell and Stalin.

tacit knowledge: in the broad sense, knowledge which is not usually mentioned explicitly, whether because it is taken for granted, or because it is about a sensitive topic. Much expertise consists of tacit knowledge, and acquiring it is an important part of doing a PhD. This topic usually isn't addressed in PhD training courses or books, and is usually left to the supervisor, if indeed anyone thinks explicitly about it at all.

there is a literature on that: a middle-key insult that means, 'That topic has been thoroughly studied by a large number of people, and you have clearly failed to do your homework and discover it; also, you have just wasted a chunk of your life reinventing the wheel'.

viva: short for Latin *viva voce*. A live interrogation, usually by external examiners, to test your knowledge of your chosen subject. The final stage of a PhD may also be used on MSc and undergraduate students on occasion. In some countries, the viva takes place as a public event open to anyone who feels like coming along to the lecture hall where it is held; in The Past, as a further aid to students' nerves, vivas were held in Latin, so if you're feeling worried about your own viva, then count yourself lucky that you aren't having it in sixteenth-century Paris.

voice: somewhere between style and viewpoint. For instance, the voice in which a paper is written may be austere, or informal, and/or authoritative. The same word is used in a different sense in traditional grammar.

Some further reading

. . . he was no more consistent than other men, and in spite of his liberal principles and his dislike of constituted authority he was capable of petulant tyranny when confronted with a slime-draught early in the morning.

Earlier in this book, we explained why, after some debate, we had decided not to include a section of further reading. This is the section that we decided not to include. It consists, like the rest of this book, mainly of things that don't usually appear in other books on this topic (some of which may seem improbable), and is intended to complement the standard-issue 'further reading' sections rather than to duplicate or to supplant them.

Phil Agre, on 'networking the network':
http://polaris.gseis.ucla.edu/pagre/network.html
Phil Agre has a site full of interesting material. This part is our favourite.

Judith Butcher, on copy-editing:
Butcher, J. (1992) *Copy-Editing: The Cambridge Handbook for Editors, Authors and Publishers*, 3rd edn. Cambridge: Cambridge University Press.
The classic book on copy-editing; invaluable for doing a professional job when the proofs come back with a note asking you to check them within two working days.

Lyn DuPré, on improving your writing:
DuPré, L. (1998) *BUGS in Writing, Revised Edition: A Guide to Debugging Your Prose*. Reading, MA.: Addison-Wesley.

A practical, nuts-and-bolts guide to English usage that combines wit with mastery.

Stephen Jay Gould's books of essays:
Useful for helping students to appreciate the scholarship of previous centuries in context, rather than as a quaint collection of mistaken and discarded beliefs.

Sir Ernest Gowers, on effective writing:
Gowers, E. (revised by Greenbaum, S. and Whitcut, J.) (2003) *The Complete Plain Words*. Harmondsworth: Penguin.
The classic advice on writing: 'Keep it simple, stupid.'

Herodotus:
Herodotus, Marincola, J.M. and De Selincourt, A. (1996 edition) *The Histories*. Harmondsworth: Penguin.
A wonderful example of uncritical but scrupulously accurate reporting. We often use Herodotus as a contrast to Thucydides for purposes such as explaining the difference between a literature report (Herodotus) and a literature review (Thucydides).

Darrell Huff, on statistics:
Huff, D. (2003 reissue) *How to Lie with Statistics*. London: W.W. Norton.
Once celebrated as 'blasphemy against the religion of statistics', this delightfully readable book is a classic on the use and abuse of statistics. Huff is a salutary reminder to *pay attention to the evidence.*

David Patterson, on 'how to have a bad career in research/academia':
http://www.cs.berkeley.edu/%7Epattrsn/talks/BadCareer.pdf
These are slides from a talk by David Patterson offering advice that is wickedly and memorably to the point.

Estelle M. Philips and Derek S. Pugh, on how to get a PhD:
Philips, E.M. and Pugh, D.S. (2000) *How to Get a PhD: A Handbook for Students and their Supervisors*, 3rd edn. Buckingham: Open University Press.
There's a good reason why this book has sold so many copies year after year. It's an excellent overview of the PhD process – indeed, we have always considered our book as a complement to Philips and Pugh.

G. Pólya, on reasoning and problem solving:
Pólya, G. (1971) *How to Solve It: A New Aspect of Mathematical Method*. Princeton, NJ: Princeton University Press.
Although an introduction to mathematical problem-solving might seem irrelevant, it's not. Good research is about good reasoning, and Pólya's book is a fine excuse to explore and reflect on strategies for problem-solving.

The **Skeptic's Encyclopedia,** on reasoning and evidence:
http://skepdic.com/contents.html
Very useful for practice in reasoning, logic and use of evidence.

William Strunk Jnr. and E.B. White, on writing right (sorry, we couldn't resist that one):
Strunk, W. and White, E.B. (1979) *The Elements of Style.* New York: Macmillan.
This is a fundamental guide to English usage. Every writer should have it, and should have read it.

Robert H. Thouless, on reasoning and thought:
Thouless, R.H. (1995) *Straight and Crooked Thinking.* London: Macmillan Publishing. This is a book about argument and intellectual engagement set in the context of human emotion and psychology. It articulates a range of pitfalls in argumentation. Students would do well to use the appendix on 'Thirty-eight dishonest tricks which are commonly used in argument' as a checklist for debugging their dissertations.

Thucydides, on rigorous thinking:
Thucydides, Warner, R. and Finley, M.I. (1954) *History of the Peloponnesian War.* Harmondsworth: Penguin.
Most students have a certain degree of condescension towards work done before they were born, and this can lead to dangerous habits and sloppy scholarship. Thucydides' writing and reasoning (for instance, his analysis of the size and significance of the Trojan War) help students understand how much there is to gain from treating the literature seriously, however old it is.

The urban legends FAQ:
http://www.urbanlegends.com/afu.faq/
Generally entertaining (though often gruesome); good for teaching students caution when deciding which statements need to be checked, and which statements are known by everyone to be true.

The Wikipedia sections on rhetoric and on logical fallacies:
http://en2.wikipedia.org/wiki/Rhetoric
http://en.wikipedia.org/wiki/Fallacy
Most students have room for improvement as regards seeing errors either in their own reasoning or in the texts they are using. The Wikipedia site is one of several modern sites which provide accessible introductions to this via understanding rhetoric and logical fallacies.

Related books from Open University Press
Purchase from www.openup.co.uk or order from your local bookseller

HOW TO GET A PhD (2nd edition)
A HANDBOOK FOR STUDENTS AND THEIR SUPERVISORS
Estelle M. Phillips and D.S. Pugh

This is a handbook and survival manual for PhD students, providing a practical, realistic understanding of the processes of doing research for a doctorate. It discusses many important issues often left unconsidered, such as the importance of time management and how to achieve it, and how to overcome the difficulties of communicating with supervisors. Consideration is given to the particular problems of groups such as women, part-time and overseas students.

The book also provides practical insights for supervisors, focusing on how to monitor and, if necessary, improve supervisory practice. It assists senior academic administrators by examining the responsibilities that universities have for providing an adequate service for research students. This is a revised and updated second edition; it will be as warmly welcomed as the first edition:

> One way of providing a more supportive environment for PhD students is for supervisors to recommend this book.
>
> *Teaching news*

> Warmly recommended as a bedside companion, both to those hoping to get a PhD and to those who have the responsibility of guiding them, often with very little support themselves.
>
> *Higher Education Review*

> This is an excellent book. Its style is racy and clear . . . an impressive array of information, useful advice and comment gleaned from the author's systematic study and experience over many years . . . should be required reading not only for those contemplating doctoral study but also for all supervisors, new and experienced.
>
> *Higher Education*

Contents
Preface – Becoming a postgraduate – Getting into the system – The nature of the PhD qualification – How not to get a PhD – How to do research – The form of a PhD thesis – The PhD process – How to manage your supervisor – How to survive in a predominantly British, white, male full-time academic environment – The formal procedures – How to supervise – Institutional responsibilities – References – Index.

224pp   0 335 19214 9 (Paperback)